Persuasive Writing

HARPERCOLLINS COLLEGE OUTLINE

Persuasive Writing

David I. Daniels
Camden County College

Barbara J. Daniels
Camden County College

Harper Perennial
A Division of HarperCollins Publishers

An American BookWorks Corporation Production

Project Manager: Judith A. V. Harlan

Editor: Robert A. Weinstein

Library of Congress Cataloging-in-Publication Data

Daniels, Barbara J., 1945–
    Persuasive writing / Barbara J. Daniels, David I. Daniels.
      p. cm.
    Includes bibliographical references and index.
    ISBN 0-06-467175-5
    1. English language—Rhetoric. 2. Persuasion (Rhetoric)
I. Daniels, David I., 1942– . II. Title.
PE1431.D35 1993
808' .042—dc20   92-54678

93 94 95 96 97 ABW/RRD 10 9 8 7 6 5 4 3 2 1

Contents

Preface vii

1 What Is Argument? 1

2 Models for Argument 29

3 Supporting and Attacking 49

4 Thinking Effectively 70

5 Defining and Classifying 97

6 Recognizing Faulty Reasoning 117

7 First Steps in Persuasive Writing 145

8 Planning a Written Argument 170

9 Choosing an Effective Style 199

10 Polishing a Persuasive Paper 220

11 Doing Research 243

12 Using Sources in a Research Paper 266

Glossary 303

Resources for Writers 313

Answers 315

Index 329

Preface

Of all the reasons for learning to argue, our favorite is the one given by Lewis Carroll's Father William when his son asked how he could eat such tough food at his age:

> "In my youth," said his father, "I took to the law
> > And argued each case with my wife;
> And the muscular strength, which it gave to my jaw,
> > Has lasted the rest of my life."

Argument is often no laughing matter. We live in a time when the level of debate on important issues appears to be sinking steadily. Thirty-second sound bites have replaced reasoned discourse as the principal vehicle for seeking public office, and advertisements are based largely on slogans and specious claims. People shout at one another across police barricades rather than discuss their differences face to face.

On the other hand, we have never been better placed to find the information we need to form well-reasoned opinions. Computers, twenty-four-hour news services, and print media are all available, providing the data we need to help us make up our minds on the issues that influence our lives. It often seems that all we lack is the will to think things through.

In your life as a student, a job holder, and an active member of your community, learning to argue more effectively can empower you. The more you understand your own point of view on an issue, the greater your chances of convincing others that you are right. And the information this book provides can protect you against the many unsound arguments you will hear and read.

We offer *Persuasive Writing* as a guide to the kind of argument that helps people make sense of the world around them. The book begins with a discussion of how argument works and then applies this theoretical knowledge to the problems of convincing others. Illustrations drawn from daily life focus the discussion on practical issues. We do not necessarily agree with the many examples of arguable claims we have included. They are intended to expose you to both sides of intriguing controversies. Numerous exercises (with answers at the back of the book) enable you to check your progress at every stage. The terms printed in bold type are defined in the glossary, and a brief summary ends each chapter.

Of the many people we wish to thank for help and support, Jack Cohen comes first to mind. As both family member and friend, he has demonstrated intelligence, enthusiasm, and generosity and has served as a model to us for many years. We dedicate this book to him.

David I. Daniels
Barbara J. Daniels

Persuasive Writing

1

What Is Argument?

You are sitting on a bus one afternoon trying to read your history assignment when the couple in front of you begin shouting at each other. "Three hundred dollars!" the man bellows. "Do you think we're millionaires?"

"What about those golf clubs you bought last week?" the woman yells back.

You try to ignore them, but soon not only you but all the other passengers are looking in their direction. Their faces turn red, and their voices quiver with emotion.

That evening the two candidates for mayor of your city appear together on television. It has been a bitter campaign, and you soon realize that Ellen Singleton, the Democrat, and Pete Sanchez, the Republican, don't like each other. They're supposed to be talking about public housing, but Singleton accuses Sanchez of trying to keep a drug treatment center out of his own suburban neighborhood, and Sanchez accuses Singleton of filing false income tax returns.

The next day you are walking your dog in the park when you pass a bench where a young man and woman are sitting. The man is waving his arms and talking very quickly, and the woman is frowning and shaking her head. As you go by, you hear the man say something about "truly great performances." The woman replies, "Vivien Leigh was okay as Scarlett, but Clark Gable was just another pretty face." You catch on that they are disagreeing about one of your own favorite movies, Gone with the Wind.

All of these people are engaging in one of the most common and natural of human activities: argument.

The couple on the bus are quarreling. A quarrel is a form of argument in which each person's goal is to get his or her way or at least hurt the other person's feelings. Quarrelers are often spiteful and intense, veering off in irrelevant directions and lashing out at each other in angry voices. As a result, quarrels are as likely to obscure the truth as to reveal it.

The two candidates are debating. In a **debate**, people (or teams) with opposing views appeal to third parties (voters or judges) to determine which side has argued a public question more effectively. As successful debaters learn to investigate and analyze issues, they develop the ability to attack their opponents' positions and the confidence to defend their own. However, because the purpose of a debate is usually to win votes or a trophy rather than to seek the truth, debaters run the risk of oversimplifying complicated questions and expressing themselves too forcefully.

The friends on the park bench might just be expressing their personal tastes. One of them might have enjoyed *Gone with the Wind* enormously and the other not nearly so much. If they merely share their responses to the movie, they are only chatting. But perhaps they began by agreeing about what makes a great movie. Then, knowing they have much the same standards, they are discussing whether or not this particular movie measures up to them. Ultimately one friend may persuade the other to share his or her evaluation of *Gone with the Wind*. This kind of productive argument is the subject of this book.

UNDERSTANDING ARGUMENT

Convincing someone to accept a point of view (and perhaps take action based on that view) is called **persuasion**. Persuasion can be carried out in numerous ways: by appeals to emotion, by manipulation, by trickery, and by argument. **Argument** is the process of making a point and trying to convince other people that the point is worthy of belief. To argue effectively, you must support your point with evidence—that is, provide people with reasons for believing it. These two components—point and support—are indispensable to every reasoned argument. A would-be argument without a point is aimless. A point without support is a slogan: It might sound good, but there's no reason to believe it.

Arguments in one form or another go on all around us. Family members, friends, acquaintances, advertisements, political speeches, and newspaper editorials compete for our attention, making conflicting claims that tug us in different directions. We feel the need for intellectual tools to help us make sense of them. Is your friend Sheila right that going to college is a waste of time and money? What was the point of the president's speech last evening? Can the Glitter Toothpaste Company prove that its product helps fight tooth decay? Understanding how arguments work won't always lead you to the right conclusions, but it can provide ways of thinking about issues that put you in a better position to judge them.

WHY ARGUE?

Your usual reason for arguing will be to convert others to your point of view. But arguments can also enable you to make up your own mind about difficult issues. A good argument helps you strengthen your convictions when they are weak or discard them when you discover that they lack objective support. As you master argument, you'll become more skillful at understanding not only your own positions but also opposing ones. As the English philosopher John Stuart Mill (1806–1873) wrote, "He who knows only his own side of the case knows little."

Making Up Your Own Mind

Arguing against either real opponents or imaginary ones can be a path to self-discovery. Understanding argument will help you distinguish important issues from trivial ones. As a skillful arguer, you'll also be less likely to judge other people's views too hastily or to fall for poorly constructed arguments. In addition, participating in a good argument will yield fresh perspectives on familiar issues and prompt you to raise new questions about them.

Sometimes arguments about abstract issues can seem remote from your everyday concerns. Determining what role the United States should play in the Middle East, for example, may not seem relevant to your career or personal life. However, like any useful skill, argumentation takes practice. By discussing Islamic fundamentalism or Palestinian rights, you can improve your ability to express and support your opinions on any subject. Understanding argument can help you clarify your goals and determine how to reach them. It can also help you find weak points in other people's positions and avoid being manipulated by others. In other words, understanding argument equips you to take control of your own life and think for yourself.

Forceful arguers often take the lead in business and community life. Whether you are making a sales presentation or arguing for a zoning change in your neighborhood, a sound knowledge of argument can help you secure a hearing for your views. The issue at stake may be as limited as how best to organize a summer softball league or as sweeping as how to reform tax laws. In either case, an effective argument can prove decisive in getting what you want.

In fact, argument is the foundation of our entire democratic system of government. One of our basic freedoms is expressed in the First Amendment to the Constitution: "Congress shall make no law . . . abridging the freedom of speech, or of the press." This amendment ensures that we can stand up for our beliefs rather than face the manipulation, censorship, and intimidation typical of authoritarian regimes. Argument, then, is one of the skills of a good citizen, and a willingness to express and listen to opinions on important issues is one of the marks of a conscientious one.

TRY IT OUT

You probably already have ideas and feelings about some controversial subjects. Perhaps you have discussed or read about these issues or seen movies or television programs that dramatized them. Identifying the issues that already interest you is a first step toward focusing your thinking and writing about debatable topics. The reactions you have now can serve as the basis for further thinking, research, and writing as you learn more about what makes an argument effective.

Listed below are some controversial issues. In the space to the left of each issue write the number that represents your feelings about it. Use the following scale:

5 = I feel very strongly about this issue. I would very much like to discuss or write about it.

4 = I have some strong feelings about this issue. Discussing it or writing about it would interest me.

3 = I'm interested in this issue, but I don't have strong feelings about it.

2 = I'm not very interested in this issue.

1 = I find this issue boring. I would not want to discuss it or write about it.

___abortion   ___business ethics

___prayer in public schools   ___education

___compulsory AIDS testing   ___birth control

___racism   ___animal rights

___reform of college sports   ___poverty

___the environment   ___the family

___euthanasia   ___homosexual rights
___censorship   ___capital punishment
___women's rights   ___divorce
___legalizing drugs   ___gun control
___pornography   ___religion

Focus your reactions to these issues by completing the following sentences:

1. The issues on the list that I feel most strongly about are

_____.

2. The issues on the list I would most like to learn more about are

_____.

3. The issues on the list that seem to be the most controversial are

_____.

4. The issues that I think will be most important in the future are

_____.

5. A question I have about one of the issues on the list is

_____

_____?

6. Other issues that could be added to the list are

_____

_____.

7. If I wrote about one of these issues today, the topic I would choose would be

_____

_____.

8. My main idea would be

_____

_____.

Persuading Others

Argument is a form of communication. Scholars who have studied communication suggest that argument is a collaborative process. When an arguer makes a point, a listener or reader participates by interpreting it and perhaps responding to it. Such interaction requires a certain amount of goodwill and reasonableness on both sides. When the participants in an argument are trying to discover the truth about an issue, both sides often change their original convictions a little. At the end they feel that beliefs which have stood the test of being challenged are stronger because of it.

Persuading others requires not only presenting and supporting your opinions clearly and forcefully but also involving your audience in the communication process. Sometimes your audience consists of people hostile to your views. But just as often you will be addressing people who either share your views or begin with no particular convictions one way or the other. Different audiences require different argumentative strategies.

PERSUADING A FRIENDLY AUDIENCE

Your audience may already be convinced that your views are correct. Speaking to a group of emergency services volunteers on the importance of knowing cardiopulmonary resuscitation or to ecologists on the need to save the rain forests may seem unnecessary. But such arguments are made to create a feeling of solidarity within a group and renew its commitment to the tasks at hand. This kind of audience needs only a bare outline of the support for its beliefs, together with a reminder of the need for hard work or self-sacrifice to achieve common goals.

PERSUADING A NEUTRAL AUDIENCE

Often, your audience will begin with no particular convictions about an issue that seems vitally important to you. This kind of audience is a good target for your persuasive skills because neutral listeners or readers do not start out with prejudices against your views. For example, suppose you know help is urgently needed to alleviate famine in a particular African country, so you decide to write an article for a local church's newsletter inaugurating a fund drive. From speaking to people informally you are aware that some church members have never heard of the country where millions are hungry, let alone thought of providing any assistance. Your first task, then, is to make the problem clear and only after explaining it, to recommend steps people can take in support of the relief efforts.

PERSUADING A HOSTILE AUDIENCE

Sometimes you may attempt to change the views of unfriendly audiences. One of the principal skills you need under such circumstances is the ability to anticipate and answer possible objections to your argument.

Suppose that as an editor of your college newspaper you decide to write an editorial about the need for more Americans to study foreign languages. Some students at your college have had unpleasant experiences with language study in high school; others are engineering or animal science majors who think they have no use for a second language and no room in their programs for language courses. Your editorial will be more persuasive if you take their objections into account.

Arguments addressed to hostile audiences are the most difficult of the three types. No matter how reasonable and well supported your argument is, hostile readers or listeners may well refuse to accept your line of reasoning and cling stubbornly to their own opinions. (The process of finding reasons to justify what one wants to believe and tricking oneself into thinking the reasons are good ones is called **rationalization**.) However, by arguing skillfully with people who oppose your views, you can at least win their respect, show them that you have reasons for believing as you do, and decrease their antagonism toward your ideas.

WHAT IS ARGUABLE?

Not all statements are arguable. Distinguishing between unarguable and arguable statements is a first step in discovering fruitful topics for discussion.

Unarguable Statements

A **fact** is an item of information that can be proven true. For example, if you disagree with your sister about how cold a day it is, rather than argue, you can look at a thermometer or catch a weather report on the radio. This process of confirming that a statement is true is known as **verification**. Facts differ from opinions in that facts can be verified, but opinions must be supported.

Or suppose you buy a candy bar and offer to share it with your friend Paula. Instead of accepting it or saying "No, thanks," Paula makes a face and says, "Don't be silly. I can't eat chocolate; I'll get acne." You and Paula may disagree about the effects of eating chocolate, but you can't argue about this point. The statement "People get acne from eating chocolate" is either true or not true. To find out, you need go no further than an up-to-date medical encyclopedia.

Suppose, on the other hand, that Paula turns down half your chocolate bar, saying, "Oh, I never eat chocolate; I hate it." You can't argue with her about that, either. You have no reason to doubt that she hates chocolate, and nothing you can say is likely to convince her that chocolate tastes good. She is expressing one of her **personal preferences**, which are opinions based entirely on one person's tastes. Personal preferences aren't arguable (there's a Latin saying *De gustibus non est disputandum*, which means, "There's no disputing about [matters of] taste").

Arguable Statements

The only time an arguable point can be based on a personal preference is when reasons can be found to support it that other people would be likely to share. For example, you could examine your preference for a particular television show and transform the statement "I like the show" into an arguable statement: "The show's excellent acting, exciting plot, and thrilling special effects make it well worth watching."

Unlike a fact or an expression of personal preference, an **arguable statement** expresses a controversial point of view that a person can support (or argue against) by providing evidence. Other people can decide that it is sound (that is, agree with it) or unsound (that is, disagree).

INFERENCES

Many arguable statements are **inferences**, which are interpretations of facts. We draw many inferences without seeming to think about them, but if necessary we could construct the chain of reasoning that led us along a path of facts to our conclusions. For example, if we see someone coming along waving a lottery ticket and singing "I'm in the money," we conclude he has just won the lottery. If we had to reconstruct our thinking, we could do so:

FACT: This man is waving a lottery ticket in the air.

FACT: This man is singing "I'm in the money."

FACT: Other people who have acted similarly in the past have done so just after winning the lottery.

INFERENCE: This man has just won the lottery.

In complicated circumstances, however, two people could interpret the same facts very differently. For example, both sides in the abortion debate accept the same facts about how a fetus develops. However, each side comes to a different conclusion about just when life begins.

JUDGMENTS

Another kind of arguable statement is a **judgment**, which is an evaluation based on ideals or philosophical beliefs. Many of the most heated arguments over public policy are over judgments. For example, in the abortion debate the prochoice side judges that the rights of a pregnant woman should take precedence over the rights of the fetal life inside her. The prolife side judges that the rights of the fetus should be paramount.

EXERCISE 1

NOTE: Answers to the exercises are provided at the back of this book.
Directions: Classify each statement below by using the following code:

A = arguable

NA = not arguable

Example: _A_ The voting age should be lowered to 16.

___ 1. A gram of fat contains nine calories.

___ 2. Florida is a better state for retirees than California is.

_____ 3. Gray is my favorite color.

_____ 4. Collecting and eating wild plants are unnecessarily risky.

_____ 5. The conductor of an orchestra is called "maestro."

_____ 6. The gunfighters of the Old West were villains, not heroes.

_____ 7. State law should prevent telephone marketers from calling people who indicate that they don't want to be called.

_____ 8. The Greeks used measurement and mathematics for keeping accounts, telling time, designing buildings, and making maps.

_____ 9. IQ scores should not be used to label and track school children.

_____ 10. This year's vacation was the best one I ever took.

COMPARING SPOKEN AND WRITTEN ARGUMENT

Arguments—arguable statements and support for them—can take many forms. For example, they can be spoken or written. These two types of arguments share many characteristics, but there are important differences between them.

Expectations for Spoken and Written Argument

In a spoken argument your opponent states his or her views and challenges those you put forward. You need to listen to what the other person has to say and be ready both to criticize his or her position and defend your own. In written argument, on the other hand, you are often responsible for presenting not only your own but also the opposing side of the issue in order to point out its weaknesses. Sometimes your written argument will be in response to something you've read that expresses the opposing side's position. But frequently you will need to foresee the opposing view and anticipate how prospective opponents might criticize your own.

An advantage to spoken arguments is that the person you're talking to can stop you if you make an ambiguous statement and ask you to clarify it. The other person's facial expressions or gestures can also indicate whether you are getting your message across. In spoken arguments, you can sometimes express uncertainty ("I'm not sure of this, but . . .") and occasionally back away from extreme statements ("Well, I didn't really mean *all* . . .").

In writing, on the other hand, you need to make your points as clearly as possible without anyone to tell you whether you have succeeded or not. You need to provide guideposts, such as transitional words and phrases (*first*, *next, on the other hand, in conclusion,* and so on), to help your readers follow your line of thought. You cannot modify your position as easily in writing once you hand your work to an instructor or get it published in a newspaper or magazine.

Standards for Spoken and Written Argument

Written arguments are generally held to higher standards than spoken ones. A spoken argument may lack a serious purpose; you and your friends may argue just to pass the time. In contrast, written arguments are often more earnest; if you take the trouble to write, you are usually trying to make an important point. Spoken arguments may include contradictions, errors, or irrelevant remarks which go unnoticed in the heat of the discussion. In speech you may get by with inadequate support for some of your statements because speakers, unlike writers, are not usually expected to provide well-organized, verifiable support for general ideas. (An exception to this occurs in debates and other formal presentations for which speakers are expected to be well prepared.) In casual conversation you may use informal words (*kids* instead of *children* or *okay* instead of *acceptable*) or even ungrammatical constructions, and usually no one will notice or mind.

When you write, readers pay closer attention to your arguments, so you are expected to polish them. In writing, weak statements are fixed on the page for opponents to spot and criticize. Contradictions, factual errors, and lack of adequate support are all easy for readers to identify. In addition, you need to use a more formal and precise vocabulary and hold yourself to higher standards of correctness. A poor choice of language or errors in grammar may brand a written argument as not worth serious attention.

By writing arguments, you can sharpen both your ideas and your skill in expressing them. When you argue a position convincingly in writing, you clarify your own thinking about an issue and may convert others to your viewpoint as well.

The chart below summarizes the differences between spoken and written argument.

Casual Spoken Argument	Written Argument
Informal word choice (including slang) is acceptable, and *you* and *I* are common.	Precise, formal vocabulary is expected, and *you* and *I* are less common than in speech.
Careful organization is not necessary.	A logical sequence of ideas is essential.
Formal transitional words (such as *nevertheless*) are uncommon.	Transitional words are common.

Casual Spoken Argument (cont'd)	Written Argument (cont'd)
Listeners let each other know (verbally and nonverbally) if they misunderstand or disagree.	Writers must anticipate readers' opposing views.
Vague or unsupported ideas may go unchallenged.	A forceful, detailed defense of one's views is expected.
Speakers can modify their views as the discussion continues.	Writers are held responsible for published views.
Contradictions and irrelevancies are often unnoticed.	High standards of coherence and correctness are required.

EXERCISE 2

Directions: Some of the statements below are typical of written argument; the others are typical of spoken argument. Identify each statement by using the following code:

S = typical of spoken argument

W = typical of written argument

Example: _S_ I think there's a good chance that pesticides could be handled better.

_____ 1. Future economic progress in developing countries will depend on the decentralization of political power, the improvement of management training, and the encouragement of public enterprise.

_____ 2. You're fooling yourself if you think you'll save money by buying a home freezer.

_____ 3. Taking care of their elderly parents is the kids' responsibility, not some doctor's or social worker's.

_____ 4. Although medical science has been highly successful in dealing with infectious diseases, controlling degenerative diseases will prove more difficult.

_____ 5. However, an analysis of the Chinese democracy movement from 1978 to 1981 provides important clues to the meaning of democracy in China today.

_____ 6. Boxing is so disgusting. How can you stand to watch it?

_____ 7. Despite extensive contact with Europeans over the last two hundred years, Pacific Islanders have played a central role in shaping their own history.

___ 8. Things are a lot worse today than they ever were. Everybody is always acting crazy.

___ 9. I'm sure parents are the best people to teach their children about sex because my parents did a good job of explaining things to me.

___10. Thus, Shakespeare's last four plays reflect a preoccupation with death, final judgment, and life after death.

Types of Spoken Argument

Many oral presentations, such as college lectures, talks at business meetings, and political speeches, are arguments. A lecture on the Civil War, for example, may contain a great deal of factual information, but the instructor uses the facts to support his or her own interpretation of what happened. During informal discussions—in town meetings, clubs, and religious groups, for example—the speakers' contributions often contain the elements of argument: a main point ("Let's rent a bus for our trip to Minneapolis this year") and support for the main point ("Last year, three cars got lost trying to follow each other through downtown traffic"; "We'll have more fun if the group stays together").

Types of Written Argument

For centuries writers have been expressing their opinions in **essays,** which are short works of nonfiction expressing a personal viewpoint. The Frenchman Michel de Montaigne (1533–1592) was the first person to call his writings *essais,* a French word meaning "trials" or "tests." By choosing this title Montaigne implied that he was striving to discover the truth about subjects open to dispute. He began writing his essays after his best friend, Etienne de La Boétie, died, which suggests that they were continuations of spoken arguments with his friend. Montaigne's essays are not organized as essays are today. **Digressions,** passages unrelated to the main idea, are common in his writing.

Since Montaigne's day essays have been written on subjects as different as roast pigs, prize fighting, and pilgrimages to Lourdes. Essays may be formal or informal, commenting on issues of lasting interest, current events, or apparently trivial incidents in the writers' lives. Regardless of the style or subject matter, an effective essay is a thoughtful expression of its author's own viewpoint. In an essay the **thesis,** or main idea, is either stated directly or strongly implied. When stated directly, the thesis is usually expressed in a sentence called a thesis statement.

Today the line between fiction and essay is sometimes blurred. Like a short story, an essay can narrate events and be interpreted in a variety of ways. Unlike a short story, however, an essay must stay close to facts. Invented conversations and falsified statistics are not acceptable.

ACADEMIC WRITING

Like professional writers, college students express their opinions in essays, which are also called themes, compositions, or papers. A professional writer sometimes produces an informal, unstructured personal essay, but a college student is expected to make a clear point and support it in an organized, well-reasoned paper. Academic writing calls for carefully written arguments presented in a formal style. Digressions, although part of the essay tradition handed down from Montaigne, are usually not appropriate.

Students also express their interpretations and judgments in **research papers**, long formal essays that include material from a variety of sources. In contrast, **reports** merely present information on specified topics; report writers aren't asked to offer their own opinions about the material. Reports are sometimes based on observation, but often they require the same kind of delving into sources that research papers do. Therefore, both reports and research papers can require students to read extensively and evaluate their source material. Neither type of paper is merely a matter of stringing quotations together.

Writing a research paper means following many of the same steps you would use to write a shorter paper: choosing a topic, making a point, and supporting it in an organized and unified way. However, a research paper is longer than an essay, so it requires significantly more time and effort. Because of its length, the research paper requires a deeper exploration of its topic, including a more detailed evaluation and more complicated fusion of varying viewpoints.

Doing research will equip you with fundamental skills and habits of mind that you can use all your life to make practical decisions and evaluate complex issues. Much intellectual work consists of reading, thinking about what you have read, and reporting on it to someone. Writing a research paper is a systematic way to master this basic strategy.

ARGUMENT IN PRINT

Written argument appears in many newspapers and magazines. In theory, news articles should not express opinions although the way information is selected and emphasized unavoidably leads to some **slanting**, which is distorting information to reflect a particular point of view. Usually, the better the newspaper or magazine, the clearer the distinction is between argumentative writing and news stories. In major newspapers most argumentative writing is found in editorials and on the **op-ed** or commentary page, a page opposite the editorials that is devoted to columnists and other contributors of interpretive essays. Op-ed pages have a wider range of style and subject matter than editorial pages; they include topics beyond current news, such as accounts of personal experiences, reflections on history, and analyses of long-term trends.

Editorials are short argumentative essays presenting and supporting the opinions of a publication's editors or of an editorial board made up of writers with varied backgrounds and viewpoints. Good editorials inform as well as persuade. Often an editorial provides some background information on a topic, beginning with a general statement or observation and moving on to the reasons supporting the generalization.

Editorials usually consist of only a few paragraphs and sometimes only a few sentences. Richard Aregood of the *Philadelphia Daily News*, a Pulitzer Prize-winning editorial writer, often produces very short editorials. One of his best known is the following, published on November 20, 1975, the day Spanish dictator Francisco Franco died:

> They say only the good die young. Generalissimo Francisco Franco was 82. Seems about right.

Aregood assumed that readers of the editorial pages (about a third of the people who read newspapers) were familiar with Franco's bloody record as the long-time dictator of Spain.

Besides editorials, an editorial page often includes letters to the editor and political cartoons. Widely differing views appear in letters to the editor, which have been published in U.S. newspapers for more than two hundred years. Many of the letters submitted are from people who make a habit of writing to newspapers. Editors prefer to present a variety of views. Therefore, not having written a letter to the newspaper before and having something distinctive to say increase your chances of being published as do making your letter short and clear and emphasizing something out of the ordinary about your viewpoint.

Argumentative writing also appears elsewhere in newspapers and magazines, such as in reviews of books and movies and evaluations of new cars. Regular contributors express their opinions in columns on politics, sports, fashions, and even good manners.

CRITICAL LISTENING AND READING

Whatever kinds of arguments you are dealing with, becoming a critical listener and reader is important in learning to understand them. Being critical in this sense does not mean faultfinding or belittling someone else's work. Another term for criticism is evaluation, so **critical listening and reading** involve looking carefully at both the strengths and weaknesses of arguments and making conscientious, impartial judgments about them.

Becoming a Critical Listener

Good listening is hard partly because we spend most of our waking hours half listening to music, radio and television programs, and the conversations of friends and family members. Such experiences lead us to expect that listening is easy. On the contrary, listening to a closely reasoned argument is very demanding, even more demanding than reading equally difficult material.

The more carefully and critically you listen, the more you can learn from oral arguments, and the more effectively you can present your own views when your turn comes to speak. You can improve your listening skills by following the guidelines below.

Prepare to listen. Before you hear a lecture or speech, try to skim articles or books on the topic (or read them carefully if you have time). In a class, assignments and lectures are designed to reinforce each other. Understanding one will inevitably make the other easier to follow. Likewise, keeping up with current issues in the news will enable you to grasp and participate in discussions of contemporary problems.

Make predictions based on where a speech will take place, what its title is, and what you already know about the speaker. For example, suppose you are planning to attend a talk sponsored by the Good Neighbors' Association entitled "Crime Prevention: Everybody's Job." Before going to hear the speaker, a local police officer named Lieutenant D'Angelo, you can ask yourself, "What are the crime problems in my neighborhood?" and "What can a private citizen do about them?" You can assume Lieutenant D'Angelo will not want you and your neighbors to risk your lives trying to fight crime yourselves. Therefore, she will probably advocate some form of cooperation between citizens and the police, such as a neighborhood crime watch. During her speech, you can check to see how well you have anticipated what she is saying.

Examine your own views. If you expect to disagree with a speaker, prepare to concentrate even harder than usual so that at the end you can summarize the presentation objectively. Be willing to explore all sides of an issue by opening your mind to new ideas. This means taking a "wait and see" attitude rather than dismissing unfamiliar viewpoints without really listening to them.

Arrive on time. Choose a place to sit that offers a minimum of distractions (a seat away from a window, for example, may help you to look up at the speaker rather than at the traffic on the street outside). If you usually sit toward the back of the room in classes or meetings, moving closer to the front should enable you to concentrate better.

Listen for a thesis—a statement of the speaker's main idea. Often, the primary point will be clear from a speech's title. Sometimes a speaker will state his or her main point at the beginning ("I'm here today to convince you that this college needs a women's studies program"). Once you've grasped the main idea, distinguishing the key supporting points from less important details will be easier.

Watch the speaker's body language (movements and gestures) and listen to his or her tone of voice for clues to which ideas the speaker feels most deeply about. Body language may also help you guess which points in the argument the speaker fears are weakest—useful information if you plan to make the case for the other side.

Take notes. Circle, capitalize, or underline the points that seem to be important to the speaker.

Keep thinking and raising questions as you listen. Plan to ask your questions later, and make notes on the points you'd like to ask about.

People are least able to listen closely when they feel strongly about what is being discussed. Discussions about abortion, for example, are often unproductive because each side is too angry to hear the other person's point of view. People with strong feelings about an issue often think they already know everything the opposition has to say and no longer bother to listen.

In heated arguments, you can increase your chances of understanding an opponent's position by restating it (a procedure advocated by the American psychologist Carl Rogers [1902–87]). Keep rephrasing the views of your opponent until your version of what has been said seems satisfactory to him or her. Using this technique will compel you to listen carefully, not just assume you know what the other side thinks.

Becoming a Critical Reader

If you try to understand written arguments by skimming or reading quickly, you might make the snap judgment that you're not a good reader or that the material you're reading is too difficult. However, just as careful writing requires rewriting, most serious reading calls for rereading. But merely rereading difficult material is often not enough. Preparing yourself to read, raising questions and reading actively to answer them, understanding an essay's structure, and ultimately drawing your own conclusions about the issues are the keys to understanding complicated arguments.

PREPARING TO READ

Do you often read in bed under a warm blanket with only a single dim light to see by? If so, you've almost certainly had the experience of falling asleep over a book. Reading novels in bed can be better than taking a sleeping pill, but reading arguments on euthanasia or foreign policy in the same setting can be almost useless. Instead, sit up in a straight chair under good lighting, and keep distractions to a minimum. This definitely means turning off the television set and perhaps the radio as well. If possible, do your most difficult reading when you are well rested.

Before reading an intricate argument, jot down notes on what you already know about the subject, such as the meaning of key terms and any other information you have gathered from classes or previous reading. Collecting your thoughts in this way will prepare you to learn new material effectively.

You may already know something about the author whose work you are dealing with, but if you don't, reading his or her biography in an introductory paragraph or on a dust jacket can help you form some ideas of what to expect. Ask yourself when, where, and for what audience the book or essay was written. For example, if you are reading the Declaration of Independence, everything you can remember about the struggle between Great Britain and its American colonies will be useful for understanding Jefferson's argument.

You can also consult a book's preface or introduction, in which authors frequently state their intentions and explain how their books are organized. Use this material to get an **overview** (a general idea of what to expect) before you start to read. Leaf through the pages of an argument, glancing at any illustrations or special features, such as checklists, summaries, or study questions to see what they reveal about the material's main ideas. At this point you should begin to raise some questions of your own based on the work's title and subtitles. For example, if an essay is called "Flag Burning Isn't the Real Issue," your initial questions might be "Why isn't flag burning a real problem?" and "If flag burning isn't the real issue, what is?" These questions will help focus your attention on key points as you read.

EXERCISE 3

Directions: Listed below are titles and subheadings of some articles, essays, and books. Use each item as the basis for one or more questions that could direct your reading. Write your questions on the lines below the items. Some suggested questions for each item are given at the back of this book.

Example: "Two Sides of Freedom"

Focus questions: <u>What are the two sides of freedom?</u>

<u>Which side seems more convincing?</u>

1. "Tumbleweeds: Old Enemy, New Ally"

Focus questions:

_____

_____

2. "A Tough Law's First Test"

Focus questions:

_____

_____

3. *Outcast Americans*

Focus questions:

_____

_____

4. "On the Brink of the Second Space Age"

Focus questions:

_____

_____

5. "Paul Gauguin, Self-styled Rebel"

Focus questions:

_____

_____

6. "How to Handle Hate on Campus"

Focus questions:

_____

_____

7. "Some Doubts on School Vouchers"

Focus questions:

_____

_____

8. "Black Poet, White Critic"

Focus questions:

_____

_____

9. "Relief for Investors"

Focus questions:

_____

_____

10. "Justice Blinded"

Focus questions:

_____

_____

READING ACTIVELY

As you reread an argument, vary your pace. The first time through, read swiftly, skipping material that does not yet make sense. Don't try too soon to make the material fit a particular pattern. Instead, be flexible enough to consider a variety of interpretations until you are sure you understand what the author means.

Your first goal should be to find the main ideas. Look for a thesis at the end of the first or second paragraph of an essay or in the conclusion. If the thesis is not stated directly, make a preliminary guess at what you think it might be. Then focus on the main reasons that seem to support the thesis. Is each supporting point discussed in a separate paragraph, or are related reasons grouped together? Look for transitional words and phrases such as *first*, *second*, *as a result*, *then*, and *on the other hand* to help you locate the main divisions of an essay.

If you can see that what you're reading is much too difficult for you, try reading something easier on the same topic. An introductory article or book (even one written for children) or an article from an encyclopedia could give you the background you need to make sense of more complex material.

When you reread an essay, pause now and then to reflect on what you are reading: Does your current interpretation of the essay match your original expectations? If not, why not? How does what you are reading relate to what you have previously learned about the topic? Now that you've read the essay once and had a chance to guess at the meanings of unfamiliar words, check your guesses in the dictionary.

Most authors of argumentative essays mention opposing viewpoints, partly to show they are familiar with the other side's position but primarily to point out why their opponents are wrong. One of the pitfalls of reading an argument is to mistake a statement of an opposing view for the author's own position. A common approach in argumentative writing is to acknowledge that the opponent's position has some validity. As a result, a hasty reader can easily think that an author's position is the opposite of what it actually is. Check your interpretation of the material against the title, which often hints at or even states the author's view.

Follow the steps described below when you read a complicated argument.

Overview:	Glance over the argument to get a general idea of what to expect.
Question:	Raise questions of your own to focus your reading.
Read:	Read for main ideas.
Recite:	State key elements of the argument orally or in writing.
Reread:	Expect to reread difficult material to understand it fully.

Review: Look back later to be sure you haven't
                    forgotten what you learned.

ANALYZING A DIFFICULT ARGUMENT

To make sense of an especially difficult argument, try expressing its author's ideas in your own words, perhaps by outlining or summarizing the main points. If you cannot find a thesis statement, try writing one yourself, being as faithful as you can to the author's ideas.

Write the thesis statement at the top of a blank sheet of paper. Then put the essay aside and ask yourself, "If this were my thesis, what evidence would I need to convince someone that it is valid?" Jot down questions and comments about what you think your supporting points would be if this really were your thesis. Don't worry yet about whether or not you have actually found the evidence in the essay. For example, suppose the thesis statement is "Americans should elect their president by popular vote rather than indirectly through the electoral college [the body that elects the president and vice president of the United States after the popular vote is counted]." Jotting down questions and comments about possible evidence might lead to a list like this:

1. Does the electoral college distort the popular vote? Find elections in which the popular vote and the electoral vote led to different results.

2. If there have been no such elections, how close has one come? What are the chances that such an election will occur in the future? If there is any likelihood of this happening, the electoral college should be abolished.

3. Why did the authors of the Constitution devise the electoral college? If their reasons don't apply to the present situation, we should abolish it.

4. Is the electoral college expensive? We might be able to save money by abolishing it.

5. Does the electoral college system lead to corruption? If fraud is even a little less likely in direct elections, the electoral college should be abolished.

Now go back to the original essay and find out whether the author has made these or similar points. Check off the points the author presented. If he or she has made points you haven't thought of, add them to your list.

Once you're confident that you understand the author's main point and the support for it, analyze the argument more closely. Mark off the argument's main divisions, noting how each paragraph contributes to its overall structure. If you think parts of the essay aren't related to the main subject, look at them especially closely. Digressions are rare in written argument; look for the connections between an author's ideas rather than dismiss apparently irrelevant passages too hastily.

As you analyze an argument, you should also evaluate the support for its main ideas. Is the evidence accurate, up to date, and convincing? Are the people described as supporting the author's position experts on the subject? Are their beliefs or those of the author stated as if they are opinions, not facts?

DRAWING YOUR OWN CONCLUSIONS

At this point you can decide whether or not you agree with the author. One way to focus your response is by jotting yes or no next to the material you definitely agree or disagree with. Then you can consider questions of approach and tone: What in the essay makes you trust or mistrust the author? Does he or she show respect for the opposition and for you, the reader? Does the author seem to treat issues fairly and completely?

At last you can evaluate the whole argument. Has the author fulfilled the purpose of the piece as you understand it? More important, has the argument made you think? Have your views on the subject of the essay changed in any way as a result of having read it? Could you write an essay of your own supporting the author's views or opposing them? Writing such a response can be the most challenging test of whether or not you have understood what you have read.

EXERCISE 4

Directions: The following argumentative essay discusses the reintroduction of wolves to Yellowstone National Park. Analyze it by carrying out the steps listed below. (Answers will vary; sample answers are included at the end of this book.)

1. Before reading the essay, answer the following questions:

   a. What do you already know about wolves? Have you heard anything about the controversy over reintroducing wolves to Yellowstone National Park? If so, what? _____

   _____

   _____

b. The title of the essay is "Reintroducing Wolves to Yellowstone." Write two questions based on this title: _____

_____

_____

_____

2. Read the first paragraph of the essay. Then either copy the author's thesis on the lines below or, if the thesis is implied rather than stated, write a sentence indicating what you think the thesis is:

_____

_____

_____

3. If this were your thesis, what support could you provide to back it up? List possible supporting points in the form of questions, comments, or both: _____

_____

_____

_____

_____

_____

4. Read on to see if the author supports the thesis in the way you expect.

5. Look for words (such as *however*) and phrases (such as *on the other hand*) that provide clues to the overall structure of the essay. Underline these transitions.

6. Draw brackets ([ ]) to show the main divisions of the essay. Label each division with a short phrase describing its contents.

7. Go back to the list you made for item three above. Add the supporting points to your list that the author made but that you did not anticipate. Evaluate any ideas on your list that you expected the author to make but which did not appear in the essay. Do you have any ideas the author does not include? _____ If so, should the author have included them? _____ Is their omission a serious weakness in the essay? _____

8. Reread the parts of the essay in which the author discusses views that oppose his or her main point. Do you think the author does a good job of responding to opposing views? _____ Why or why not?

_____

_____

9. Evaluate the evidence that supports the essay's thesis by answering the following questions:

Does the support seem accurate? _____

Is the support convincing? _____

Is the person described as supporting the author's views an expert on the subject? _____

Does the author express beliefs as if they are opinions rather than facts?_____

10. Go through the essay again, writing "yes" in the margin next to the ideas you agree with and "no" next to the ideas you disagree with. Briefly explain your views.

_____

_____

_____

_____

11. Evaluate the essay as a whole by answering the following questions: Does the essay make its point effectively? _____

Why or why not?_____

_____

_____

_____

_____

REINTRODUCING WOLVES TO YELLOWSTONE

1.   Despite vigorous opposition from local interests, the National Park Service is preparing to reintroduce wolves into Yellowstone National Park and, inevitably, into the sheep- and cattle-raising country surrounding it. The movement to bring wolves back is part of a general policy of restoring wild areas as fully as possible to their natural state. Returning wolves to the park would reestablish conditions as they existed when it was opened in 1872. Despite the occasional problems this reintroduction may cause, it deserves vigorous public support.

2.   Before the Europeans settled North America, wolves roamed in great numbers all across the continent. Whenever new settlers arrived, however, one of their first priorities was to eradicate wolves, animals they considered threats to their livestock and even their children. Between 1870 and 1877, hunters killed 55,000 wolves every year in the United States.

3.   Even though Yellowstone, America's oldest national park, was designated a permanent wilderness area, the public's fear of wolves extended the slaughter within its boundaries. Bounty hunters eliminated wolves from Yellowstone during the 1920s by an extensive program of shooting, trapping, and poisoning. The first justification for reintroducing them is therefore historical: with less than 1 percent of the land within U.S. borders still in its natural state, restoring the park's ecosystem to its original condition would be an invaluable reminder of life as it existed before the coming of European settlers.

4.   A second and more important reason to reintroduce this last missing component of the original habitat is that wolves *belong* in the ecosystem, indirectly benefiting the very species on which they prey. That wolves help keep deer, elk, and bison herds at sustainable sizes, preventing deaths by starvation during occasional bitter winters, is well documented. According to L. David Mech (a biologist with the U.S. Fish and Wildlife Service and the author of the book *The Wolf: Ecology and Behavior of an Endangered Species*), after wolves arrived at Isle Royal National Park, an island in Lake Superior, by crossing the frozen lake from Canada during an especially severe winter, the size of the moose herd actually grew. By keeping moose numbers down initially, the wolves prevented overgrazing, which in turn allowed plant life to regenerate, eventually increasing the herd's food supply.

5.   A third reason for supporting the efforts to reintroduce wolves to Yellowstone may be the most important of all. The modern ecology movement, uniting millions of people all over the world, has gained many victories so far. Ultimately, however, human regard for nature will be tested by our willingness to live together with other species even when we must endure inconveniences to do so. Reintroducing wolves to Yellowstone National Park may cause some problems, but if our respect for nature is genuine, the risk is well worth taking.

6.   The Yellowstone reintroduction program is not unique. For example, wolves have been successfully reintroduced into

the Alligator River National Wildlife Refuge in North Carolina with no problems for surrounding animal or human populations. In Minnesota, the only area in the lower forty-eight states where large numbers of wolves still exist in the wild, ecologists and cattle raisers alike are largely satisfied with the present situation. Minnesota wolves, whose prime food source is deer, kill relatively few domestic animals. Those wolves that do are promptly destroyed. As a result, many Minnesota farmers seem willing to coexist with wolves—a great success story for an animal with such a bad reputation.

7. Objections to the Yellowstone reintroduction program have come from hunters, ranchers, and other residents of the areas surrounding the park. Hunters fear that wolves would keep down the deer and elk populations; because hunting is an important element in the economies of many western states, local public officials and businesspeople have similar concerns. Experience suggests that in times of plenty, there will be more than enough game to satisfy both two- and four-footed hunters. However, after especially bitter winters, when the number of game animals diminishes and the wolf population remains stable, continued hunting by wolves does delay the herd's regrowth. Nevertheless, the improved wilderness management to be gained by the wolves culling out old and diseased animals more than compensates for their continued hunting during occasional periods of scarcity.

8. The most vocal protests against wolf reintroduction to Yellowstone have come from cattle ranchers whose herds graze the public lands adjoining the park. Some mistakenly think the federal Endangered Species Act prohibits killing wolves that attack cattle. Others believe wolves take far more cattle than they do (in Minnesota, wolves kill approximately one in every 2,000 cattle and one in every 1,000 sheep every year). Funds have been established to compensate ranchers for lost livestock; however, to receive compensation they are obliged to prove that wolves did kill their cows or sheep. Often acceptable proof, or even the carcass itself, is lacking. On the other hand, these ranchers graze their cattle on public lands at very low cost and should be willing to endure an occasional loss to continue enjoying what would still be a highly favorable financial arrangement.

9. Some concerned local residents believe that wolves in Yellowstone will kill people as well as cattle. Montana senator

Conrad Burns has warned that "there'll be a dead child within a year" after wolves are reintroduced to Yellowstone. In fact, wolves seldom attack human beings, and the attacks that do occur are very rarely serious. Attacks by bison, animals with no reputation whatever for ferocity, would continue to pose a far greater danger to visitors even if wolves were brought back to the park in large numbers.

10.   The conflict pitting the interests of modern ranching and recreation against those who want to preserve remnants of the great wilderness that once was North America is far more bitter than it needs to be. Sensible wildlife management can assure that wolves and human beings share one of the last great natural areas on earth. Our willingness to coexist with our fellow species is being tested by the controversy over reintroduction of wolves in Yellowstone. Support for the wolf is a small but important symbol of our commitment to the planet.

Understanding argument helps people make up their own minds about issues and solve practical problems. Argument also entails trying to change the views of audiences that may be supportive, neutral, or even hostile. Facts and personal preferences are not arguable, but inferences (interpretations of facts) and judgments (evaluations based on ideals or philosophical beliefs) are. In spoken argument, vague claims, contradictions, and informality are acceptable, but written argument calls for formal word choice, clear organization, detailed support, and high standards of correctness. Written arguments include a wide range of forms: essays, research papers, editorials, letters to the editor, columns, and op-ed features. To understand an oral argument, a critical listener prepares carefully, predicting main ideas and taking his or her own views into account. Similarly, a critical reader prepares to study an argument by getting an overview of difficult material, raising questions, and predicting what the argument will be about. Then he or she reads to find answers to the questions, evaluates opposing viewpoints, and draws conclusions.

CHAPTER EXERCISE

I. MATCHING

Directions: Match each term in the list below with its definition by writing the correct letter in the space provided. Some of the terms on the list will not be used.

TERMS:

A. argument
B. digression
C. editorial
D. essay
E. fact
F. inference
G. judgment
H. op-ed

I. overview
J. personal preference
K. rationalization
L. report
M. research paper
N. slanting
O. thesis
P. verification

DEFINITIONS:

_____ 1. the process of making a point and trying to convince others that it is worthy of belief

_____ 2. the process of tricking ourselves into finding reasons to justify what we want to believe

_____ 3. an item of information that can be proven true

_____ 4. the process of confirming that a fact is true

_____ 5. an opinion based on an individual's tastes

_____ 6. an interpretation of one or more facts

_____ 7. an evaluation based on ideals or philosophical beliefs

_____ 8. a short work of nonfiction expressing a personal viewpoint

_____ 9. material that is off the subject

_____10. a statement of the main idea of an essay or speech

_____11. a long formal paper which supports a thesis and is based on a variety of sources

_____12. a paper that does not necessarily support a thesis but presents information based on sources

_____13. a short argumentative essay presenting a newspaper's views on a controversial issue

II. MULTIPLE CHOICE

Directions: On the line at the left write the letter of the phrase that best completes each item.

_____14. The best approach to take when presenting an argument to a hostile audience is to

A. renew the group's commitment to a common purpose.

B. show that you have reasons for your views and try to win the audience's respect.

C. ridicule the prejudices that prevent the audience from listening carefully to your views.

_____15. The following are arguable:

A. inferences and judgments.

B. reports and letters.

C. facts and personal preferences.

_____16. The aims of studying argument include learning to

A. avoid falling for poorly constructed arguments.

B. intimidate other people.

C. justify what we want to believe.

_____17. A research paper is similar to a report in that both of them

A. are merely a matter of stringing quotations together.

B. involve wide reading and evaluation of sources.

C. are short papers that do not rely on outside sources.

_____18. Unlike spoken arguments, written arguments are more likely to include

A. vague or unsupported ideas.

B. informal word choice, including slang.

C. formal transitional words.

_____19. Critical listening does not include

A. belittling a speaker's ideas, especially when he or she does not support a thesis with convincing evidence.

B. preparing ahead of time by reading related material and making predictions about what a speaker will say.

C. making conscientious, impartial judgments after evaluating both sides of an issue.

_____20. A good approach to analyzing a difficult argument is to

A. make up your mind to read it only once, very slowly and carefully.

B. try to think of support the author could provide for a thesis and then look to see if he or she has done so.

C. start by reading it very slowly and carefully, looking up every word you don't know and jotting down notes on the definitions.

2

Models for Argument

The editorial in today's Daily Express *arguing that colleges and universities must raise tuition 5 percent has made you very angry. You can't afford another tuition hike yourself, and you're sure many people like you would stop attending college altogether if tuition were increased. You believe that forcing people away from college would be very short-sighted: Won't that hurt the state's economy in the long run? You sit down at your computer determined to write a letter to the editor. But what form should your argument take?*

Your problem, constructing an effective argument, has concerned writers and speakers for centuries. Since the time of the ancient Greeks, philosophers have tried to discover properties shared by all arguments. They reasoned that if they could identify the forms that sound (flawless) arguments must take, independent of their subject matter, they would have a powerful tool for judging whether any argument was convincing or not. These forms would provide models for constructing new arguments as well as ways to test existing ones.

THE CLASSICAL TRADITION

In 399 B.C. the Greek philosopher Socrates (c. 469–399 B.C.) was put on trial in Athens for not believing in the gods and for teaching young people not to believe in them either. The proposed penalty was death.

Socrates believed it was his mission to find the wisest man on earth. He thought if he could determine who was wisest, that person could tell him how to live a good life. So he questioned men with reputations for wisdom, invariably discovering that they weren't as wise as they thought they were. Socrates concluded that he himself was wisest because he didn't know anything and knew he didn't, while everyone he questioned didn't know anything but thought he did. This strategy made Socrates extremely unpopular.

Socrates' question and answer technique is called Socratic dialogue in his honor. Socratic dialogue is not only a teaching method but also one of the oldest models for argument. Socrates was so skillful at asking just the right questions that he often led his opponents into making contradictory statements, either convincing them to change their original positions or, just as often, making them angry.

Socrates' trial was very unlike a modern court trial in that ancient Greece had no professional judges or lawyers. The jury that decided his case consisted of about 500 Athenian citizens chosen by a kind of lottery. The trial began with Socrates' accusers stating their case. Then Socrates presented his defense. Afterward, the jury voted and, by a narrow margin, found him guilty. In a second vote they condemned him to death. Socrates' ideas ultimately triumphed: *The Apology*, a book by his pupil Plato (c. 427–347 B.C.) which recreates Socrates' speeches to the jury, is a great work of literature that is still influential today. Its title may seem to suggest that Socrates apologized for his behavior, but *apology* in this sense means "defense"; thus Plato's book presents an explanation and justification of Socrates' life and ideas. Besides expressing Socrates' views in *The Apology*, Plato wrote about his own philosophical ideas, some of which were critical of the Athenian democracy, the form of government responsible for the death of his teacher.

Civil cases in ancient Greece, in which one person sued another over a plot of land or a goat, worked in much the same way as Socrates' trial. Every Greek man who found himself in court (Greek women took no part in legal proceedings) had to act as his own lawyer. Because the ability to argue convincingly was very valuable, some professional teachers called Sophists charged high fees to teach people how to win their cases, whether or not they were in the right.

DISTINGUISHING BETWEEN INDUCTION AND DEDUCTION

Along with devising answers to practical questions about how to argue effectively in court, the ancient Greeks studied argument from a philosophical point of view. One of their important contributions was distinguishing between two contrasting ways of drawing conclusions: induction and deduction.

Induction

Students in basic philosophy classes are often startled when their instructor asks them why they believe the sun will rise tomorrow. When they answer, "Because it has always risen in the past," they have performed an act of **induction**, the process by which we reach general conclusions based on particular facts, examples, or other information. To decide whether or not the sun will rise, the students drew a conclusion about the future based on what happened in the past.

Induction is common to both human beings and other animals. The British philosopher Bertrand Russell (1872–1970) gives the example of a chicken that has always been fed by the same person. When the chicken sees that person coming, it expects food. Unfortunately for the chicken, one day the person comes along and, instead of feeding it, wrings its neck. This illustrates that conclusions based on inductive reasoning are only probable, never certain. The frequent occurrence of an event in the past is not proof that it will occur again in the future. Nevertheless, the more times it has occurred in the past, the more likely it is to occur again when conditions are similar.

THE SCIENTIFIC METHOD

Arguments based on induction are familiar and convincing because most people have been exposed to the scientific method, a systematic approach to knowledge that involves testing a **hypothesis** (a tentative assumption) by collecting evidence. When a great deal of trustworthy supporting evidence is found, the hypothesis is judged likely to be true and is reclassified as a theory or law. Respect for this way by which scientists pursue new knowledge has built confidence in the inductive approach—the support of a general idea by collecting an abundance of evidence.

Although the general conclusions presented in persuasive writing have often been reached through induction, they are not necessarily given last. Instead, main points are often presented early in articles and essays and at the beginnings of paragraphs. The material that follows is the specific evidence upon which the generalizations were based.

EVALUATING INDUCTIVE REASONING

Good persuasive writing depends on strong links between specific details and the generalizations they support. We evaluate an inductive argument by examining these links. When there is enough specific support, and we regard it as typical of all the support that could be provided, we conclude that the argument is sound. On the other hand, if the evidence offered in an inductive argument does not seem characteristic of all the possible evidence or if a writer has not provided clear links between the evidence and the conclusions, we rightly distrust the argument. Inductive reasoning is especially prone to the error of ignoring conflicting information. Someone who is seeking support for a particular point of view may find it all too easy to locate that support despite an abundance of evidence to the contrary.

Deduction

The ancient Greeks were not wholly satisfied with inductive reasoning. They wanted to believe that ideas could be proven true—that they could make statements to which there were no possible exceptions. Some Greeks excelled in mathematics and were delighted with the idea that mathematical statements (such as $1 + 1 = 2$) were true in all circumstances. But statements about numbers, while interesting, did not give them sufficient scope to make as many true statements about daily life as they wished to.

SYLLOGISMS

Socrates' student Plato had a student of his own named Aristotle (384–322 B.C.), who also became a famous philosopher. Aristotle thought he had solved the problem of making true statements about the real world by using syllogisms. A **syllogism** is a concise form of argument in which two statements lead logically to a third statement, called a conclusion. The first two statements in a syllogism are **premises**, sentences which state points that are the basis for a conclusion. If a syllogism is correctly written, and its premises are true, then its conclusion must be true. The process of drawing conclusions from the relationship between premises is called **deduction**. In a way, induction and deduction are opposites: induction moves from specific statements to a general conclusion while deduction moves from general statements to a specific conclusion.

Modern students of logic have reduced Aristotle's twelve kinds of syllogisms to four, of which we are discussing only the most important type here. The most famous of all syllogisms consists of the following statements about Aristotle's teacher's teacher, Socrates:

All men are mortal.

Socrates is a man.

(Therefore) Socrates is mortal.

The first statement, "All men are mortal," is called the **major premise** because it is the more general of the two statements used as the basis of the argument. In a correctly written syllogism, the major premise contains the word or words in the predicate (the last part) of the syllogism's conclusion ("mortal"). The second statement, "Socrates is a man," is called the **minor premise**; it is a more specific statement, here an assertion about a specific individual. The minor premise contains the grammatical subject of the conclusion ("Socrates"). "Socrates is mortal" is the **conclusion**; it is the part of the syllogism that follows logically from the premises. If the premises are true, the conclusion must also be true.

The syllogism about Socrates is illustrated in the following diagram, in which the largest circle represents the largest category ("mortal"). The second category, "all men," is represented as a smaller circle within the larger one because the category of all men is part of the larger category of mortals. The smallest circle, Socrates, fits inside the circle "all men" because the syllogism asserts that Socrates is included within that category. Taken together, the three circles illustrate that if the Socrates circle belongs inside the "all men" circle, it must also belong inside the "mortal" circle:

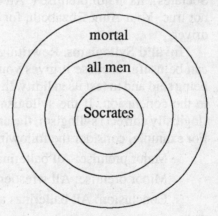

The syllogism about Socrates' mortality contains three terms—men (or man), mortal, and Socrates. **Terms** are the grammatical subjects or predicates of the statements in a syllogism. In a correctly written syllogism each term appears twice. The proper arrangement of terms in this syllogism can be shown by giving them letters:

men/man = A

mortal = B

Socrates = C

The syllogism can then appear in the following form:

Major premise: All A's are B's.

Minor premise: All C's are A's.

Conclusion: All C's are B's.

Referring to Socrates (one person) as "All C's" may seem strange but becomes easier to accept if we think of Socrates as a class or group of people consisting of only one member.

Unsound Syllogisms. Arranging an argument into a syllogism does not prove its conclusion is correct unless the premises are true. Suppose you are riding to work with your friend Alfred and the car in front of you is going so slowly that other drivers are passing it on the right. You notice that the creeping car is being driven by one of your neighbors, a retired man named Gil. Alfred turns to you and says, "Old people should have their licenses taken away! Then guys like him wouldn't be cluttering up the roads." Alfred's comment can be expressed as a syllogism:

All old people (A) are bad drivers (B).

Gil (C) is an old person (A).

Gil (C) is a bad driver (B).

This syllogism is in proper form (the same form as the syllogism about Socrates). Its major premise ("All old people are bad drivers"), however, is not true. Your Aunt Elizabeth, for example, is eighty-two and an excellent driver.

Invalid Syllogisms. Rewriting an argument in the form of a syllogism can be useful because it gives you a chance to determine what is actually being said and to test its validity. In a **valid** syllogism the premises must lead to the conclusion. If the syllogism does not follow the pattern of a valid (logically correct) syllogism, the argument is invalid (not logically correct). For example, consider the following invalid argument:

Major premise: All ballerinas wear tights.

Minor premise: All wrestlers wear tights.

Conclusion: All ballerinas are wrestlers.

This argument is invalid because many kinds of people wear tights besides ballerinas and wrestlers, as the following diagram indicates:

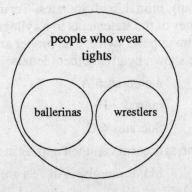

The ballerinas and wrestlers are not overlapping groups. This argument follows an invalid pattern:

> All A's are B's.
>
> All C's are B's.
>
> (Therefore) All C's are A's.

You can reject the conclusion of a syllogism such as this one without entering into debates over the differences between ballerinas and wrestlers because you know that if the form of an argument is invalid, so is its conclusion.

Enthymemes. A syllogism in which one of the premises or the conclusion is not stated is called an **enthymeme**. Enthymemes are common in informal arguments. For example, suppose one of your friends says, "Roberta's a northerner. You can't expect her to appreciate barbecued ribs." The major premise of this argument is implied rather than stated directly. Filling out the enthymeme results in the following syllogism:

> Unexpressed major premise: A northerner can't appreciate barbecued ribs.
>
> Minor premise: Roberta is a northerner.
>
> Conclusion: Roberta can't appreciate barbecued ribs.

Stating the major premise enables you to judge whether or not you consider it convincing.

EXERCISE 1

Directions: Fill in the missing terms in the syllogisms below.

Example:

All members of the Redstone Chamber of Commerce are local business people.

Marta is a member of the Redstone Chamber of Commerce.

Marta is a local business person.

1. All the fourth graders are learning to play musical instruments.

Juan is a fourth grader.

Juan_____.

2. All the quilts with the double wedding ring pattern are hand-made.

This quilt _____.

This quilt is handmade.

Directions: On the lines below write the premises that are not expressed in the following enthymemes.

Example:

Willow High School's sex education courses are worthwhile. They urge abstinence from sexual intercourse before marriage.

Unexpressed premise: <u>Sex education courses that urge abstinence from sexual intercourse before marriage are worthwhile.</u>

3. Louise is sophisticated. She's traveled abroad several times.

Unexpressed premise _____

_____

4. Naturally Martin drinks too much. Everybody in fraternities drinks too much.

Unexpressed premise_____

_____

5. Sammy is divorced. Of course he's a lonely person.

Unexpressed premise_____

_____

Although deductive reasoning is often helpful, not all arguments can be reduced to syllogisms. In real-life arguments, induction and deduction often occur together, each method supporting the other.

UNDERSTANDING STEPHEN TOULMIN'S IDEAS ABOUT ARGUMENT

For many centuries European students of logic did little more than refine Aristotle's methods. Only in the last 100 years have philosophers moved slowly away from methods inherited from the ancient Greeks. The British philosopher Stephen Toulmin (b. 1922) wrote a book published in 1958 called *The Uses of Argument.* In it he presents a model for analyzing arguments that strikes many modern thinkers as more useful and flexible than classical argument.

Toulmin's Model

Toulmin uses the labels claim, data (or grounds), and warrant to describe arguments. A **claim** is an arguable statement, and **data** are evidence used to support a claim. A **warrant** is a general statement that provides a link between the data and the claim.

Toulmin proposes the following basic model:

DATA ———┬——— *so* CLAIM
                        since

WARRANT

Here is a simple argument diagrammed according to Toulmin's model:

DATA ————┬———— CLAIM

Grass can require as much as eighteen gallons of water per square foot during the growing season	*so* owners of lawns should switch to ground cover, wildflowers, trees, and wood chips.

WARRANT

since

people should conserve water.

QUALIFIERS

Real-life arguments aren't usually as simple as this diagram suggests. Toulmin points out that in real life, claims are often qualified. A **qualifier**, a word such as *probably* or *many*, limits the scope of a claim. The addition of a qualifier can make a claim more believable. For example, the claim "Campus police should carry guns" ignores the fact that some campus police are not fully trained in the use of firearms. Therefore, the qualified claim "Most campus police should carry guns" or even "Some campus police should carry guns" would enlist more support.

TRY IT OUT

Try your hand at qualifying the claims below by selecting appropriate qualifiers from the following list. A qualifier may be used more than once.

almost certainly	often
apparently	presumably
appear(s) to	probably
frequently	seem(s) to
main	sometimes
many	somewhat
most	usually

Example: High schools do not <u>appear to</u> equip graduates with the job skills they need.

1. _____ no decision deserves more careful thought than the decision to have a baby.

2. Opening mail to search for illegal drugs _____ violates a basic right to privacy.

3. A parent should _____ not alter a child's diet without consulting a doctor.

4. _____ anthropologists today lack confidence in their ability to examine other cultures objectively.

5. A child's popularity does not _____ have much effect on his or her happiness as an adult.

6. Hate groups _____ abuse the constitutional right to free speech.

7. Serious eating disorders _____ cannot be overcome without medical help.

8. The present system of campaign financing is _____ ineffective.

9. The _____ quality travelers need is the ability to adapt to the unpredictable.

10. The Muslim religion today _____ has the power both to unite the Arab world and to divide it.

RESTRICTIONS

Some claims also have **restrictions**, statements of conditions under which they do not apply. For example, the claim "Owners of lawns should switch to ground cover, wildflowers, or trees and wood chips" might contain the restriction "unless water is plentiful in their region of the country."

BACKING

Toulmin also shows that warrants may require **backing**, support that convinces people to accept them. The warrant in the argument about lawns ("People should conserve water") is backed by ample experience of the great inconvenience and even danger that water shortages can cause.

A model of the argument about lawns might look like this with the addition of a qualifier, restriction, and backing:

DATA ——————— CLAIM

| Grass can require as much as eighteen gallons of water per square foot during the growing season | *so* owners of lawns should *probably* (**qualifier**) switch to ground cover, wildflowers, or trees and wood chips *unless* water is plentiful in their region of the country. (**restriction**) |

WARRANT

since

people should conserve water

because

water shortages cause great inconvenience and
even danger to a community. (**backing**)

Applying Toulmin's Model

Toulmin's model can help us understand the structure of many real-life arguments. For example, suppose that because Amalya has been late for work every day this week, she suggests to a group of friends that the speed limit on the highway between her home and job should be raised to sixty-five miles an hour from the present limit of fifty-five. As evidence, she mentions that the engineers who designed the road planned it to be safe at sixty-five miles an hour. She also remarks that slower truck traffic means higher transportation costs for consumer goods. Finally, she has recently seen a newspaper survey showing that most drivers support faster speed limits. Set up according to Toulmin's model, her argument would look like this:

DATA——————— CLAIM

| Engineers who designed the road planned it to be safe at sixty-five mph, slower truck traffic means higher transportation costs for consumer goods, and most drivers support faster speed limits, | *so* the speed limit on the Coast Highway should be raised to sixty-five mph. |

Suppose that when Amalya says, "You know, the state government should raise the speed limit on the Coast Highway to sixty-five," Curtis answers, "That's the worst idea I've heard today." Curtis knows she's right about how the road was designed and about transportation costs. He's also seen the newspaper survey, so he can't dispute that. In fact, Curtis accepts all Amalya's data. Because Curtis accepts the data and still disputes the claim, he must disagree with the warrant. Like many warrants, the warrant for this argument was not expressed. Stated, it would be something like, "For economy and convenience, highway speed limits should be set as high as possible."

"What if fifty people a year die in traffic accidents because of the higher speed limit?" Curtis asks. "Is that acceptable?"

"No," Amalya answers, "but who says fifty people a year would die?"

"How about if one person dies?" asks Curtis. "Is that acceptable?" Curtis is disputing the warrant underlying Amalya's argument by suggesting that safety should be a more important consideration in setting highway speed limits than economy and convenience.

Toulmin's model provides a general framework within which to think about arguments like this one. A closer examination of his key concepts of claim and warrant provides a good practical basis for an analysis of persuasive writing. (Data will be discussed in chapter 3.)

More About Claims

A claim is an arguable statement that often appears in the form of a thesis, a clear expression of an argument's main idea. A thesis statement usually appears toward the beginning of a written argument so that readers will find it easy to see how the evidence the writer presents supports the claim. Because a claim is also the conclusion of an argument—the point that the writer has been trying to prove—it often appears (expressed in different words) in the conclusion as well.

Claims can be divided into three types: claims of fact, claims of value, and claims of policy.

CLAIMS OF FACT

Many facts are easily verified; all people have to do is look them up. Suppose, for example, that you disagree with a friend about the location of Timbuktu. (You say it's in Africa; your friend claims it's an imaginary city.) Instead of arguing, you go to an encyclopedia and look up the answer: it turns out that Timbuktu is a city in Mali, a country in Africa.

However, some statements that seem factual have not yet been proven either true or false. They require either more data or more thorough analysis to establish whether they are true or not. These **claims of fact** are arguable statements about information that can be proven true or false. But unlike straightforward factual statements, claims of fact are difficult to verify. For example, in 1905 a fierce epidemic of yellow fever erupted in Panama. The United States had begun building the Panama Canal in 1902, and American health officials were already on the scene. They made the claim of fact that the germ causing yellow fever was carried by mosquitoes. At the time, many people thought this idea was ridiculous. They not only argued against the claim but actually tore the screens from doors and windows to show their contempt for it. Only after strong measures were taken to control mosquitoes and the epidemic ended was the claim widely accepted.

Some statements about the future, such as "The temperature will hit ninety today," are not likely to be good subjects for argument because all we need to do is wait to find out if they are true or not. Unless we must make a decision based on the temperature, we are usually content to wait and see.

In other cases we simply cannot afford to wait. A bad outcome may be inevitable *unless* we take action. For example, the stringent building codes in California cities are based on the claim of fact that a major earthquake will take place there sometime in the near future.

CLAIMS OF VALUE

If someone says that bubble gum is her favorite flavor of ice cream, she is expressing a personal preference that is not arguable. But some statements that express preferences can be argued. They are classified as claims of value. In a **claim of value**, a writer or speaker makes a judgment about whether something is good or bad, right or wrong, or worthwhile or not worthwhile and asks other people to share that belief. Someone who says "Watching baseball on television is a waste of time" is making a claim of value.

People who argue about claims of value need to answer two questions:

1. What are the standards by which we can judge something?
2. Does this particular example measure up to the standards we have agreed upon?

Someone wishing to argue that watching baseball on television is a waste of time needs to establish standards by which we can judge whether or not a particular activity is a waste of time. He might argue, for example, that any activity is a waste of time which does not improve a person either mentally, morally, or physically and that watching baseball does none of these things. A person who wishes to dispute this claim might attack these standards, perhaps arguing that they are too narrow ("Self-improvement isn't the only important goal in life").

On the other hand, if both sides accept the standards, the side disputing the claim must show that watching baseball on TV meets these standards. Perhaps he might argue that baseball improves people mentally by helping them relax so they can return to more important tasks with renewed alertness and enthusiasm.

CLAIMS OF POLICY

A person making a **claim of policy** is arguing that something should either be done or not done, for instance, that a company should install new equipment to improve productivity. Arguing a claim of policy involves first convincing people that the prevailing situation is bad or could be improved. Next, it requires showing that the suggested remedy will improve matters.

One kind of claim often shades into another, making it difficult to tell them apart. A claim of value such as "Watching baseball on television is a waste of time" suggests a claim of policy: "People shouldn't spend so much time watching baseball on television."

Notice that thesis statements are sometimes made up of two or more different types of claims. For example, the thesis "Public libraries are a precious resource for our citizens and should be protected from budget cuts, even when money is tight" is both a claim of value and a claim of policy.

EXERCISE 2

Directions: Each of the sentences below is a claim (a thesis). Classify each claim by using the following code:

$$F = \text{claim of fact}$$
$$V = \text{claim of value}$$
$$P = \text{claim of policy}$$

Example:

__P__   Our state should drop out of the nationwide English and mathematics testing program.

_____ 1. The city council should budget money to repair existing pools and recreation facilities before building new ones.

_____ 2. Careful copies of fine antique furnishings are as beautiful as the antiques themselves.

_____ 3. Federal laws restricting pornography will be passed this year.

_____ 4. The FCC ought to prevent stations from advertising junk food on television shows aimed at children.

_____ 5. The county court system should be provided with more space for courtrooms.

_____ 6. A pregnant woman who drinks any alcoholic beverages can harm her unborn child.

_____ 7. The city council ought to pass a regulation that prevents local high school students from parking in front of residents' homes.

_____ 8. Ancient Greek coins are miniature masterpieces of classical art.

_____ 9. Friendships between women make their lives more rewarding.

_____ 10. The interstate highway system encouraged the growth of
suburbs, spurred the development of the trucking industry,
and increased air pollution.

More About Warrants

In every argument certain basic beliefs underlie the claims of both sides.
For example, in a discussion of capital punishment, both sides are committed
to the belief that human life is precious. To someone who does not accept
this fundamental premise, capital punishment would not be worth arguing
about; there would be no point to preserving the lives of people convicted
of murder, avenging their victims, or deterring future murders if life itself
was not valuable.

Basic assumptions called warrants provide necessary connections between claims and the data that support them. Toulmin refers to a warrant as
a "bridge" because it links a claim and its support, just as a bridge links one
bank of a river to the other. Warrants are broad, general ideas that apply in
a number of situations, and they are usually accepted without proof. Here is
a model for one side of an argument about the ethics of undercover police
operations:

DATA ——————— CLAIM

Some people are induced to commit crimes they would not have committed had the police not led them into temptation,	*so* the government should not permit police officers conducting undercover operations to trick people into committing crimes

WARRANT

since

police officers should be held to a high standard of honesty.

This warrant, the assumption that police officers should be held to a high
standard of honesty, is one that most people share.

Sometimes not one but several warrants underlie an argument. For
instance, the claim "Families should be limited by law to no more than two
children" is based on assumptions about the undesirability of increased
population and the desirability of involving government in family planning.

STATED WARRANTS

Thomas Jefferson clearly states his warrants toward the beginning of
the Declaration of Independence:

> We hold these truths to be self-evident, that all men are created
> equal, that they are endowed by their creator with certain
> unalienable Rights, that among these are Life, Liberty and the
> pursuit of Happiness.

Jefferson's truths are strong warrants, assumptions that readers are likely to accept easily. Warrants are strong if they are relevant to the claims they support and logically consistent with them.

As is true of all parts of an argument, a warrant is stronger if it is chosen with the convictions of the audience in mind. For example, most people on both sides in the debate over the death penalty believe that cruel and unusual punishment is morally wrong, making this idea an effective foundation for an argument. However, a warrant may not be shared by all readers. George III, the King of England at the time of the American Revolution, almost certainly would not have accepted Jefferson's idea that all men were created equal. But Jefferson was not writing the Declaration of Independence to convince George III; his intended audiences were residents of the American colonies, open-minded English citizens, and inhabitants of neutral countries such as France.

Arguments in which the two sides do not accept each other's warrants, or even realize what they are, usually lead nowhere. It is far better to discuss the warrants directly and come to some kind of consensus on them if possible than to argue at cross purposes. If you believe that your readers may not share your basic values and beliefs, stating your warrants directly should strengthen your argument.

UNSTATED WARRANTS

Most of the time warrants are not supported or even stated directly because writers assume that everyone (or almost everyone) already agrees with them. Sometimes a writer may not even be conscious of the assumptions that form the basis for his or her argument. This is especially likely when the hidden assumptions behind a claim are **stereotypes**, oversimplified generalizations based on insufficient evidence. People often base their thinking on unexamined stereotypes about gender roles or nationalities. **Ethnocentrism**, the assumption that the values of one's own culture apply throughout the world, can also lead to flawed arguments. For example, the claim that women are safer drivers than men would be meaningless to many Saudi Arabians, who believe that women should not be permitted to drive. The warrant behind the claim that women are safer drivers than men is that all trained, responsible adults should be allowed to drive; this is accepted in most of the world's cultures, but not all.

When the basic assumptions behind an argument are unflattering to its author or even dishonorable, he or she may intentionally conceal them. Part of your challenge as a critical thinker and writer is to explore the largely unacknowledged assumptions at the heart of many arguments. Unfortunately, such assumptions are easier to spot in other people's arguments than in your own. However, identifying the basic beliefs that underlie your argument will help you make sure that they would stand up to examination.

EXERCISE 3

   Directions: Match the claims below to the warrants on which they are based by writing the letters where they belong in the spaces at the left. In each case choose the best warrant. Some of the warrants on the list will not be used.

Example:

 __G__ Older children should not be obligated to discipline their
           younger brothers and sisters.

Warrants

   A. People who risk their lives to preserve law and order deserve
        special legal safeguards.

   B. In the United States the issue of race cannot be ignored.

   C. Human beings are more important than other animals.

   D. The more independent a country is the better.

   E. People deserve equal treatment under the law.

   F. Art should challenge people, not merely make predictable ap-
        peals to their emotions.

   G. Parents have the main responsibility for controlling their
        children.

   H. The government should not interfere with people's basic rights.

   I. Educated people should be well rounded.

   J. Freedom of the press is a basic human right.

   K. People should be encouraged to own their own homes.

   L. The environment should be protected.

   M. Exercise is good for people.

Claims

 _____ 1. Before industrial sites can be sold, official evaluation of
           potential environmental damage should be mandatory.

 _____ 2. First-time home buyers deserve special tax breaks.

 _____ 3. All college students should be required to take several
           liberal arts courses.

 _____ 4. The United States should not depend on oil produced in
           other countries.

 _____ 5. There are moral, scientific, and practical reasons for con-
           tinuing to experiment on animals.

 _____ 6. White-collar criminals should be given the severe sentences
           they deserve.

_____ 7. A person convicted of killing a police officer deserves the death penalty.

_____ 8. Many of the works of art in the City Museum's current show are shallow and sentimental.

_____ 9. The state department of transportation should encourage bicycling by paving highway shoulders.

_____10. High school newspapers should not be subject to censorship by teachers, principals, or school boards.

The Greek philosophers Socrates (c. 469–399 B.C.), Plato (c. 427–347 B.C.), and Aristotle (384–322 B.C.) established influential models for the study of argument. The Greeks distinguished between two ways of drawing conclusions, induction and deduction. Induction is the process of drawing general conclusions based on particular facts, examples, or other evidence, and deduction is the process of drawing conclusions from the relationships between premises. Deductive arguments usually take the form of syllogisms.

Modern philosophers have developed new ways of thinking about arguments. Stephen Toulmin (b. 1922) proposed a model that includes a claim (an arguable statement), data (evidence to support the claim), a warrant (a link between the data and the claim), a qualifier (a limitation of the claim), restrictions (exceptions), and backing (support for the warrant). Claims can be classified as claims of fact, claims of value, or claims of policy.

CHAPTER EXERCISE

I. MATCHING

Directions: Match each term on the list below with its definition by writing the correct letter in the space provided. Some of the terms on the list will not be used.

TERMS:

A. backing	H. hypothesis
B. bias	I. induction
C. claim	J. major and minor premises
D. data	K. qualifier
E. deduction	L. restriction
F. enthymeme	M. stereotype
G. ethnocentrism	N. syllogism

O. terms   Q. warrant

P. valid

DEFINITIONS:

_____ 1. drawing conclusions based on specific examples

_____ 2. drawing conclusions based on the relationships between two premises

_____ 3. a tentative assumption

_____ 4. an argument arranged in the form of two premises and a conclusion

_____ 5. sentences in a syllogism which state points that are the basis for a conclusion

_____ 6. logically correct

_____ 7. a syllogism with a missing part

_____ 8. an arguable statement

_____ 9. evidence used to support a claim

_____10. general assumption that links a claim and its supporting data

_____11. word such as *probably* that limits a claim

_____12. support for a warrant

_____13. statement of a condition under which a claim does not apply

_____14. oversimplified generalizations based on insufficient evidence

_____15. assuming that the values of one's own group apply everywhere

II. MULTIPLE CHOICE

Directions: On the line at the left write the letter of the phrase that best completes each item.

_____16. The Greek philosopher Aristotle

    A. included warrants, restrictions, and backing in his model for argument.

    B. was condemned to death for teaching young people the principles of argument.

    C. used the syllogism as a concise way of expressing a logical argument.

_____17. The scientific method

    A. is a form of deductive argument.

    B. was introduced in Plato's *Apology*.

    C. involves testing a hypothesis by collecting evidence.

_____18. The Toulmin model for analyzing arguments

    A. demonstrates what is wrong with relying on specific evidence.

    B. includes claims, data, and warrants.

    C. is based on premises and conclusions.

_____19. A syllogism is unsound if one or more of its premises are

    A. not true.

    B. unstated.

    C. specific.

_____20. The three kinds of claims are

    A. claims of fact, claims of value, and claims of policy.

    B. major claims, minor claims, and concluding claims.

    C. qualifications, restrictions, and backing.

3

Supporting and Attacking

You are strolling down the street one sunny afternoon when a complete stranger approaches you and whispers, "Hey, want a hot tip on the fifth race at Breezy Park today?"

You have never bet on a horse race in your life and don't intend to start now. Moreover, you suspect he might be about to offer his so-called "hot tip" in exchange for cold cash. Instead he continues, "Baby Doll's a sure thing. If you don't take all the money out of your bank account and bet it on Baby Doll to win, you'll be sorry for the rest of your life. Trust me." And, having patted your arm reassuringly, he walks away.

This accommodating stranger has made a claim of policy ("You should bet your life savings on Baby Doll in the fifth"), but he has given you no reason whatsoever to act on it.

UNDERSTANDING DATA

People make unsupported claims all the time ("Sudso Powder is the most powerful clothes detergent you can buy," "Cats are perfect pets," "We should vote for Wilson Weddington"), but in a well-constructed argument, claims must be supported. You can support claims by providing data (also called evidence): facts, examples, statistics, and expert testimony.

Facts

Although many facts are easily verified and therefore don't make good claims, they can be used to support claims. The more widely accepted a fact is, the greater its value as support. In an argument about gun control, for example, well-informed people on both sides of the issue would regard the following statements as facts:

1. The Second Amendment to the U. S. Constitution states, "A well regulated Militia, being necessary to the security of a free State, the right of the people to keep and bear Arms, shall not be infringed."

2. In the 1939 case *U.S. v. Miller*, the U. S. Supreme Court ruled unanimously that only people on active duty in a militia have the constitutional right to bear arms.

3. The earliest gun-control laws in the United States were passed in the South during the decades following the Civil War.

One or all of these facts could be used to support several different claims about gun control, but people on both sides of the argument, whether or not they accept a particular claim, would accept the facts themselves.

Examples

Closely related to facts are examples (specific illustrations of more general points). The following are examples illustrating the fact that the earliest gun-control laws in the United States were passed in the South after the Civil War:

1. In 1870 Tennessee passed a law banning the sale of all but the most expensive kind of handguns.

2. In 1893 Alabama put a heavy tax on the sale of handguns.

3. In 1902 South Carolina passed a law banning the sale of handguns to all but "sheriffs and their special deputies."

How this fact and these examples might be used to support a particular claim is shown later in this chapter under "Expert Testimony."

Hypothetical Examples

Examples cited in support of a claim are mostly drawn from real life. However, another kind of example is also useful at times. A **hypothetical example** is an incident or circumstance that did not occur but might have occurred or could occur at any time. Suppose someone is arguing in favor of allowing business people to possess handguns to defend themselves against robbers. She tells the following story:

Say you own a gas station on a highway outside of town. One morning about four o'clock, two men come in. They look suspicious, so you open the drawer behind the counter where you keep your gun. One of the men pulls a large hunting knife out of his jacket and says, "Okay, hand over all your cash." Instead, you

take your handgun out of the drawer. The two men take one look
at it and run away.

This incident never happened. You probably don't own a gas station and
may never have worked in one. Still, it's the kind of occurrence that well
might happen to someone, and the story enables you to put yourself in the
station owner's place and understand why a person who works alone late at
night might want to own a handgun.

An argument consisting entirely of hypothetical examples might leave
the audience wondering why no real-life examples could be found to support
the claim. Nevertheless, hypothetical examples are often very effective in
supporting claims in persuasive writing. For example, in a paper on gun
control your friend might express her hypothetical example in the following
form: "A gas station owner who had used a gun to fend off would-be thieves
would probably oppose more stringent gun-control laws."

STATISTICS

Statistics represent information in the form of numbers (either totals or
percentages). If a writer tried to narrate all the incidents he or she had read
about in which a person was killed accidentally with a handgun, readers
would soon grow weary. But pointing out that "last year there were eighty-
five accidental deaths in our city due to handguns" uses the cumulative
weight of all those accidental deaths to make the point without going into
unnecessary detail.

The following statistics are typical of those often cited in gun-control
arguments:

1. About 22,000 people are killed by handguns each year.

2. About 12,000 of these deaths are suicides.

3. The National Rifle Association has about 3,000,000 members.

An argument containing numerous statistics such as these can be difficult to grasp. Therefore, writers need to put statistics in context and
interpret them. For easier reading, statistics are often presented in the form
of a chart or a graph.

Including statistics in an argument offers both opportunities and pitfalls.
Statistics tend to be convincing because they're associated with science in
many people's minds; a number such as 10.797 seems precise, so readers
may find it believable without examining it closely. On the other hand,
readers uncomfortable with mathematics may skip over statistical data.
Others may have heard of Darrell Huff's book *How to Lie with Statistics*
(1954) and fear that they'll be fooled in some way.

Your attitude toward statistics should be somewhere between uncritical
acceptance and total skepticism. As a reader, you can examine the source
and meaning of statistics you're being asked to accept. And as a writer, you

can provide the information your readers need to judge your statistics accurately.

WHAT IS THE SOURCE?

In general, the more reliable the source of a statistic, the more you can trust it. Government agencies, universities, and eminent scientists, for example, are likely to publish more trustworthy statistics than companies with products to sell or special interest groups. Because some writers have been known to make up statistics to bolster their arguments (a very unethical practice), you should be very suspicious of a statistic for which no source is indicated.

HOW WERE THE DATA COLLECTED?

Many statistics are derived from surveys. Those involving large numbers of participants are usually more reliable than those involving fewer people. The samples must also be representative, that is, the individuals answering questions must be typical members of their group. Suppose, for example, someone was trying to determine how much sexual harassment occurs in a company with 6,000 workers. Asking three employees if they have ever been sexually harassed would be inadequate because the sample is too small. Asking 100 male employees between the age of forty and fifty would not lead to accurate results either because they are unlikely to represent the work force as a whole.

WHAT DO THE STATISTICS REALLY INDICATE?

Sometimes a statistic is an average figure: "In 1993 the average income of the 101 employed residents of Smithville was $60,000 a year." Statisticians use three kinds of averages, called the mean, the median, and the mode. What most people think of as the average is really the **mean**, the amount found by adding a group of numbers and dividing the sum by the number of items in the group. The mean income for all the employed residents of Smithville is found by adding all their incomes and dividing by 101. The **median**, the middle number in a series, is found by listing all their incomes in order from highest to lowest. The income of the fifty-first resident is then the median (fifty make more money than she does and fifty make less). The **mode**, the number that occurs most frequently in a group of numbers, is found by putting Smithville residents with identical incomes into groups. The income of those people in the largest group is the mode.

These three ways of computing an average can lead to very different results. Suppose four residents of Smithville are partners in the local factory while all the others work there. The six-figure incomes of the partners help bring the mean up to $60,000. The median income, however, is $29,000, while the mode (the income of the people on the assembly line) is $24,000 a year. Knowing whether the mean, the median, or the mode is being used can therefore be crucial to understanding an argument.

Expert Testimony

Often someone provides several facts, examples, or statistics and then says or writes, "The facts speak for themselves." Occasionally a fact's bearing upon an argument is self-evident, but far more often it needs to be interpreted. Interpretations can be arrived at by applying general knowledge and common sense, but for some specialized subjects we need the help of experts to interpret data correctly. **Expert testimony** consists of judgments and interpretations of data by qualified people.

Anyone can express an opinion about how he or she thinks a fact should be interpreted, but some people have studied particular issues far more carefully than others. If you had to have your appendix removed, you would most likely want a doctor to do it, and if you had your choice, you would want one who had performed many successful appendectomies in the past—a surgeon rather than a general practitioner. Similarly, if you were concerned about the effects of a new clean air act, you would probably trust the opinion of a scientist who had spent his or her life studying air pollution more than that of a shoe salesperson or a school teacher.

The fact that "the earliest gun-control laws in the United States were passed in the South during the decades following the Civil War" may not seem especially significant in an argument over whether a new handgun law should be passed. But gun-control expert Don Kates and others have used it to support their claim that gun-control laws are racially motivated. They suggest that Southern legislators wanted to keep guns out of the hands of poor blacks, making it harder for them to defend themselves against the Ku Klux Klan and other hate groups. Kates explains that the "special deputies" mentioned in the 1902 South Carolina law who could still buy guns legally were mostly members of the Ku Klux Klan. According to him, some recent gun-control laws are also racially motivated.

We can't be experts on all the subjects we write about, but fortunately when we argue, we can enlist experts on our side. Referring to authorities who support our positions can be very convincing.

Evaluating Data

The facts, examples, statistics, and expert testimony with which you support your claims should be the strongest you can find. However, when you are judging other people's arguments, examining the support for their claims will sometimes reveal surprising weaknesses. The following sections offer guidelines that should help you both strengthen the support for your own claims and detect inadequate support when you analyze the arguments of others.

EVALUATING FACTS, EXAMPLES, AND STATISTICS

Some statements presented as facts are untrue—that is, they are not facts at all but errors. A single error does not wholly invalidate an argument (how much damage it does depends on how important the statement is to the argument as a whole), but if you find one inaccuracy, such as a misspelled name, incorrect date, or dubious statistic, you may suspect that other statements presented as facts are also doubtful.

Facts, examples, and statistics should also be as up to date as possible. An argument about U. S. policy toward eastern Europe should include data drawn from recent events, not those of the 1970s and 1980s. Even if the old information is still relevant, an audience will expect to learn how developments in the last few years have affected the situation.

You should also judge whether facts, examples, and statistics are relevant to the main point of an argument. Suppose that in a discussion of airport security against terrorism, someone suggests that thorough searches of all passengers and baggage are necessary to prevent terrorists from smuggling weapons or bombs aboard planes. Another person points out that the long delays involved in truly thorough searches would make air travel intolerable. "Yes," someone else remarks, "and security searches aren't the only reasons for delays. Just last week, I flew to Denver, and air traffic was so congested . . ." Traffic congestion at airports usually has nothing to do with terrorism, so the example of the flight to Denver has no place in this argument.

EVALUATING EXPERT TESTIMONY

The first question to ask about expert testimony is whether a person whose opinions are used to bolster an argument is really an expert. Someone who has earned an advanced degree in a particular field is likely to know a great deal about it, as is a person who has written a book or series of articles on a subject.

However, sometimes people who lack the necessary qualifications pose as experts. Television commercials for over-the-counter drugs often present an actor dressed in a white coat to suggest that he or she is a doctor. (A particularly dishonest trick is to use an actor who plays a doctor in a popular daytime drama to do a commercial for aspirin, cough medicine, or a similar drug.) Often celebrities such as athletes or movie stars endorse products or political candidates. This kind of endorsement is known as a **testimonial**. When genuine experts in one field endorse products or ideas in another field, they hope that their prestige will lend additional weight to their views. Nuclear scientists, for example, are entitled to express their opinions about world peace (or any other nonscientific topic). However, their views are not more worthy of attention than those of nonscientists except on scientific subjects and may be less important than the views of people who have studied the issues involved in achieving world peace—foreign policy experts, for example.

Experts are often paid for their opinions as compensation for the years of study needed to acquire their expertise. But sometimes experts employed by people or groups seeking opinions that favor their own interests feel pressure to provide the interpretations their employers want. For example, research scientists working for the tobacco industry consistently produce reports maintaining that no relationship can be proven to exist between smoking and illnesses such as cancer, emphysema, and heart disease. As this example implies, experts are sometimes open to a charge of **conflict of interest,** a clash between an expert's responsibility to seek the truth and his or her personal benefit. Expert testimony can also be **biased**, that is, distorted by prejudice. For instance, an expert on education who hates and fears homosexuals probably could not give an objective opinion on how a particular homosexual schoolteacher was performing in a classroom.

Often the same information is interpreted very differently by different people. When the people are all experts, it can be difficult to choose which one to believe. For example, at a trial in which a defendant pleads not guilty by reason of insanity, both the defense and the prosecution call psychiatrists to the witness stand. These psychiatrists have all examined the defendant, but those called by the prosecution have concluded that he or she is sane according to the legal definition of sanity and those called by the defense that he or she is insane. At the end it's up to the members of the jury, none of whom is a psychiatrist, to decide which side's experts are interpreting the facts correctly.

One way to resolve the problem of disagreement among authorities is to compare the credentials of the experts on each side. If the better qualified experts are mostly on one side, we can presume that they are correct. However, one person may be correct even when many others with equal or better qualifications disagree. Louis Pasteur (1822–1895), for example, believed that microorganisms caused disease even when the entire medical profession believed otherwise. His theory proved to be sound, and now his views are almost universally accepted.

TRY IT OUT

Some short argumentative writing is very convincing; as you read it, you find yourself nodding in agreement, perhaps wishing that you could express yourself so effectively. Other times you may want to sharpen your pencil and get to work on a thoughtful—or scathing—response to what you have read. Try your hand at interpreting, evaluating, and perhaps responding to the following letters to the editor of a local newspaper.

PART I. MAIN IDEAS

State the main idea (claim) of each letter in a single sentence.

1. My best friend's father was killed by a drunk driver last year. She served only three months of her six month sentence and is free today. The judge was lenient with her because she had children to care for. But what about my friend? She needs her father just as much as the woman's children need their mother. In the interest of fairness we must make sure that drunk drivers who kill are given the long jail sentences they deserve.

    Claim: _____

    _____

    _____

2. What makes good students? We shouldn't pretend we don't know. The best test scores come from schools and communities where there is little educational innovation but many stable families. Students do well not where more money is spent but where homes contain newspapers, books, and parents who take the time to check homework assignments. Yes, we need dedicated, well-qualified teachers, but we don't need the expensive and wide reforms proposed this week by our governor.

    Claim: _____

    _____

    _____

3. To explain the increase in crime in this city, we need go no further than the cuts in federal funding we have experienced during the last few years. We lost more than 50 percent of the budgets of two effective crime-fighting programs, one dedicated to the treatment of drug addicts and the other to the rehabilitation of youthful offenders. If federal money had been available when we needed it, we wouldn't require the costly crime-fighting measures now being implemented.

    Claim: _____

    _____

    _____

4. I've heard enough about women's demands for equal rights. Ask the women you know. They'll tell you that what they really want is a man to make decisions for them. Women should be subject

to men in all things, especially in the home, and it's time that our everyday lives reflected this fact.

Claim: _____

_____

_____

5.   After sixteen years as a pediatrician, I can report that doctors know too well the sad facts of child abuse you reported in your recent article "Children at Risk." How ironic that large numbers of people are galvanized by the abortion controversy, yet so few dedicate themselves to the well-being of children.

Claim: _____

_____

_____

6.   Years ago I served as a Peace Corps Volunteer in Somalia. I was twenty-four. At that time I had little sense of what the world was like outside my small southern city. Yet as a volunteer I learned the crucial importance of dedication to something beyond the self. This is a life-transforming lesson young people can learn today—if we support the proposed two-year national service program. As volunteers fighting poverty, illiteracy, and poor health, young people can make a big difference. The need is urgent, yet the volunteers will surely gain more than they give.

Claim: _____

_____

_____

PART II. EVALUATION

1. Which letter did you find most persuasive? _____ Why? _____

_____

_____

2. Which letter do you think is the least effectively written? _____
Why?_____

_____

3. Which (if any) of the letters are overly simple or unnecessarily vague?_____

_____

4. Which (if any) of the letters would be more convincing if better supporting facts, examples, and statistics were added to them? _____

_____

5. Do you think any of the letters contain material that could be eliminated? _____ If so, what? _____

_____

_____

6. Is there a letter you would find more convincing if its claim were qualified or restricted in some way? _____ If so, rewrite the claim.

_____

_____

Now try writing a letter on a topic of your own choice and submitting it to a newspaper or magazine.

EXERCISE 1

Directions: Each group of statements below contains a claim (a thesis), part or all of the data supporting the claim, and a warrant (an assumption that provides a link between the claim and its support). Write the word that identifies each statement in the space at the left:

claim = claim or thesis

data = evidence or support that backs up the claim

warrant = the basic assumption that connects the claim and its support

EXAMPLE:

warrant   A. The choice of a conservative candidate is evidence of political sophistication.

data   B. Conservative candidates have been elected as mayors of large Arizona cities and as members of Congress from the state.

claim   C. In the last ten years Arizona voters have become more sophisticated politically.

_____   1A. Programs to aid poor children must become a top priority in the United States.

_____   1B. A country can be judged by the way it treats its children.

_____   1C. More than one-third of all the poor people in the United States are children.

_____   2A. Unnecessarily long delays in obtaining chest X-rays and monitoring vital signs caused the death of Warren Lee in the Cherokee County Hospital emergency room last month.

_____ 2B. Hospital emergency rooms should be equipped and administered to save lives whenever possible.

_____ 2C. Action must be taken to improve service in Cherokee County Hospital's emergency room.

_____ 3A. Rather than use chemical pesticides, gardeners should purchase and release beneficial insects to destroy pests.

_____ 3B. Pesticides are losing effectiveness as resistant strains of insects develop.

_____ 3C. Nonchemical gardening methods are preferable to chemical methods.

_____ 4A. As much as one-quarter of health-care spending by employers is due to preventable illnesses.

_____ 4B. Companies should penalize employees who have poor health habits.

_____ 4C. Companies do not have an unlimited responsibility to pay employees' medical bills.

_____ 5A. The amount of lead in imported dishes should be restricted by law.

_____ 5B. Even low levels of lead can slow a child's development and cause brain damage.

_____ 5C. The government has a responsibility to protect citizens from serious health risks.

_____ 6A. Babies deserve drug-free lives.

_____ 6B. A drug-addicted baby is born every two hours in this city.

_____ 6C. Prenatal counseling should be provided at every city-run drug treatment center.

_____ 7A. Some laws mandate the death of all pit bull terriers whether or not they have attacked anyone.

_____ 7B. Like humans, animals have the right to be considered innocent until proven guilty.

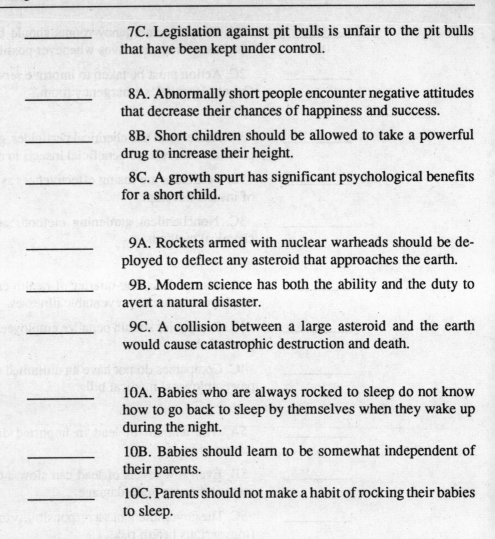

_____ 7C. Legislation against pit bulls is unfair to the pit bulls that have been kept under control.

_____ 8A. Abnormally short people encounter negative attitudes that decrease their chances of happiness and success.

_____ 8B. Short children should be allowed to take a powerful drug to increase their height.

_____ 8C. A growth spurt has significant psychological benefits for a short child.

_____ 9A. Rockets armed with nuclear warheads should be deployed to deflect any asteroid that approaches the earth.

_____ 9B. Modern science has both the ability and the duty to avert a natural disaster.

_____ 9C. A collision between a large asteroid and the earth would cause catastrophic destruction and death.

_____ 10A. Babies who are always rocked to sleep do not know how to go back to sleep by themselves when they wake up during the night.

_____ 10B. Babies should learn to be somewhat independent of their parents.

_____ 10C. Parents should not make a habit of rocking their babies to sleep.

REFUTING AN OPPONENT'S ARGUMENT

A **refutation** provides reasons for rejecting all or part of an opponent's argument. It is a way of discrediting opposing views. In some arguments one side tries to prove a claim and the other side needs only to refute it, not prove a claim of its own. A good example of this is a criminal trial in which the prosecutor provides evidence to show that the defendant is guilty. The defense attorney, meanwhile, does not need to show that another person committed the crime or even that the defendant is innocent, only that the prosecution's evidence is inadequate to prove guilt beyond a reasonable doubt. Thus, defense in a criminal trial consists entirely of refutation.

When the two sides in an argument make opposing claims ("Vote for Sheila O'Malley"; "Vote for Wilson Weddington"), refutation also plays a role ("Don't vote for my opponent because . . ."). Most readers expect written arguments of either type to state opposing viewpoints fairly and refute them convincingly. They assume that the chances of determining the truth are greater when opposing views are weighed against each other. Arguments that do not include refutation are vulnerable to the criticism that the writer is not aware of, doesn't understand, or refuses to acknowledge the other side of the case.

Some writers feel uncomfortable about attacking an opponent's views because doing so seems disagreeably close to launching a personal attack. Readers can also feel uneasy about a refutation if it appears aimed at another person rather than at his or her ideas. However, a refutation offered in a rational tone can avoid offense and contribute to a discussion's value by helping readers determine which viewpoint is the right one. An argument that has stood up to a determined attempt at refutation is almost always stronger than one that has never been challenged. As the English statesman Edmund Burke (1729–1797) put it, "He that wrestles with us strengthens our nerves, and sharpens our skill. Our antagonist is our helper." People whose views differ from our own may be our opponents, but they are not necessarily our enemies.

A person familiar with the give and take of refutation is unlikely to feel daunted by new ideas or to fall for the dubious claims of a dynamic speaker or writer. A knowledge of how sound arguments are structured can provide the clues needed to find weak points in an opponent's position. The claim itself, the data that supports it, and the assumptions behind it (the warrants) can all be criticized, as well as the manner in which the argument is presented. A number of ways to refute an opponent's argument are suggested below.

Attacking Claims

Show that your opponent's claim is vague, overstated, or self-contradictory. For example, someone might argue that all Americans are victims of crime because we are all heavily taxed to pay for police, courts, and prisons. This claim is vulnerable to criticism because the word *victim* is vague. We usually use the phrase *crime victims* to describe people who have been robbed, injured, or murdered. After hearing this objection, the person who made the original claim might alter it to the more reasonable statement that all Americans are harmed by crime to some extent.

Suggest that a claim is unreasonably broad. You can undermine an opposing claim by showing that it needs to be limited in some way. For example, to argue that all animals have the same rights as human beings would strike most readers as preposterous once you extended the argument to include microscopic animals. You could point out that the original claim should at least be restricted so that it refers to some animals or many animals, not all of them. This way of demonstrating the unreasonableness of an opponent's claim is sometimes known by its Latin name **reductio ad absurdum** (literally "reduction to absurdity"). It consists of pretending to accept a claim and then extending it to nonsensical lengths. Using *reductio ad absurdum* has its dangers, however. Any technique that appears to misrepresent or ridicule your opponent runs the risk of offending your audience.

Point out that opposing ideas are not practical. Many claims call for action of some sort; perhaps putting your opponent's claim into practice would be far too expensive or difficult. For example, someone might suggest that because nonsmokers are harmed by second-hand smoke, the government should make tobacco smoking illegal. You might grant that second-hand smoke is damaging to nonsmokers but point out that a law against all tobacco smoking would be unenforceable. Other claims can be refuted by pointing out that the motives behind them are praiseworthy, but the timing or approach is wrong.

Present your own proposal. Suppose someone suggests that citywide curfews would be a good way to reduce juvenile delinquency. You might counter by proposing that offering idle teenagers recreational or job opportunities would be more effective in combatting juvenile crime.

Attacking Support

Demonstrate that the support for your opponent's claim is inadequate, irrelevant, or untrue. Often too little evidence is provided to support a claim. For example, someone might say that Madame Ouspenskaya, his favorite fortune teller, has supernatural powers. "Why, she told me that within a year I would meet the woman of my dreams, and only eight months later I met Elizabeth, my fiancée." You might point out that one successful prediction, which may well be due to coincidence, does not add up to a very strong case for supernatural powers.

In some cases there may be plenty of data to support a claim, but some of the data are outdated or incorrect. For example, the claim that your city should build more emergency shelters for homeless people may be valid, but it cannot be adequately supported by statistics dating from 1985. The local economy may have improved since then, and there may be fewer homeless people on the streets. Or your opponent may have seriously underestimated the cost of such shelters to an already overburdened local government.

Sometimes an argument is intentionally based on falsified data, but more often inaccuracies are a matter of carelessness, not dishonesty. To help readers check, sources for any evidence that is not easily verifiable should be carefully indicated. If a writer fails to provide information about his or her sources, you can point this out in your refutation since it may mean that the facts themselves are not reliable.

Find counter examples that outweigh your opponent's. Suppose someone asserts that because women are sensitive, responsible, and warm, they naturally take better care of children than men do. He provides examples of single mothers raising happy and well-adjusted sons and daughters. In your response you can provide counter examples of men who are compassionate and responsible with children, including instances of single fathers whose offspring have achieved success comparable to that of children raised by their mothers.

Explain that your opponent has misinterpreted the data used to support his or her claim. You can show why you disagree with conclusions based on statistics and other facts or explain that information your opponent considers central to his or her argument is really trivial or meaningless. For example, if someone argues that women in the military should not be allowed to participate in armed combat because most women are physically weaker than men, you might point out that physical strength is seldom required in modern warfare.

Using the same evidence your opponent does but showing that it leads to a very different conclusion is an approach known as **turning the tables**. Suppose someone claims that because statistics show rape has increased 50 percent in your city over the past year, the police must be doing a poor job of protecting women from sexual attack. You might point out that the police force's new rape crisis unit has encouraged victims to report rapes in unprecedented numbers; according to your interpretation, the 50 percent increase in reported rapes actually represents police success in getting victims to come forward.

Point out errors in reasoning. For example, your opponent may claim that two situations are alike that you judge to be very different or suggest a connection between them that you consider dubious. Someone might argue that pupils who fail a standardized math test should repeat the fifth grade "because people who can't do their jobs in the business world are fired, not promoted, and kids have to learn that it's a cold, cruel world out there." In your refutation you could point out that the fifth grade and the business world aren't really very much alike. (Various kinds of faulty reasoning are discussed in chapter 6.)

Challenge the experts your opponent quotes in support of his or her argument. You can question how well qualified these experts are or quote equally well-qualified specialists who hold contradictory views. You can also show that the testimony of some experts is influenced by conflict of interest or bias.

Attacking Warrants

Criticize the assumptions that underlie your opponent's argument. You may be able to show that the basic principles or moral judgments that provide the foundation for the argument are wrong. For example, someone might argue that Senator Browning would make an excellent president because he is an extremely pleasant, amiable man who has many friends and few enemies, even after twenty-five years of public life. Underlying this argument is the assumption that being pleasant, amiable, and well liked are important qualifications for being president. You might suggest that this assumption, whether your opponent expresses it openly or not, is unrealistic. You might continue by saying that in the choice of a president, intelligence and distinguished public service should weigh far more heavily than a gift for friendship.

Attacking Presentations

Point out problems with your opponent's approach. This can mean indicating misjudgments in emphasis or claiming that an argument reveals a bias offensive to you and potentially to other readers. For example, someone who begins a line of argument "Any fool can see . . ." is trying to browbeat his audience while inadvertently suggesting that his case may not be as strong as he wants it to appear. The list below provides additional hints for writing refutations.

MORE TIPS ON WRITING REFUTATIONS

1. Summarize your opponent's views fairly rather than assume that your readers are familiar with them. Aim to be open-minded, honest, and courteous.

2. Be careful to do more than merely state your opponent's views. Expressing opposing views without explaining what is wrong with them reinforces your opponent's argument rather than attacks it.

3. Refute important points, not trivial details or mere slips. Concentrating your refutation on unimportant details gives the impression that you can't tell which ideas are crucial or that your opponent's argument is basically correct.

4. If some of the opposing views are convincing, acknowledge that you agree with them, up to a point. This gives your readers the impression that you're being reasonable.

5. Provide enough refutation of opposing views so that your readers won't miss it. A sentence or two is usually not enough.

6. Locate your refutation toward the beginning of your essay or toward the conclusion, so readers are more likely to notice it.

7. If your views are apt to be unpopular, be especially careful to provide a detailed, well-organized refutation of the position taken by your opponent.

8. Know your material. Successful refutation is not a matter of verbal trickery but of thoroughly understanding both sides of an issue.

EXERCISE 2

Directions: On the lines that follow each statement, suggest one or more ways you could refute it. There is no single refutation of each statement, but some possible approaches to each one are given at the back of this book.

Example:

The high crime rate today proves that parents are not strict enough with their children.

<u>Suggest other causes for the high crime rate. Explain that using the word "proves" overstates the case.</u>

<u>Give examples of strict parents who do not have law-abiding children.</u>

1. Astrology is certainly valid because my horoscope always gives me good advice.

_____

_____

2. College professors should not lecture because their lectures are always so boring and repetitive that they never teach anybody anything.

_____

_____

3. The minimum wage should be doubled immediately.

_____

_____

4. If drugs were made available to addicts at a low cost, the crime rate would go down and the power of organized crime would lessen.

_____

_____

5. Only idiots believe that car theft can be stopped.

_____

_____

6. If more people don't start participating in recycling programs, the city government should take every nonparticipant to court at once.

_____

_____

7. Our national anthem should be replaced because it is too hard to sing.

_____

_____

8. Most mothers of young children work because they believe they have the right to indulge themselves by buying luxuries with the money they earn.

_____

_____

9. Car and truck traffic should be prohibited in the central business districts of major cities.

_____

_____

10. The popular music of today is not nearly as good as the music of the fifties.

_____

_____

*S*upport for claims is made up of data: facts, examples, statistics, and expert testimony (judgments and interpretations of facts by qualified authorities). Hypothetical examples (incidents or circumstances that did not occur but might have), while less effective than real-life examples, can be very persuasive. Statistics, which present factual information in the form of numbers (totals or percentages), must be examined closely to determine their sources and their significance. Data used as support in an argument should be accurate, up to date, and relevant. Written arguments are strengthened by the inclusion of refutations, which present reasons for rejecting all or part of opponents' arguments. Refutations include attacks on claims, data, warrants, and the ways arguments are presented.

CHAPTER EXERCISE

I. MATCHING

Directions: Match each term on the list below with its definition by writing the correct letter in the space provided.

TERMS:

A. biased
B. conflict of interest
C. expert testimony
D. hypothetical example
E. mean
F. median

G. mode
H. *reductio ad absurdum*
I. refutation
J. statistics
K. turning the tables

DEFINITIONS:

_____ 1. incident that did not occur but could have

_____ 2. information in the form of numbers

_____ 3. judgments and interpretations by qualified people

_____ 4. an amount found by adding a group of numbers and dividing the sum by the number of items in the group

_____ 5. the middle number in a series

_____ 6. the number that occurs most frequently in a group of numbers

_____ 7. clash between an expert's responsibilities to the truth and his or her own benefit

_____ 8. distorted by prejudice

_____ 9. the part of an argument that provides reasons for rejecting an opponent's argument

_____10. a way of discrediting an opponent's claims by extending them to nonsensical lengths

_____11. showing that evidence supporting an opponent's claims can be interpreted in the opposite way

II. MULTIPLE CHOICE

Directions: On the line at the left write the letter of the phrase that best completes each item.

_____12. To be most effective, facts that support a claim should be

A. expressed as modes, not means or medians.

B. easily verified.

C. accepted by people on both sides of an argument.

_____13. Hypothetical examples used in an argument should

A. be drawn from real life.

B. seem as if they could occur.

C. be interpreted by experts.

_____14. The number indicating the salary earned by the largest number of people in a group of workers is known as the

A. mean.

B. median.

C. mode.

_____15. Readers evaluating the use of statistics derived from a survey should be sure that

A. the statistics are not presented in the form of a chart or graph.

B. the group of people questioned is large enough and is representative.

C. the statistics were gathered by a special interest group.

_____16. In an argument facts, examples, and statistics should be

A. drawn from testimonials.

B. drawn from a single source.

C. accurate, up to date, and relevant.

_____17. When experts in a field disagree, nonexperts should

A. examine the experts' credentials.

B. believe only people who are experts in another field.

C. conclude that none of the experts is reliable.

_____18. The *reductio ad absurdum* approach can be used to

A. reduce one's own proposal to a one-sentence thesis.

B. suggest that a claim is unreasonably broad.

C. show that an opponent's claim is practical, at least in part.

_____19. Turning the tables is a way of showing that

A. an opponent's claim is irrelevant.

B. an opponent's argument is not well organized.

C. an opponent has misinterpreted evidence.

_____20. A good refutation

    A. expresses an opponent's views fairly without commenting on them.

    B. presents a personal attack on an opponent.

    C. attacks an argument's claim, support, warrants, or presentation.

4

Thinking Effectively

*R*aymond has been an excellent executive assistant at Winslow Electric for two years. His second annual evaluation was so favorable he was promoted to management trainee.

Unfortunately for Raymond, his new supervisor isn't easy to please. When she asked him to evaluate a long memo from the research and development division, Raymond wasn't sure what she expected of him. He asked her to explain what she wanted, and she answered, "I want you to decide whether or not it makes sense. You know, analyze the ideas and criticize them."

Raymond took the report home that evening and read it. It all seemed sensible enough, but he suspected that if he simply told his boss that everything looked good, she would ask him some questions he couldn't answer. He decided to read it again, this time trying to understand how the writers had arrived at their ideas. Eventually he could identify the thinking patterns that had led them to their conclusions. Most of these patterns seemed logical, but, to his surprise, Raymond found that he could challenge some of the authors' findings. With this first step he has begun to acquire the most important skill he would need in his business career: the power to think for himself.

Like Raymond, you can become a better thinker. This chapter discusses effective thinking patterns—comparison and contrast, cause and effect, analysis and synthesis, evaluation, and recommendation—that are natural and common ways of arranging information and drawing conclusions. Becoming familiar with them will improve your ability to understand other people's reasoning and develop ideas of your own.

Constructive thinking patterns don't often occur in isolation. Most of your thinking and writing will involve complex combinations of skills, such as identifying the causes of a problem, ranking them in order of importance, and evaluating possible solutions before choosing the best one. The ways of thinking described in this chapter are not accompanied by simple rules that specify exactly what to do. Most problems require you to adopt flexible approaches, not follow elementary paint-by-number routines. As a result, flexibility and a willingness to accept uncertainty are fundamental to becoming a clearer thinker. Studying each of the patterns in turn will give you the confidence to apply them as you need them.

COMPARING AND CONTRASTING

Comparing and contrasting involve showing how two or more objects or ideas are similar and different. Comparison emphasizes similarities ("Japanese and British car factories are alike in many ways") and contrast emphasizes differences ("The communication styles of men and women differ dramatically"). A comparison can also point out equivalences ("Beethoven's music was as inventive as Mozart's"). Usually comparisons and contrasts are intertwined so that similarities, differences, and equivalences are described and illustrated within a single argument.

You can choose from a wide range of topics to compare and contrast. Comparisons can focus on different time periods ("Pittsburgh is a much cleaner city now than it was forty years ago"), places ("Yellowstone National Park is more beautiful than the Grand Canyon"), or competing theories ("The American tradition of violence began with the growth of cities, not with the westward movement"). Whether a comparison is worth making, however, depends on a writer's purpose and audience. A comparison is interesting if it makes people see new connections between objects or ideas and important if it changes their attitudes and actions.

Pointing out all the ways two topics are alike or different is usually impossible, so the writer of a comparison-contrast argument has to be selective, emphasizing the most meaningful similarities and differences. An argument can mention obvious points without elaborating on them or even omit them entirely if readers can be trusted to take them for granted. As a rule, the more similar two objects or ideas seem, the more provocative contrasting them will be. Likewise, the more unlike they are, the more interesting an essay comparing them will be. However, surprising and disputable similarities or differences require elaborate support. For example, if you compared Jesse Jackson's campaign for the presidency with

John F. Kennedy's, you might want to show that in some parts of the country during the 1950s prejudice against Roman Catholics was almost as strong as prejudice against African Americans decades later. This idea would be surprising to some of your readers, so you'd need to offer convincing evidence in its support.

Comparisons and contrasts can be tricky because no two topics are completely alike or completely unlike each other. One way to deal with this problem is to concede the differences between the items you're comparing and the similarities between those you're contrasting. Acknowledging contradictory evidence in this way establishes your reasonableness, making your claims more credible.

One type of comparison, an analogy, raises yet another problem of credibility. An **analogy** compares things or ideas that are not ordinarily associated with one another. Arguments based on analogies can be striking and imaginative. The claim that "like drivers' licenses, marriage licenses should come up for renewal every few years" could provoke some lively discussion. However, analogies are difficult to defend. They are always open to the charge that the features singled out are not actually similar. (People needn't renew their driver's licenses if they don't want to, but they haven't made lifetime commitments to their cars, either.) Ordinarily, analogies are convincing only when there are a significant number of meaningful parallels between the subjects being compared.

Organizing Comparison Arguments

Some comparison arguments divide their subjects in half, with the first half devoted to one of the topics being compared and the second half to the other. For example, an article comparing the way history textbooks have treated religion over the years could have two parts, one discussing religion in older history books and the other religion in contemporary texts. Comparing wholes with wholes works best when the topics are not complicated, when they do not divide easily into parts, and when the parts are unimportant.

Treating one half of a comparison first and then moving on to the other half makes readers sort out resemblances and differences for themselves. First dividing each subject into parts and then comparing them part by part usually works better. For example, someone supporting the claim that alcohol does more harm than marijuana could devote half an essay to the harm caused by alcohol and the other half to the harm caused by marijuana. However, a clearer way to organize the argument would be to begin by comparing accidents caused by both marijuana and alcohol, then covering medical problems caused by both substances, and finally concluding with a comparison of the social problems they cause. This part-by-part comparison works well when topics are complicated and easily divided into recognizable parts.

Visualizing Comparisons and Contrasts

A good way to plan a comparison and contrast argument is to draw two large overlapping circles. In the overlapping area, jot down notes on points the two topics have in common, and in the areas that do not overlap make notes on characteristics they do not share. This kind of diagram will help you visualize the relationships between your ideas. The following simple comparison illustrates this technique:

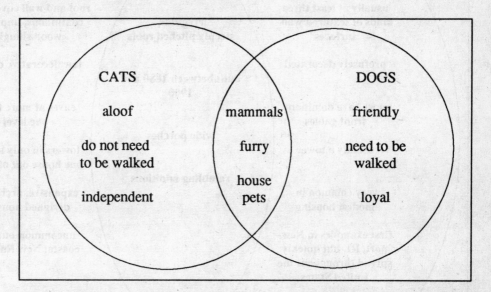

Diagramming your material can be a great help when your subject matter is complicated or unfamiliar. For example, the diagram on the following page compares and contrasts two American housing styles from the end of the nineteenth century:

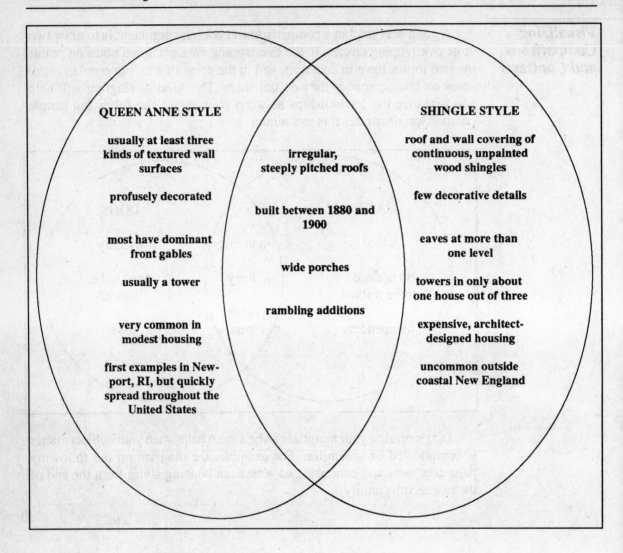

QUEEN ANNE STYLE

usually at least three kinds of textured wall surfaces

profusely decorated

most have dominant front gables

usually a tower

very common in modest housing

first examples in New-port, RI, but quickly spread throughout the United States

irregular, steeply pitched roofs

built between 1880 and 1900

wide porches

rambling additions

SHINGLE STYLE

roof and wall covering of continuous, unpainted wood shingles

few decorative details

eaves at more than one level

towers in only about one house out of three

expensive, architect-designed housing

uncommon outside coastal New England

TRY IT OUT

Try using overlapping circles to plan a comparison. In the parts of the circles that do not overlap, make notes about the distinctive qualities of your topics. In the overlapping segment note the traits they have in common.

Choose a topic of your own or select one from the following list:

   high school and college

   living alone and sharing an apartment

   watching sports in person and watching them on TV

   two actors, two politicians, or two sports teams

   friendship and love

Topic 1
_____
_____
_____

Topic 2
_____
_____
_____

Common Traits
_____
_____
_____
_____
_____
_____

_____
_____

_____
_____

solar energy and energy from fossil fuels

dying at home and dying in a hospital

working for a family member and working for a person who isn't related

owning a car and owning a motorcycle

promotions based on merit and promotions based on seniority

After you fill in the diagram, indicate your conclusions by checking one of the lines at the left:

_____ The similarities between my topics are more significant than the differences.

_____ The differences between my topics are more significant than the similarities.

Express your main ideas about your comparison in a single sentence:

_____

_____

_____

Using Comparatives and Superlatives

Comparing often requires using comparative and superlative forms of adjectives and adverbs. These words are usually formed by adding *-er* (*faster, harder, sooner*) or *-est* (*fastest, hardest, soonest*) but can also be formed with the words *more, most, less* and *least* (*more difficult, least challenging*). Notice that using a comparative or superlative involves not one, but two claims. For example, arguing that one compact disc is more poorly produced than another makes two claims: that both were poorly produced and that one was more poorly produced than the other. Be sure to provide evidence for both claims when both require support.

Below are lists of words that usually indicate comparisons and contrasts.

WORDS SIGNALING COMPARISON ARGUMENTS

alike	equivalent
analogous	identical
as . . . as	like
comparable	likewise
consistent with	parallels
correlates with	resembles
corresponds to	same
equally	similar
equals	similarly
equates with	

WORDS SIGNALING CONTRAST ARGUMENTS

conflicts with	distinct
contradicts	diverges
contrasts with	diverse
conversely	however
departs from	inconsistent with
deviates from	less
different	more
differentiates	nevertheless
differs	on the other hand
disparate	on the contrary
dissimilar	unlike

MAKING CAUSE-EFFECT ARGUMENTS

A **cause-effect argument** explains why something has happened or probably will happen. A cause and effect relationship assumes a time sequence: first you flick a switch, and then a light goes on, so you conclude that flicking the switch caused the light to go on. When you explore causes and effects, you seek answers to questions about past events or future trends. For example, cause-effect arguments can support claims such as "Social policies in South Africa have hindered efforts to control tuberculosis" or "Our band's fund-raising drive will succeed if we publicize our best program, the free summer concerts." A knowledge of cause and effect relationships is a strong basis for practical planning and problem solving. In fact, understanding the causes of a problem is the only sound basis for proposing a solution to it.

Basic to cause-effect arguments is the "if . . . then" sentence pattern: "*If* you pledge a fraternity, *then* your social life will improve." You can discuss causes and effects in chronological order with the causes first ("Navajo religious symbols and ceremonies [the causes] give worshippers a sense of harmony with the universe [the effect]"). You can also describe an effect and then trace it back to its causes ("A shopping mall is an unsatisfactory place for young people to congregate [the effect] because of a mall's anonymity, predictability, and emphasis on consumerism [the cause]").

An argument can pay equal attention to a cause and its effects or stress one more than the other. Or an entire argument can be devoted to proving that a cause-effect relationship does *not* exist. Arguments can also focus on how effects should be encouraged or discouraged, explaining ways to increase or decrease particular effects.

To use cause-effect analysis for problem solving, start by examining the nature of the problem: Who suffers as a result of it? In what way? Similarly, you should look closely at the cause of the problem. If the effect is caused by a person, what are his or her motives? Is the harm that results intentional or unintentional?

Sufficient Causes

Having identified a cause, you should determine whether that cause alone is strong enough to bring about the effect. A cause adequate by itself to produce an effect is a **sufficient cause**. When a sufficient cause occurs, its effect must follow. Some events do have single sufficient causes (heating water causes it to boil, for example), but a situation complicated enough to be arguable rarely involves a single cause. Effects such as increased drug abuse or high unemployment usually result from complex combinations of causes. One of those causes, occurring without the others, would not have much of an impact.

Immediate and Remote Causes

You can sometimes attribute an effect to a chain of causes, each one related to the next. Causes closest in time to the effect they produce are **immediate causes**, while those further back along the chain are **remote causes**. For example, the remote causes for a series of murders might be the severe abuse and abandonment experienced by the serial killer as a child while the immediate cause could be a seemingly minor event such as the murderer's being fired from a job or quarreling with an acquaintance.

Assuming that one event caused another because it occurred first is natural but chancy. Night follows day, for example, but day doesn't cause night. At one college, enrollment increased soon after tuition charges went up. Did the increase cause more people to attend the college, perhaps because they believed that a higher-priced education was more valuable? It's more likely that the increased enrollment was caused by other factors such as a new advertising campaign and a changing local economy. Assuming that since one event preceded another, the first event necessarily caused the second is called the *post hoc* fallacy, which is discussed in chapter 6.

Reciprocal Cause-Effect Relationships

Mistaking an effect for a cause is another pitfall of cause-effect arguments. The subjects taught at a local school, for example, might be identified as the cause of certain attitudes and incidents in a community when the viewpoints of community members have actually shaped the school's programs. The school-community relationship is more likely to be reciprocal. **Reciprocal cause-effect relationships** are situations in which effects act upon their causes. In other words, the school influences the community, but the community also influences the school.

Social trends are often reciprocal. For instance, as people begin to move to a dilapidated neighborhood and work hard to remodel their houses, small businesses follow, making the area more attractive and causing more people to move in. The original cause (the first urban pioneers) leads to an effect (a better neighborhood) that has a reciprocal effect on the cause, resulting in more people being attracted to the neighborhood.

Sign Arguments

Signs are indications assumed to accompany certain events or situations. For example, people usually assume that a flock of geese flying overhead is a sign of the changing seasons and that staggering and talking incoherently are signs of drunkenness. The claim is often made that a sign proves the existence of the event or situation it usually accompanies. But sign arguments are convincing only when there's no plausible alternative interpretation of the signs. In fact, geese may flock at other times than during spring and fall migration, and a staggering, incoherent person may be suffering from a heart attack rather than the effects of alcohol. Thus, sign arguments should be regarded with some suspicion. Arguments in which clear cause-effect relationships can be established are always more convincing than those that depend on signs.

Below is a list of words that usually indicate cause-effect relationships.

WORDS SIGNALING CAUSE-EFFECT ARGUMENTS

activates	if . . . then
affects	impels
as a result	improves
because of	incites
brings about	increases
catalyst	induces
causes	influences
consequence	initiates
contributes	inspires
creates	leads to
decreases	motivates
depends on	necessitates
destroys	origin
determines	originates
effect	outcome
engenders	outgrowth
follows from	precipitates
generates	produces

prompts	sign of
provokes	source
reason for	suffices
responsible for	triggers
result	

EXERCISE 1

Directions: List possible immediate and remote causes for each situation below. To identify each cause you believe could be classified as sufficient, write an *S* in the space at the left. To identify each reciprocal cause, write an *R* in the space at the left. Many causes you list will be neither sufficient nor reciprocal. There are no specific correct answers, but possible responses are given at the back of this book.

EXAMPLE:

Situation: After repeated efforts a college student is still unable to find a summer job.

Possible immediate causes:

_S_   Because of a recent layoff in a local business, many highly qualified people are competing for jobs usually held by students.

_____   The student was late for one of his job interviews.

Possible remote causes:

_R_   The student has no work experience.

_____   The student has not developed the skills desired by local employers.

1. Situation: A forest fire destroys 5,000 acres of woodland in a national park.

Possible immediate causes:

_____ _____

_____

_____ _____

_____

Possible remote causes:

_____ _____

_____

_____ _____

_____

2. Situation: A van runs off a road into a ditch.

Possible immediate causes:

_____ _____

_____

_____ _____

_____

Possible remote causes:

_____ _____

_____

_____ _____

_____

3. Situation: A college student does well in a calculus course.

Possible immediate causes:

_____ _____

_____

_____ _____

_____

Possible remote causes:

_____ _____

_____

_____ _____

_____

4. Situation: A man trespassing on a neighbor's property is bitten by the neighbor's dog.

Possible immediate causes:

_____ _____

_____

_____ _____

Possible remote causes:

_____ _____

_____

_____ _____

5. Situation: A gang member shoots a member of a rival gang.

Possible immediate causes:

_____ _____

_____

_____ _____

Possible remote causes:

_____ _____

_____

_____ _____

6. Situation: Many fish suddenly die in a river near a large city.

Possible immediate causes:

_____ _____

_____

_____ _____

Possible remote causes:

_____ _____

_____ _____

_____ _____

7. Situation: A teenager buys a pair of athletic shoes.
    Possible immediate causes:

_____ _____

_____ _____

_____ _____

    Possible remote causes:

_____ _____

_____ _____

_____ _____

8. Situation: An old building collapses.
    Possible immediate causes:

_____ _____

_____ _____

_____ _____

    Possible remote causes:

_____ _____

_____ _____

_____ _____

9. Situation: A women's softball team wins a championship game.
    Possible immediate causes:

_____ _____

_____ _____

_____ _____

Possible remote causes:

_____   _____

_____

_____   _____

_____

10. Situation: A local Italian restaurant suddenly becomes more popular.
    Possible immediate causes:

_____   _____

_____

_____   _____

_____

Possible remote causes:

_____   _____

_____

_____   _____

_____

ANALYZING AND SYNTHESIZING

Children often amuse themselves by taking things apart and recombining the parts in new and imaginative ways. The same thought processes that lead a child to disassemble a favorite toy and try to put it back together in a different way have also led to some of the most important discoveries and inventions in human history.

Analysis

Analysis comes from a Greek word meaning "break up." **Analyzing** means breaking a whole into its parts, identifying the parts, and describing how they relate to each other. For example, chemical analysis consists of separating a compound into its elements and examining the relationships between them. Analysis can also involve identifying the components of a computer system or the characteristics of jazz and determining how the elements work together to form a coherent whole.

Many kinds of academic and practical problems can be solved by analysis. It helps you understand a subject by forcing you to look closely at details until you perceive the larger patterns that govern their interrelationships. When you analyze an argument, for example, you break it up into its components—claim, data, and warrants—to see how the parts are related to each other.

Analysis is not a matter of breaking a topic into parts according to a fixed pattern, like cutting a pie into slices. On the contrary, it requires seeing a problem as a whole so that your grasp of the issues is neither fragmented nor incomplete. A thorough analysis should take account of all the elements of a situation, not just those that support an overly simple or rigid interpretation.

Moreover, analysis alone doesn't always provide solutions to complex problems. Analyzing is like dismantling a car engine that won't start, discovering and replacing a defective part, and restoring the engine to working order. But a good mechanic might also begin with two hopelessly defective engines and use parts from each to build one that works, creating a new synthesis. **Synthesizing** (which comes from a Greek word meaning "put together") creates new meaning by restructuring information in terms of broad connections among its parts.

One of the most famous scientific ideas in history is a product of synthesis. At the beginning of the sixteenth century, the Polish astronomer Nicolaus Copernicus (1473–1543) reexamined ancient theories about planetary motion. Since the time of the ancient Greeks, astronomers had believed that the earth stood motionless at the center of the universe, and the sun, other planets, and stars revolved around it. A great deal had been discovered about the movements of the planets, all interpreted according to the belief that the earth did not move. Copernicus asked himself if this data could be interpreted in a new way: what if the sun were at the center and the earth and other planets revolved around it? In 1514 he outlined his new system, which was far simpler than the old one, and started a revolution in astronomy.

Copernicus was faced with a choice between two explanations of a complicated situation, each of which was satisfactory in its own terms. When faced with a choice between two apparently valid explanations, perhaps he remembered a principle attributed to one of the great philosophers of the Middle Ages, the Englishman William of Occam (c. 1290–c. 1349). Occam wrote, "It is vain to do with more what can be done with fewer." In other words, when faced with two good explanations for an event or situation, the simpler one is better. This principle is called **Occam's Razor** because it cuts away unnecessary complications.

True synthesis involves a unified, coherent reinterpretation in which both the separate elements and the entire situation make sense in a new way. Therefore, synthesis requires more than a superficial grasp of a subject. Comprehensive knowledge is needed to incorporate information into a unified theory. Forming a new synthesis also means finding a fresh viewpoint, a new way of seeing.

Creating an original way to organize and interpret information may sound like a formidable challenge, but in fact you already synthesize information whenever you master new facts and ideas, adapt them to your personal needs, and make them your own. Cultivating an open, even playful, approach to new ideas should help you find creative ways of synthesizing. Because a new synthesis is likely to be unfamiliar to your listeners or readers, you will need to state it clearly and provide abundant illustrations and evidence to support it. Also, you should beware of falling in love with your own (or anyone else's) synthesis: a compelling new theory can blind you to alternative interpretations that work as well or better.

Below are lists of words that usually indicate analysis and synthesis.

WORDS SIGNALING ANALYSIS

analyze	ingredient
characteristic	made up of
component	parts
constituent	portion
dissection	section
divide	segment
division	separate
element	split
factor	

WORDS SIGNALING SYNTHESIS

associate	pattern
combine	reexamination
connect	relate to
correlate	resemble
integrate	restructure
interpret	unite
interrelationship	work together
link	

EXERCISE 2

Directions: Identify the statements below as analysis or synthesis by underlining the correct words at the left.

Example:

<u>analysis</u>　　synthesis　　Many small businesses lack skilled managers, adequate financing, and long-term business plans.

analysis   synthesis   1. In the United States sports are characterized by competitiveness, hard work, and discipline.

analysis   synthesis   2. Self-publishing, small presses, or subsidized publishing were crucial to the early careers of the literary giants Joyce, Eliot, Woolf, and Nabokov.

analysis   synthesis   3. Despite their violence, fairy tales give children a way of relating fictional conflicts to the inner dramas of their lives.

analysis   synthesis   4. Africa actually bears little resemblance to the image of the continent presented in most movies.

analysis   synthesis   5. The elements of street life, especially prostitution, drugs, and pregnancies, pose dangers and difficulties for runaway teens.

analysis   synthesis   6. The efforts of the great world powers in the face of war can be interpreted as attempts to confine the conduct of war within definite boundaries.

analysis   synthesis   7. The mosaics in Ravenna are related in style and subject matter to the mosaics in Venice.

analysis   synthesis   8. Most societies are divided into two classes, an elite class that rules and an underclass that is ruled.

analysis   synthesis   9. Changing ideals of masculinity and femininity work together to shape the modern quest for perfect health.

analysis   synthesis   10. The social structures of ancient Egypt and Rome can be correlated to answer fundamental questions about how and why societies change.

EVALUATING

Evaluating means judging what something is worth. It requires going beyond personal taste or conviction to arguing that others should share the same viewpoint. For example, someone could argue the claim that "from the nineteenth century until today, British government policy in the Middle East led to one disaster after another."

Evaluations can be moral, ethical, aesthetic, or practical, but the principles for supporting any kind of evaluation are roughly the same. To form sound value judgments, you need to establish **criteria**, standards used as the basis for your evaluation. (The main criterion for judging a professional football coach, for example, is his win-loss record.) Determining your criteria and arranging them in order of importance are useful steps in any kind of evaluation.

Evaluations sometimes begin as snap judgments, conclusions based on very little observation or analysis. Snap judgments are not necessarily bad, but taking the time to equip yourself with more information always helps. Premature evaluations, made before evidence has been gathered and sifted, can easily be flawed. Becoming conscious of the emotional basis for personal preferences can help to keep your expectations or feelings from having too much influence on your evaluations.

Moral Evaluations

Moral evaluations are judgments about whether particular kinds of conduct are right or wrong. Many moral standards are generally agreed upon; for example, most people believe that stealing and murder are wrong. However, new kinds of conduct, for which standards have not yet been established, are often the basis for arguments: If a married couple is unable to have children, is artificial insemination morally acceptable? Is research conducted on aborted fetal tissue morally wrong?

Ethical Evaluations

Both morals and ethics refer to standards of conduct; however, **ethics** usually applies to standards in business and in professions such as medicine and law. For example, suppose that five vice presidents conspire to defraud their company. The company president states, "I trusted those men and women; I was fooled as badly as everyone else." Should she be held responsible for not supervising her subordinates more closely? Or a psychiatrist knows that one of his patients is potentially extremely violent, yet the ethics of the psychiatrist's profession prevent him from disclosing information acquired in therapy sessions. What should the psychiatrist do?

Aesthetic Evaluations

Aesthetics is a branch of philosophy concerned with determining standards of beauty and excellence in the arts. "Donatello was the greatest sculptor of the Italian Renaissance" is an example of an aesthetic evaluation.

Like other kinds of evaluation, aesthetic evaluation requires the establishment of criteria. Judging a contemporary work of art by the same criteria as a portrait by Rembrandt would be neither useful nor fair. An aesthetic judgment is based in part on whether a work of art does what it is intended to do. Therefore, one of the first steps in an aesthetic evaluation is classifying the subject correctly: Is it realistic, impressionistic, or abstract? Does it appeal to the senses or to literary and historical associations or to both?

Reference works are available to tell you what experts think are the appropriate criteria for a specific type of work you're evaluating. You may choose to develop criteria on your own, but if you do, you're obliged to explain and support them. As you learn more about your subject, you may well find that your first impression is not one you want to support, so you'll benefit from remaining flexible.

Practical Evaluations

Evaluations can also be practical. The thesis of a memo to the fire chief, "Holly Street between Fifth and Sixth avenues is the best location for the new fire house," is a claim that evaluates the worth of several possible locations and argues for one over the others. Policy decisions, whether in the public or the private sector, usually combine one or more practical evaluations with calls for action. For example, the evaluation "Beanbag cushions are not safe beds for infants" leads easily to the thesis "Beanbag cushions should not be used as beds for infants." Likewise, "Young people are losing respect for their elders" can be restated as "Young people should show more respect for their elders." These conversions move the claims out of the realm of judgment and into that of direct action.

Organizing an Argumentative Evaluation

When you write an argumentative evaluation, you may decide to provide some background information, but your argument will be more effective if you avoid the temptation to supply lengthy summaries or obvious descriptive details. Assume that your reader has at least a superficial familiarity with your subject and include only material that directly supports your thesis.

Some evaluations require support from outside sources. For example, if you claim that Charles Dickens is the best-loved writer in the English language, you might support your view with statistics revealing how well Dickens's books sell each year or results of opinion polls in which people consistently name Dickens as a favorite author.

Below is a list of words that usually indicate evaluations.

WORDS SIGNALING EVALUATIONS

accurate	forceful	outstanding
bad	good	practical
better	great	preferable
biased	greatest	productive
constructive	harmful	promising
convincing	honorable	proper
defective	immoral	satisfactory
disaster	important	significant
disastrous	impressive	sound
effective	inferior	spurious
erroneous	injustice	superior
ethical	judge	suitable
exceptional	just	unethical
fair	least	unfair
faulty	mediocre	unsatisfactory
finest	moral	worse
flawed	most	worst

RECOMMENDING

Recommending means proposing changes in people's attitudes or actions: "Teachers should recognize that their main task is training students to learn on their own." Recommendations for action are claims of policy. Most recommendations contain the word *should* or an equivalent such as *must* or *ought* because recommendations tell what should be done to prevent or solve a problem. The proposed solutions may be partial or complete, temporary or permanent. They may be positive, suggesting ways to improve a bad situation, or negative, warning against a particular course of action by pointing out its drawbacks.

Recommendations sometimes take the form of advice about how to do something, such as how to start a play group for neighborhood children. Such advice should be clear, accurate, and organized in easy-to-follow, step-by-step order. However, how-to advice should not be oversimplified; a writer ought not to imply, for example, that choosing a nursing home for an aged parent is a simple process.

Choosing a Topic

The first step in making a recommendation is identifying a problem that interests you. You could start with a situation you already know well, such as a difficulty at your job. On the other hand, studying an unfamiliar problem, such as possible future objectives for the U. S. space program, could prove extremely interesting. If you choose a problem you believe is important, you'll probably be willing to spend extra time devising strategies to solve it.

A recommendation usually includes the following elements:

1. a description of what is wrong
2. a proposal for action to solve the problem
3. an explanation of the benefits that would result from adopting the proposal
4. a refutation of possible objections to the proposal

Describing What Is Wrong

The description of the current situation should prove that there is a compelling need for change. For example, you could show that sales have been rapidly decreasing at the delicatessen where you work, and customer complaints have been mounting.

Making a Proposal

Wording your proposal properly can be tricky. A general claim, such as "Giorgio's Delicatessen should offer higher quality food and better service to its customers," is usually less effective than a more specific recommendation. Suggesting that "the prepared foods sold at Giorgio's Delicatessen should be made fresh every day, and a manager should be on duty at all times to deal with customer complaints" would be more useful. However, making the more specific claim commits you to discussing the deli's procedures and management policies in detail.

The next step is to convince readers that your proposed solution will work. You might point out that if your suggestions were followed, fewer customers would complain about their sandwiches and salads, and when occasional customers did complain, someone authorized to take effective action would be on hand to deal with them. One way to show that a proposal is practical is to discuss a **precedent**, a past occurrence that can help justify your recommendation. Perhaps you know from talking with a friend that a delicatessen owner across town had problems similar to Giorgio's and solved them by following recommendations like yours.

Explaining the Benefits of Your Proposal

It helps to be as explicit as you can about the benefits that would result from your proposal, specifying who would gain and how. Satisfied customers and increased sales would obviously benefit the deli's owner, but the changes you propose would also help employees enjoy their jobs and feel more secure about them. As additional support, besides showing how the situation would improve if your advice is followed, you can predict that it will worsen if your remedies are not adopted.

Refuting Opposing Views

To convince others that your solution is sound, you should show that you've considered alternative solutions and have good reasons for ruling them out. For example, cutting prices might lead to a temporary increase in business, but customers would still be dissatisfied with stale food, and revenue would probably go down in the long run.

You can make your claim more credible by admitting that your recommendations have their disadvantages, such as increased costs. Because complicated problems rarely have single solutions, you will be more convincing if you don't exaggerate the benefits that adopting your proposal will bring. For example, even if a manager is always present, she still may not be able to satisfy every customer or increase sales dramatically.

When you make a recommendation, you're asking people to change their attitudes or their actions or both. Any change, even an apparently simple one, can seem threatening, so you should expect some resistance to your proposal, no matter how reasonable it seems to you. Your task is to fashion a well-argued case to win people over to your view and inspire them to cooperate in making the changes you suggest.

Below is a list of words that usually indicate recommendations.

WORDS SIGNALING RECOMMENDATIONS

advise	modify	reorganize
advocate	must	replace
alter	ought	repudiate
approve	proposal	request
change	propose	restore
commend	recommend	revitalize
correct	recommendation	sanction
cure	reform	should
endorse	reject	suggest
help	relieve	support
improve	remedy	urge

EXERCISE 3

Directions: Underline the words in the statements below that identify them as recommendations.

Example: The British royal family <u>should</u> be less extravagant in times of unemployment and hardship.

1. The trend toward increased smoking among citizens of developing nations must be halted.

2. The United States should have occupied all of Iraq in the 1990 Persian Gulf War.

3. Our research team endorses the proposal that international law devote more attention to the rights of aliens.

4. I support public arts programs that bring young artists to the attention of a wide audience.

5. The budget deficit ought to be closed through a combination of reduced government spending and increased taxes.

6. The peacekeeping and humanitarian tasks of the U.S. military should not take precedence over defense initiatives.

7. The ad hoc committee on corporate gifts urges that company charity be devoted mainly to programs that directly benefit employees or help educate future members of the work force.

8. More public money must be devoted immediately to the repair of bridges, highways, and railroads.

9. International commodities markets ought to be stabilized.

10. Companies selling Christmas products should not send out catalogs as early as the end of the summer.

Comparison and contrast, cause and effect, analysis, synthesis, evaluation, and recommendation are natural and common thinking patterns used for arranging information and drawing conclusions. Comparison and contrast arguments show how two or more objects or ideas are similar or different while cause-effect arguments identify immediate, remote, and sufficient causes as well as reciprocal causes and effects. Analysis involves breaking a whole into its parts, identifying the parts, and describing how they relate to each other while synthesis is the creation of new meaning by restructuring information in terms of broad connections among its parts. Evaluating, which means judging what something is worth, can be based on aesthetic criteria (standards for judging beauty and excellence in the arts) as well as on moral, ethical, or practical considerations. Recommending entails describing something that is wrong, proposing action to solve the problem, explaining the benefits that would result from adopting the proposal, and refuting possible objections.

CHAPTER EXERCISE

I. MATCHING

Directions: Match each term on the list below with its definition by writing the correct letter in the space provided. Some of the terms on the list will not be used.

TERMS:

A. aesthetics

B. analogy

C. analyzing

D. cause-effect arguments

E. comparing and contrasting

F. criteria

G. ethics

H. evaluating

I. immediate cause

J. moral evaluations

K. precedent

L. reciprocal

M. recommending

N. remote cause

O. sign

P. sufficient cause

Q. synthesizing

DEFINITIONS:

_____ 1. showing how two or more objects or ideas are similar and different

_____ 2. a comparison of things or ideas not ordinarily associated with one another

_____ 3. explanations of why events have happened or probably will happen

_____ 4. adequate by itself to produce an effect

_____ 5. cause close in time to an effect

_____ 6. cause distant in time from an effect

_____ 7. indication assumed to accompany an event

_____ 8. breaking a whole into parts, identifying the parts, and describing the relationships between them

_____ 9. creating new meaning by restructuring information

_____10. judging what something is worth based on moral, ethical, aesthetic, or practical considerations

_____11. standards of conduct in business or in professions such as medicine and law.

_____12. judgments about whether particular kinds of conduct, especially the conduct of individuals, are right or wrong

_____13. a branch of philosophy concerned with determining standards of beauty and excellence in the arts

_____14. standards used as the basis for evaluation

_____15. proposing changes in people's attitudes or actions

II. MULTIPLE CHOICE

Directions: On the line at the left write the letter of the phrase that best completes each item.

_____16. In reciprocal cause-effect relationships

    A. effects influence their causes.

    B. a single cause is enough to bring about an effect.

    C. the cause is distant in time from its effect.

_____17. Analyzing an argument involves

    A. proposing changes in people's attitudes or actions.

    B. breaking the argument into its parts.

    C. using circle diagrams for notes on the argument's key points.

_____18. According to the principle known as Occam's Razor,

    A. the simpler of two good explanations is the better one.

    B. analysis alone does not always provide solutions to complex problems.

    C. part-by-part comparisons are more effective than comparisons of wholes.

_____19. Ethical evaluations differ from aesthetic evaluations in that ethical evaluations

    A. derive from synthesis, but aesthetic evaluations derive from analysis.

    B. are based on criteria, but aesthetic evaluations do not require criteria.

    C. relate to standards of conduct in a business or profession, but aesthetic evaluations relate to excellence in the arts.

_____20. A recommendation should include

    A. a simple solution to a complicated problem.

    B. an aesthetic judgment.

    C. an explanation of the benefits that would result from adopting a proposal.

5

Defining and Classifying

"*W*hat do you mean by 'superpower'?" asked Carol.

"What do you mean, 'What do you mean?'" Nita replied angrily.

"You just said, 'The U.S. and Japan are superpowers, and superpowers have a moral responsibility to aid developing countries.' I agree that the U.S. is a superpower because it has the strongest military force in the world. But Japan's military is strictly limited by its constitution. You can only call it a superpower if you're using the word very differently from the way I do." Carol turned to her friend Jack for support, but he didn't say anything.

"Why are you asking the meaning of a word in the middle of a discussion?" complained Nita. "I think you're just trying to change the subject."

"If Japan is a superpower," Jack piped up, "how would you classify China?"

"How can we know what category China belongs in," Carol said, "until we understand what the categories are? We have to define superpower first . . ."

Although Nita doesn't think so, the precise meaning of *superpower* may be crucial to her discussion with Carol and Jack. They need to consider some puzzling questions: Have some of the states that made up the former Soviet Union remained superpowers because they still possess large military forces? Is Japan, without a large military force but with tremendous economic clout, a superpower? And in what category does China, with its huge population but outmoded technology, belong?

DEFINING

All sorts of arguments call for clear definitions since the same words can suggest different ideas to different people. However, this doesn't mean that you need to define every term you use before you start arguing. You can probably assume that listeners or readers will readily understand what you mean by "the homeless" or "immigration." But as your arguments become more difficult or technical, you're more likely to need precise definitions.

Defining is establishing what a word or phrase means. The word "definition" comes from the Latin word *definire*, "to put boundaries around." Definition is frequently an essential first step that establishes the boundaries within which an argument will take place. This is why the first speaker in a formal debate always begins with definitions.

In order for listeners or readers to see the point of a thesis, they may require definitions of one or more key terms. For example, to follow an argument about genetic engineering, readers need to know what it is. (Genetic engineering involves altering inherited characteristics of plants, animals, or perhaps even people.) Such a preliminary definition in an argumentative paper may take only a few words, a line or two, or as much as several paragraphs. After the necessary definitions have been clarified, most arguments focus on support for the principal claim, not support for the definitions.

People who need definitions usually begin by consulting a dictionary. In fact, a good way to start defining a word is by consulting several dictionaries and comparing their entries. Differences between them can provide starting points for your argument. If you quote from a dictionary, tell your readers which one you're using (rather than just calling it "the dictionary") since dictionaries differ. The name Webster's is not copyrighted and can be used for any dictionary, so using a Webster's dictionary does not guarantee that a definition is accurate.

Moreover, even accurate dictionary definitions are often not precise enough to use in arguments. A single word may have several different meanings, only one of which is relevant to your purpose. For example, one meaning of the word *justice* is "the establishment of rights according to the rules of law." But if you want to argue that the rules of law are biased against rape victims and are therefore unjust, you need to establish that justice means something more like "fair treatment."

Using Key Terms to Control Arguments

Definitions are extremely important in argument because controlling the definitions of key terms often means controlling the argument itself. Occasionally, both sides struggle so hard to use a term in the way they prefer that its real meaning gets lost in the process. For example, when government policies associated with the term *liberalism* are unpopular, politicians are eager to brand their opponents liberals without ever pausing to define the term. Two politicians, each intent on convincing the voters that the other one is too liberal, may find little time to discuss the issues at stake in the campaign.

Understanding Denotation and Connotation

The meaning of a word independent of its emotional associations is called the word's **denotation**. However, many words (such as *liberal* in the previous example) have not only meanings but also a whole complex of feelings associated with them. A word such as *mother* suggests to most people not only its denotation, "female parent," but also the love and warmth they feel for their own mothers. *Mother* is therefore a word that usually conveys strong positive feelings. The positive or negative feelings associated with a word are called its **connotation**.

EXERCISE 1

Directions: The lists below contain groups of words with similar meanings. Distinguish the words that have positive connotations from those that have negative connotations. Use the following code:

+ positive connotation

− negative connotation

Example:

__+__ antique __−__ dilapidated __−__ outmoded __−__ dated

1. ___ domineering ___ forceful ___ confident ___ overbearing
2. ___ abundance ___ plenty ___ glut ___ bounty
3. ___ open ___ responsive ___ hypersensitive ___ touchy
4. ___ bony ___ gaunt ___ slim ___ slender
5. ___ apathetic ___ dull ___ lazy ___ imperturbable
6. ___ devour ___ feast ___ dine ___ gorge
7. ___ prudent ___ miserly ___ thrifty ___ stingy
8. ___ fool ___ humorist ___ buffoon ___ wit
9. ___ dictator ___ tyrant ___ leader ___ commander
10. ___ gall ___ impudence ___ daring ___ spunk

In arguments the connotations of key terms often count as much as their denotations. In the abortion debate, for example, people on the side originally labeled "antiabortion" soon decided that the term was too negative. They began to call themselves "prolife," which sounded better and briefly gave them a considerable edge in the battle for public opinion. This left the proabortion forces in a quandary. However, by inventing the term "prochoice," they put the debate back on a more equal footing. The sides maintain the same positions they always have; only the names have changed.

Using Various Methods of Definition

You can approach definition in various ways depending on how much explanation and illustration you think readers will need to understand your argument.

FINDING SYNONYMS

Finding a synonym—a word with the same or nearly the same meaning as the word you are defining—is the quickest and simplest approach to definition. For example, if you are discussing aggression, you can briefly define it as "hostility." Expressions that seem equivalent, however, rarely mean exactly the same thing. For instance, aggression usually implies forceful action while hostility can suggest feelings of hatred with or without the use of force. Even when words do have the same meanings, their connotations are likely to differ; as a result, kinds of definitions other than synonyms are often required.

WRITING FORMAL DEFINITIONS

Writing a **formal definition** consists of putting the word you're defining into a class or category and then telling how it differs from others in the same class. For instance, you could define *terrorism* as "violence used to intimidate governments into granting political demands." Here, the first part of the definition places terrorism in a category (violence) while the rest of the definition shows how terrorism differs from other kinds of violence such as riots, brawls, and murders. When you write your own formal definitions, try not to make the category in the first part of the definition too broad. In other words, beginning to define terrorism by calling it an action would not narrow the definition enough.

PROVIDING EXAMPLES

Sometimes examples are added to a formal definition. For instance, *Webster's Ninth New Collegiate Dictionary* offers the following formal definition of *pornography*: "the depiction of erotic behavior (as in pictures or writing) intended to cause sexual excitement." To further clarify, an author might mention several examples of pornography, such as X-rated movies, photographs of sexual activity, or sexually explicit magazines.

On some occasions examples can take the place of formal definitions. For instance, in a meeting protesting the sale of sexually explicit magazines in local stores, a person who waves a copy of an objectionable publication is providing an example of pornography rather than defining it. She is assuming that under the circumstances the example alone so effectively illustrates what pornography is that a formal definition is unnecessary.

LISTING ATTRIBUTES

Another substitute for a formal definition is a list of the attributes (qualities) of the object or idea you are defining. Thus, in an argument about gender roles, a "real man" might be defined as someone who bears the major financial responsibility for his household, faces threats with resourcefulness and physical courage, and has a powerful and dominating personality.

EXPLAINING ETYMOLOGIES

Definitions sometimes rely on **etymology**, the history of words. The word *etymology* itself combines two Greek words, *etymos* ("true") and *logos* ("word"), so an etymology in a sense is the truth about a word. Sometimes etymologies can be surprising and even amusing: few people suspect that the word *sincere* is composed of the Latin words *sine* ("without") and *cera* ("wax"). It originally meant "solidly or honestly made" because Roman carpenters sometimes disguised worm-eaten furniture by filling the holes with colored wax. Eventually, *sincere* came to describe honest expressions of feeling or belief about any subject.

Etymology can sometimes suggest ways to remember unfamiliar concepts. For example, the word *chiaroscuro* names a way of painting in which forms are depicted by light and shade with little or no regard to color. This is easier to remember if you know that the term combines the Italian words for light, *chiaro* (related to the English word *clear*), and dark, *oscuro* (related to the English word *obscure*).

You can sometimes use etymologies as support for an argument. Suppose you wanted to argue that *euthanasia* (allowing or helping terminally ill people to die in order to relieve their suffering) should be legal. The original meaning of its Greek components (*eu-* meaning "good" or "easy" and *thanatos* meaning "death") might contribute to your case by showing that the goal of euthanasia is a good death.

However, the fact that a word had a certain meaning at some point in its history does not suggest that it must mean the same thing today. Words sometimes shed meanings the way snakes shed skins. For example, a thousand years ago in England a person who killed someone had to atone for the crime by paying the victim's family. In Old English law the word *murder* meant not killing itself but hiding a victim's body to avoid paying compensation.

DEVISING ANALOGIES

A rule going back at least as far as Aristotle suggests that definitions should not be based on analogies (comparisons of things or ideas that are not ordinarily associated with one another). Certainly, using an analogy that suggests irrelevant similarities between two subjects would not be useful. However, an analogy can sometimes make the meaning of a term more vivid. Suppose a Republican senator wishes to attack some costly legislation proposed by the Democrats. He or she might claim that "entitlements are like daggers aimed at the heart of our efforts to balance the budget." Saying that entitlements (rights to benefits specified by a law) are like daggers does not define them but does indicate their potentially destructive character.

ANNOUNCING STIPULATIVE DEFINITIONS

To avoid getting sidetracked by disagreements about the meaning of key terms, you can try the shortcut of announcing a definition that you do not plan to explain or defend. A definition announced in this way is called a **stipulative definition**. (*Stipulate* was originally a legal term that meant demanding a specific clause be included in an agreement.)

You can stipulate a definition if you intend to use a word in only one of its meanings (as we use the term *argument* in this book to mean "the process of making a point and trying to convince other people that the point is worthy of belief"). In such cases a clear announcement of just how you propose to use a term will avoid confusion later. Or you might need a stipulative definition because a term ordinarily covers too wide a range. For example, in discussing better medical care for the elderly, you may need to state precisely what you mean by the elderly. "The elderly are people over the age of seventy" would be a possible stipulative definition. Your readers may well disagree. They may believe everyone over sixty-five is elderly or subscribe to the cliché "You're only as old as you feel," but at least they know what you mean by the term.

When stipulating a definition, try not to choose a meaning your readers would consider peculiar. In their book *Current Issues and Enduring Questions*, Sylvan Barnet and Hugo Bedau illustrate this point by reminding their readers of the old riddle: "If you call a dog's tail a leg, how many legs does it have?" The answer is four, not five. Stipulating that a tail is a leg doesn't make it one. Therefore, you should make sure that the meanings you stipulate are ones that your readers are likely to accept.

Stipulative definitions should be used with care. Remembering unusual definitions is extra work for readers, so the more stipulative definitions you use, the more difficult it becomes to follow your argument. Another pitfall to avoid is trying to introduce a stipulative definition rather than clarifying and supporting a claim. For example, the definition "By *abortion* I mean the murder of unborn babies" requires the same explanation and support as any other claim. It is, in fact, a thesis sentence in disguise.

Avoiding equivocation. If you use stipulative definitions, try to continue using terms as you said you would. Suppose at the beginning of a memo you announce that you're using the word *incompetent* to describe any accountant who has not yet passed the examination to become a Certified Public Accountant. If you later call a veteran CPA incompetent because he failed to detect fraud during an audit, you have used the same word in two senses, a practice that is at best confusing and at worst deceitful. Using the same word in two senses with the effect of confusing an argument is called **equivocation**, a kind of flawed reasoning that is also discussed in chapter 6.

Writing straightforward titles. If you stipulate a definition for a particular term, you should probably avoid using that term in your title. As a rule, a title should be straightforward, allowing a prospective reader to see at a glance what sort of essay you have written. Imagine readers beginning a magazine article entitled "Revolution in South Africa." They soon discover that the writer is describing the decision of a South African fashion designer to raise skirt lengths from down around the ankle to well above the knee (using revolution to mean "drastic change"). They have a right to be annoyed and may stop reading as soon as they discover they have been tricked.

USING NEGATION

If you consider a term important enough to define, you probably believe that people too often misunderstand what it means. Thus, you can reasonably dedicate all or part of a definition to explaining what the word does *not* necessarily mean. **Negation** (pointing out what something is not) allows you to correct commonly held but limited or erroneous views of how a word should be understood. For example, you might begin by stating that when many people hear the word *technology*, they think of such high-tech inventions as the computer or the fax machine. You could then show that some technological innovations which have improved our lives are very simple: the zipper, the tea bag, and the ballpoint pen. By describing these simple but useful technological developments, you can broaden and deepen your readers' understanding of a familiar term.

Negation can also be used to distinguish a word from other closely related words. For example, you could compare *love* to esteem, devotion, infatuation, passion, and lust, discarding each of these terms as an unsatisfactory synonym before providing your own definition. A related approach involves contrasting a term with its opposite (*love* with *hate*, for example) in order to clarify the word's true meaning.

RELYING ON EXPERT TESTIMONY

Expert testimony consists of judgments by qualified people. The technique of enlisting experts to support a claim takes an interesting turn when definitions are at stake. If you need a definition of *relativity*, it would be especially convincing to quote Albert Einstein; if your essay requires a definition of *philosophy*, world-famous British philosopher Bertrand Russell would be an excellent person to provide it.

However, some famous people have defined terms in wildly eccentric ways. Someone seeking the meaning of *religion* would probably not take Karl Marx's definition ("Religion is the opium of the people") at face value. Another example is the definition of true art as "the communication of religious feelings" in the book *What Is Art?* by the great Russian novelist Leo Tolstoy. Unfortunately, his definition excludes all of his own novels, including his most famous one, *War and Peace*.

Writing Persuasive Definitions

Most definitions in arguments lay the groundwork for understanding a writer's main point. In some cases, however, an entire argument may be devoted to establishing the definition of a term. A **persuasive definition** is an argument that a term *should* have a particular meaning. Such a claim may be based on a redefinition of a familiar term, as in the thesis, "Anyone who punishes a child physically for whatever reason is guilty of child abuse." Attempting to show that the commonly accepted definition of *child abuse* is too narrow requires the same sort of evidence needed to support any other claim.

Sometimes a persuasive definition will seem too narrow or odd for readers to accept. Suppose you argue that a true politician is one who is constantly in touch with his or her constituents. Your readers may judge your definition to be inaccurate since it ignores political leaders who focus on making laws rather than on meeting the immediate needs of voters in their districts. To anticipate such objections, extended persuasive definitions include refutations of opposing views, just as other kinds of argument do.

Long persuasive definitions are sometimes divided into parts so that their different aspects can be developed separately. For instance, suppose you were writing a persuasive definition of *censorship*. You could develop your thesis by first discussing censorship of pornography, then censorship of religious dissent, and lastly censorship of political opinion.

Inventing a new term is another approach to persuasive definition. For example, the writer Marie Winn uses the phrase "TV addict" to describe someone whose life is warped by an insatiable need to watch television. You could follow Winn's lead by providing your own persuasive definition of worry addicts, exercise addicts, or music addicts. Or you could invent and define your own entirely new term, such as "social pollution" or "freedom engineering."

Below is a list of words and phrases that usually indicate definitions.

WORDS AND PHRASES SIGNALING DEFINITIONS

characterized by	hints at	means
connotation	implication	refers to
connotes	implies	represents
defined as	indicates	significance
definition	in the sense of	signifies
denotation	is, are	suggests
denotes	is derived from	synonym
equivalent to	meaning	synonymous with

TRY IT OUT

Try your hand at definition using some of the techniques described in this chapter. Choose a word from the list of abstract words below or a similar word of your own and define it by filling in the blanks. Feel free to consult a dictionary when you need to. Answers will vary, but a sample set of definitions for the word *dedication* is given at the back of this book.

beauty	leadership
commitment	maturity
egotism	originality
faith	prejudice
friendship	satisfaction
heroism	security
infatuation	sophistication
joy	success

Synonym

1. A good synonym for _____ is _____.

Examples

2. Some examples of _____ are _____

_____

_____

_____

_____.

Attributes

3. Some attributes (qualities) associated with _____ are

_____

_____

_____

_____ .

Negation

4. Although some people think differently, _____ is not

_____

_____

_____

_____ .

Etymology

5. The word _____ comes from the _____
   language(s) and originally meant _____

_____

_____ .

Do you think this etymological information will help you write a
definition of the term as it is currently used?

_____ yes _____ no

Stipulation

6. If I needed a stipulative definition of _____ to use in
   an argument, I would define it as _____

_____

_____ .

Formal Definition

7. _____ is _____

(category) _____

_____ (how it differs from others in the same category).

Evaluation

Now reread your definitions and circle the one you think defines the
word most effectively.

EXERCISE 2

Directions: Identify the methods of definition illustrated in each item below. Write the letter of the correct choice in the space at the left.

Example: __C__ The word *prissy* is a combination of prim and sissy.

      A. stipulative definition

      B. definition by synonym

      C. definition by etymology

      D. definition by attributes

_____ 1. *Deleterious* means "harmful."

      A. definition by examples

      B. definition by negation

      C. stipulative definition

      D. definition by synonym

_____ 2. Papal infallibility does not mean that the Pope can never make a mistake.

      A. definition by synonym

      B. definition by examples

      C. definition by attributes

      D. definition by negation

_____ 3. Fatuous people repeatedly act foolishly, yet they never recognize themselves as fools.

      A. definition by attributes

      B. definition by expert testimony

      C. definition by etymology

      D. definition by analogy

_____ 4. The word *shambles*, which once meant a slaughterhouse, now refers to any scene of death, destruction, or extreme disorder.

      A. definition by negation

      B. definition by expert testimony

      C. stipulative definition

      D. definition by etymology

_____ 5. A socially responsible company avoids polluting the environment and sells goods or services that contribute to the dignity and meaning of life.

   A. definition by analogy

   B. formal definition

   C. definition by attributes

   D. definition by synonym

_____ 6. By lies I mean only those false statements that are intended to harm others.

   A. stipulative definition

   B. definition by analogy

   C. definition by examples

   D. definition by etymology

_____ 7. According to the poet Archibald MacLeish, "Living an art" means "living for it, not by it or in it, so that what remains in the end is the enlargement of the art, not the [person]."

   A. definition by etymology

   B. formal definition

   C. definition by analogy

   D. definition by expert testimony

_____ 8. For a newly divorced person, dating is like jumping into a swimming pool with a bored shark.

   A. definition by analogy

   B. definition by attributes

   C. formal definition

   D. definition by examples

_____ 9. Community involvement means participating in literacy programs, serving on the school board, voting in local elections, coaching children's sports teams, and attending the annual Fourth of July celebration.

   A. definition by expert testimony

   B. definition by negation

   C. definition by examples

   D. definition by synonym

_____ 10. Prison psychosis is a mental disorder brought on by incarceration or the dread of incarceration.

    A. formal definition

    B. definition by analogy

    C. definition by expert testimony

    D. definition by examples

CLASSIFYING

Often, the only way we can deal with large numbers of facts is to sort them into categories. By doing so, we discover that individual facts are related to one another. Grouping objects and ideas into categories based on characteristics they have in common is known as **classifying**. Once we succeed in sorting information into plausible categories, we can begin to see how the categories themselves are related.

A simple example of classification is the arrangement of merchandise in a supermarket. If the dry cereal, say, could be anywhere in the store, next to the oranges or in with the pet food, and all the other products were shelved equally at random, shopping would take all day. The store's classification of related items (produce, fish, cereal, and so on) into groups, each in its own section of the supermarket, provides an orderly way for customers to shop.

Classification involves not only grouping ideas into categories but also labeling the groups. In classification arguments, writers divide a body of material into groups, label each group, and describe specific members of each group to convince readers that their categories are reasonable. For example, if you were to write a classification argument about the people who come into a building supply store, you would describe typical representatives of certain groups (experienced do-it-yourselfers, bunglers, and beginners, for example) in a way that justifies your labels.

Writers of classification essays often argue that one of their categories is clearly preferable to the others. For instance, in his essay "Three Kinds of Resistance to Oppression," Martin Luther King describes three categories: surrender, violence, and nonviolent resistance. King shows that he understands the desire of oppressed people to give up or fight back, but he strongly urges them to choose the third course of action, nonviolent resistance. Persuasive classification essays can also propose ways to improve existing categorization schemes: "Bazaars should not be classified as flea markets unless at least half the goods for sale are not new."

Understanding Flexible and Inflexible Categories

Classification systems often include both flexible and inflexible categories. For example, when sorting poems into categories, recognizing sonnets is relatively easy since the characteristics of a sonnet are inflexible (sonnets are fourteen-line poems that have ten syllables in each line and rhyme according to certain established patterns). The prose poem, on the other hand, is a flexible category, somewhat like prose (written in paragraphs) and somewhat like poetry (written in powerful, rhythmic language). Based on this definition, some people would argue that particular passages from the Bible or a novel by Alice Walker are prose poems, but others would disagree. This potential for disagreement could be the basis for an argumentative essay.

Some areas of knowledge require precise, inflexible classification systems that scholars use as the basis for their communication with each other. These formal classification systems have two main requirements: their categories must include every possible object or idea to be classified, and the categories must not overlap. Plants are classified according to such a formal classification system; all plants fit into the scheme, and every plant belongs in only one category. For example, a sunflower belongs to the aster family, Queen Anne's lace belongs to the carrot family, and a lady's slipper belongs in the orchid family.

Informal classification systems are less rigid. When you devise your own informal classification scheme, you may choose only categories that interest you and allow some overlapping among the categories. For example, you could write an essay in which you divide ways to control stress into categories such as biofeedback, systematic relaxation, and exercise. You could decide to ignore other categories—tranquilizers and psychotherapy, for instance. In examining your categories, you might realize that techniques such as biofeedback and systematic relaxation have characteristics in common. You would then have the option of deciding whether their similarities are important enough to justify combining two or more categories into one.

Organizing a Classification Argument

As you develop your classification system, you will probably shift examples or ideas from one category to another and back again, perhaps several times. You may divide one old category into two new ones and rearrange whole groups under new headings. Your goal in making such changes should be to provide readers with manageable chunks of information. This means creating categories that are neither too numerous nor too large. For example, an account of the seventeen ways you think the welfare system perpetuates dependence might confuse your readers, but a two-part classification of the same material would most likely oversimplify it. Probably four or five categories would be easiest for readers to understand and remember. Once you've developed a good classification system, organizing your material should be straightforward, with one section of your persuasive essay devoted to each of the categories you've devised.

Below is a list of words that usually indicate classification.

WORDS SIGNALING CLASSIFICATION ARGUMENTS

branch	classify	pigeonhole
categorize	family	sort
category	group	taxonomy
class	grouping	types of
classification	kinds of	variety

EXERCISE 3

Directions: Sort the list of words below into categories by writing them in the chart where they belong. Some of the words on the list will not be used. Use a good dictionary to look up words that seem unfamiliar.

bindweed	flounder	horsemint
bird	fly	ibis
bridge	game	lace-wing
carp	garnet	midge
cribbage	grasshopper	mineral
dandelion	haddock	quartz
diamond	hearts	spoonbill
fish	heron	wildflower

Categories	Members of the Categories			
Example: dog	beagle	bloodhound	collie	dachshund
1.	egret			
2.		canasta		
3. insect				
4.			mica	
5.				grayling

EXERCISE 4

Directions: The items below illustrate critical thinking strategies. Identify the main strategy used in each item by writing the correct letter in the space at the left.

Example: ___C___ Hunting wasps are more intelligent than other insects.

A. definition

B. classification

C. comparison and contrast

D. cause-effect

_____ 1. Lawrence of Arabia was a misunderstood military genius.

A. recommendation

B. evaluation

C. definition

D. cause-effect

_____ 2. The personnel department of this company divides members of our work force into three categories: skilled, semi-skilled, and unskilled.

A. classification

B. cause-effect

C. comparison and contrast

D. definition

_____ 3. The federal government should have less influence over scientific research.

A. analysis

B. classification

C. comparison and contrast

D. recommendation

_____ 4. In sensational criminal cases, the chances for a fair trial are destroyed by lurid media coverage.

A. cause-effect

B. recommendation

C. definition

D. classification

_____ 5. Creationism is the doctrine that the world and its inhabitants were created by God out of nothing.

A. classification

B. definition

C. evaluation

D. analysis

_____ 6. Shyness results from a lack of social skills.

A. comparison and contrast

B. recommendation

C. cause-effect

D. definition

_____ 7. The treatment of Japanese Americans during World War II was a tragic injustice.

A. recommendation

B. comparison and contrast

C. analysis

D. evaluation

_____ 8. The characteristics of the great sixteenth- and seventeenth-century navigators were competitiveness, scientific curiosity, desire for adventure, and greed.

A. cause-effect

B. recommendation

C. analysis

D. comparison and contrast

_____ 9. Dorothy Sayers's contributions to modern advertising are more significant than her theological writing or her popular detective novels.

A. recommendation

B. cause-effect

C. definition

D. comparison and contrast

_____10. A reexamination of the career of Marcus Garvey provides a useful perspective on African-American politics today.

A. synthesis

B. classification

C. definition

D. analysis

*D*efining *is establishing what a word or phrase means in order to set the boundaries within which an argument will take place. The methods of definition include finding synonyms, writing formal definitions, providing examples, listing attributes, explaining etymologies (histories of words), devising analogies, announcing stipulative definitions (statements that words will be used in particular ways), using negation (explanations of inaccurate ideas about words), and relying on expert testimony. An entire argument can be devoted to a persuasive definition, an assertion that a term should have a particular meaning. Classification arguments involve grouping objects and ideas into categories according to characteristics they have in common and labeling the groups; these arguments often assert that one of the categories is preferable to the others.*

CHAPTER EXERCISE

I. MATCHING

Directions: Match each term on the list below with its definition by writing the correct letter in the space provided.

TERMS:

A. classifying   F. etymology

B. connotation   G. formal definition

C. defining   H. negation

D. denotation   I. persuasive definition

E. equivocation   J. stipulative definition

DEFINITIONS:

_____ 1. establishing what a word or phrase means

_____ 2. the meaning of a word independent of its emotional associations

_____ 3. feelings associated with a word

_____ 4. putting a word into a category and telling how it differs from others in the category

_____ 5. history of words

_____ 6. an announcement that a speaker or writer will use a term in a specific way

_____ 7. using a term in two senses

_____ 8. pointing out what something is not

_____ 9. argument that a term should have a particular meaning

_____10. grouping objects and ideas into categories based on characteristics they have in common

II. MULTIPLE CHOICE

Directions: On the line at the left write the letter of the phrase that best completes each item.

_____11. When quoting a definition from a dictionary, a writer should

A. be sure to use a Webster's dictionary.

B. identify the specific dictionary he or she is using.

C. begin with the words "The dictionary says . . ."

_____12. "Eleanor Roosevelt was a great American" defines "great American" by means of an

A. attribute.

B. etymology.

C. example.

_____13. The advantage of a stipulative definition is that

A. its writer does not explain or defend it.

B. it allows a term to be used in several senses within the same argument.

C. it emphasizes the word's connotation, not its denotation.

_____14. Classification arguments should

A. always be based on inflexible categories.

B. contain separate sections, each devoted to a different category.

C. contain as many categories as possible.

III. TRUE OR FALSE

Directions: On each line at the left write T if an item is true and F if it is false.

_____15. When choosing words, writers should consider both the words' denotations and their connotations.

_____16. Finding a synonym is the simplest and most straightforward approach to defining a word.

_____17. Expert testimony should never be used to provide a definition.

_____18. A persuasive definition can present an extended redefinition of a word, including a refutation of opposing ideas about what the word means.

_____19. Writers of classification arguments should be careful not to imply that one category is superior to any other.

_____20. Inflexible classification schemes must include every possible item to be classified and must not have overlapping categories.

6

Recognizing Faulty Reasoning

"*A*rguing with Sheila is so frustrating," Larry complained. "What she says seems to make perfect sense, but you wouldn't believe some of the conclusions she comes to."

"Such as?" Fran asked.

"The other day she tried to convince me that everybody in Italy speaks English. She argued that on her trip this summer she tried speaking Italian to several people, and they all answered her in English. I just know she's wrong, but how can I prove it? I've never been to Italy."

"You haven't been around much at all, have you?" Fran asked, smiling.

Sometimes you may feel that an argument has gone astray but you can't explain what went wrong. Although your opponent's line of reasoning seems valid, on closer inspection you notice that the conclusions don't really make sense. Learning to identify unsound ways of reasoning can help you sort out such puzzling situations.

This chapter emphasizes **fallacies**, mistakes in reasoning that often occur in persuasive writing. The term fallacy comes from the Latin word *fallere*, which means "to deceive." Usually fallacies are intentionally used to deceive. Sometimes, however, writers or speakers may be deceived themselves, falling into patterns of faulty thinking without being aware of them. Either way, fallacies distract from careful analysis of issues and hinder thoughtful problem solving.

While some authors use the term *fallacy* in the restricted sense of "constructing a faulty syllogism," most use it to indicate a wide variety of errors in reasoning. In practical argument, whether a particular mistake in reasoning has traditionally been identified as a fallacy or as some other kind of error makes little difference; it's more important to avoid a mistake than to classify it.

The Greek philosopher Aristotle (384-322 B.C.) was one of the first to identify and describe fallacies. Over the centuries people lost interest in his works, and most of them disappeared from western Europe. However, they were preserved and studied among Arabs and Byzantine Greeks, then rediscovered by Europeans in the twelfth century A.D. By then, Latin was the international language of scholarship, so Aristotle's works, including his list of fallacies, were translated into Latin. As these Latin versions were studied over hundreds of years, scholars added items, also in Latin, to Aristotle's original list. As a result, many of the fallacies have Latin names. This chapter explains the main types of faulty thinking so that you can identify them in other people's arguments and avoid them in your own.

FAULTY GENERALIZATION

As you may recall from chapter 2, induction proceeds by examining a selection of specific examples and drawing general conclusions based on them. For example, scientists trying to determine the effects of air pollution on certain plants might expose hundreds of plant specimens to polluted air under controlled conditions and tabulate the results. If the pollution causes all or most of the specimens to die, the scientists could then make valid generalizations about the bad effects of pollution. However, reaching proper conclusions can sometimes be tricky; misunderstanding how induction works can lead to hasty or unqualified generalizations.

Hasty Generalizations   A **hasty generalization** is a conclusion based on too few specific examples. In ordinary language, forming a generalization too hastily is called "jumping to conclusions." Theoretically, the greater the number of well-chosen examples, the more likely it is that a sound generalization can be drawn. The technique used to predict the outcome of a presidential election illustrates this point: pollsters try to foresee the result by asking a representative group of people how they intend to vote. If the people asked are typical of all who will vote, and if the group is large enough, the prediction has a good chance of being accurate.

When the number of examples on which people base generalizations is too small, they can easily draw the wrong conclusions. Hasty generalizations can lead to stereotyping as well as to a wide variety of other inaccurate inferences. For example, suppose a person sees a ten-year-old Vietnamese-American violinist on television. He remembers his mother-in-law's next door neighbors, a Chinese-American couple whose six children all take music lessons. He may jump to the hasty conclusion that all Asian-American children are musical.

Unqualified Generalizations

A qualifier is a word or phrase that limits or modifies another word or group of words. An **unqualified generalization** is a statement without any qualifiers (such as "probably" or "usually") to limit it; the unqualified generalization therefore allows for no exceptions. Such overstatements are sometimes referred to by the Latin phrase *dicto simpliciter*, "something said [too] simply." They are accurate only most or some of the time rather than all of the time. For example, the statement "Killing is morally wrong" is true in an overwhelming majority of instances but may not cover cases of killing in self-defense or killing an enemy soldier in time of war. In the more cautious statement "Killing is almost always morally wrong," the words "almost always" qualify the generalization, making it more acceptable to many people than the original version.

OVERSIMPLIFICATION

Assuming that situations are simpler than they really are can encourage people to draw erroneous conclusions and propose faulty solutions to perplexing problems. This section describes ways in which complicated arguments are sometimes oversimplified: the either-or dilemma, the *post hoc* fallacy, the slippery slope fallacy, the argument from ignorance, and the practice of special pleading.

The Either-Or Dilemma

The **either-or dilemma** (also known as the false dilemma) suggests that only two possibilities exist when in reality there may be several. (A dilemma is a choice between two unsatisfactory possibilities.) For example, new developments in biology have made it possible to alter the genetic structure of fruits and vegetables. However, some people fear that these so-called Frankenfoods (a reference to the monster in Mary Shelley's novel *Frankenstein*) can pose unpredictable health risks. Suppose someone argues that unless genetic engineering is prohibited by law, our foods will inevitably be unsafe. This suggests that society must *either* outlaw genetic engineering altogether *or* face disastrous threats to our food supply. The more likely solution of testing genetically engineered foods to establish that they are safe before putting them on the market is a third choice the speaker has failed to consider.

Thinking in terms of either-or dilemmas can lead people to try drastic solutions to problems or give them up as unsolvable when better courses of action are available all along. When you suspect that a complex argument has been reduced to an either-or dilemma, searching for alternative possibilities is a useful strategy.

The Post Hoc Fallacy

Establishing cause-and-effect relationships is a natural and valuable kind of thinking, but such relationships are often more complicated than we suppose. *Post hoc, ergo propter hoc*, a Latin phrase meaning "after this, therefore because of this," refers to people's habit of assuming that because one event happened before another, the first event caused the second one (the *post hoc* fallacy). The old joke "Of course it's raining; I just washed my car, didn't I?" is based on a humorous application of the *post hoc* way of thinking. Although washing an automobile cannot possibly cause a rainstorm, pretending it does is a way of making light of this familiar coincidence.

The humorist Mark Twain (1835–1910), writing of his experiences during the Civil War, uses *post hoc* thinking as the basis of another joke:

> I joined the Confederacy for two weeks. Then I deserted. The Confederacy fell.

The suggestion that his deserting caused the Confederacy's defeat is funny because the supposed cause is far out of proportion to its alleged effect.

Post hoc thinking can also lead to serious errors. Suppose someone has just been hired as a clerk in a department store. When a series of employee thefts is discovered, the manager turns to the new person and says, "Since we never had any trouble with theft before you arrived, you must be responsible. You're fired." If the manager's conclusion is based only on the fact that the thefts were detected shortly after the new employee was hired, he is committing the *post hoc* fallacy. A long-time employee, faced with mounting debts, might have begun stealing after years of honesty. Or the thefts might have been going on for months before the new person was hired but were not detected until afterward. The new employee may be guilty (in other words, there may be a real cause-effect relationship between the hiring and the thefts). However, better evidence is needed for the manager's conclusion than one event happening shortly before the other.

The Slippery Slope Fallacy

Sloping ramps are often easier to climb than stairs, but when they are slippery, one false step can send people sliding to the bottom. The **slippery**

slope fallacy is the assumption that an early error (like a false step at the top of a slippery slope) will inevitably lead to a bad outcome. The slippery slope fallacy is also called "the domino theory" because one tipped domino can push over a whole line of other dominos.

Slippery slope thinking is tempting because slippery slopes do exist— sometimes one small act of weakness or dishonesty is only the start of a situation that worsens steadily over time. It isn't always easy to distinguish between a situation in which one false step does lead inevitably to a negative outcome and a situation in which it doesn't. However, asking whether, given the first step, the second one is really inevitable will usually point to the correct conclusion.

An example of a puzzling argument based on slippery slope thinking is the National Rifle Association's apparent view that any law restricting a citizen's right to own a weapon is only the first step in a plan to confiscate all weapons. Some members of the association have argued, for example, that a law restricting sales of automatic or semiautomatic rifles will lead inevitably to a law prohibiting would-be hunters from owning any rifles at all.

Arguing from Ignorance

Suggesting that a claim must be true because no one can prove that it's false or false because no one can prove that it's true is **arguing from ignorance**. For example, some people maintain that President John F. Kennedy's assassination must have been the work of a conspiracy because no one has ever proven beyond doubt that Lee Harvey Oswald, the man accused of firing the fatal bullet, acted alone. They are arguing that since no one can prove there wasn't a conspiracy, there must have been a conspiracy. The trouble with arguments from ignorance is that they work just as well both ways. Notice that the reverse of the conspiracy theory is just as unconvincing as the original: Lee Harvey Oswald must have acted alone because no one has ever proven beyond doubt that he was part of a conspiracy.

An argument from ignorance relies on shifting the **burden of proof** (the obligation resting on a person who makes a claim to support it with evidence) from the person making the claim to his or her opponent. The term burden of proof often occurs in law courts: a prosecuting attorney must prove that someone accused of a crime is guilty; that is, the burden of proof rests on the prosecution. Americans regard the contrary idea—that an accused person is guilty until proven innocent—as a characteristic of law under a dictatorship. Not only in court but in any argument, insisting that an opponent prove one's claim is wrong dodges the responsibility to provide support for that claim.

It's valid to argue that if no evidence exists to support a claim, it probably isn't true. However, a person arguing from ignorance is doing the opposite:

he or she is suggesting that a claim is true because no evidence exists to disprove it. For example, suppose a friend tells you that little green men live in his garden. After looking under every bush, you find no little green men and naturally conclude that none exist. If your friend says, "I know little green men live in my garden because nobody has ever proven convincingly that they don't," he would be arguing from ignorance.

Special Pleading

Sometimes an arguer could make a very solid case for a claim if it were not for one or two inconvenient facts. Presenting only favorable information and ignoring equally valid material that would weaken a case is **special pleading**. For example, a salesperson stressing a used car's shiny new paint while ignoring its faulty brakes is engaged in a form of special pleading.

Special pleading can also mean inventing reasons that a rule applying to everyone else should not apply to oneself (pleading that one's own case is special). Drivers who grumble when other people park illegally ("Can't they see they're blocking the street?") can usually find a good reason when they want to violate the parking regulations ("I'll only be a few minutes"; "I'm late already, and there's really no place else to park"). Bertrand Russell made fun of this practice by showing how the same characteristic can be described in different terms depending on whether a person was referring to him or herself or to someone else:

I am firm; you are stubborn; he [or she] is pig-headed.

TRY IT OUT

We commonly use special pleading to cast ourselves in a favorable light while describing other people in less positive terms ("I am solidly built; you are chubby; he or she is fat"). Try your skill at detecting special pleading by finding words to complete the sentences below.

PART I

Describe one of your own qualities in a flattering way, use a less positive word for the same quality in the person to whom you're speaking, and choose a negative term to describe a third person who possesses the same quality. Use a dictionary or a thesaurus (a book of synonyms) to help you. Answers will vary; sample answers are given at the back of this book.

    Example: I am __compassionate__. You are soft-hearted. He or she is a pushover.

I am . . .	You are . . .	He or she is . . .
1.	thin	skinny
2. curious	inquisitive	
3. casual	haphazard	
4. striking	noticeable	
5. thrifty	frugal	
6. sensitive		cranky
7. beautiful		pleasant looking
8.	eccentric	bizarre
9. firm	strict	
10.	aggressive	brutal

PART II

Now think of your own examples of special pleading. Write your ideas in the spaces below:

I am _____.   You are _____.

He or she is _____.

I am _____.   You are _____.

He or she is _____.

EXERCISE 1

Directions: The items below illustrate faulty reasoning. Identify the main flaw in reasoning in each item by writing the correct letter in the space at the left.

Example: __B__ There is no evidence that rock music doesn't cause suicide, so it must be the reason for the increasing number of suicides among teenagers.

    A. special pleading

    B. argument from ignorance

    C. slippery slope fallacy

_____ 1. I'm sure that children's spiritual and religious lives are deeper and more meaningful than those of adults. I've known two children who were very devout.

    A. hasty generalization

_____ B. *post hoc* fallacy

C. slippery slope fallacy

_____ 2. You have a choice: Love America or leave it.

A. argument from ignorance

B. *post hoc* fallacy

C. either-or dilemma

_____ 3. Buying a gun is the first step in an inevitable descent into a life of crime.

A. slippery slope fallacy

B. special pleading

C. argument from ignorance

_____ 4. Theresa lost touch with her old friends when she moved to California; life in the West makes people heartless.

A. *post hoc* fallacy

B. argument from ignorance

C. slippery slope fallacy

_____ 5. Although most security guards should pass background checks, I have such an excellent work record I don't need to be subjected to one.

A. argument from ignorance

B. *post hoc* fallacy

C. special pleading

_____ 6. Strenuous exercise is beneficial to health.

A. either-or dilemma

B. unqualified generalization

C. slippery slope fallacy

_____ 7. There has never been any proof that Washington did not stay overnight in this house, so that shows he did sleep here.

A. argument from ignorance

B. slippery slope fallacy

C. *post hoc* fallacy

_____ 8. Nursing home aides deserve better pay. My cousin is a nursing home aide, and nobody works harder than he does.

A. slippery slope fallacy

B. hasty generalization

C. *post hoc* fallacy

_____ 9. Parents should help with their children's homework.

A. unqualified generalization

B. argument from ignorance

C. special pleading

_____10. Ancient Rome was either an ideal republic or a center of depravity and corruption.

A. special pleading

B. either-or dilemma

C. argument from ignorance

INTENTIONAL VAGUENESS

If arguers express beliefs in vague or unclear ways, they decrease their chances of eventually reaching agreement. Suppose a critic attacks a best-selling novel on the basis that the characters are not "true to life." The author retorts that they are all modeled on her relatives and that she has toned down their eccentricities rather than exaggerated them. "Well, they don't seem real to me," the critic answers, shaking his head. This criticism is vague; the critic needs to quote specific episodes in the novel and explain why he feels real people would not act like the characters in the book. Among the means of obscuring an argument by keeping it intentionally vague are glittering generalities and equivocation.

Glittering Generalities

Sometimes vague words or phrases are used as part or all of the evidence that supports a thesis. When these vague words or phrases are positive, they are called **glittering generalities**. Advertisers who make extravagant claims for products or services are said to be relying on glittering generalities because all of the general terms they use are so positive they seem to glitter like fake diamonds. Vague words and expressions such as *great, healthy*, and *the best you can buy* cast a warm glow over products or services without really claiming anything. Effective selling sometimes involves a certain amount of exaggeration, such as "You can't find a better vacuum cleaner on the market." However, some exaggerated claims are so misleading that using them is unethical or even illegal. Vague claims should never be enough to distract a buyer from evaluating a product fairly.

When one person uses vague language and another attaches a precise meaning to it, confusion is almost inevitable. Suppose that during a financial crisis, the president of a company calls a meeting of the executives and says, "Now it's time to put aside our differences and pull together." The sales manager, who has just received a hard-won increase in salary, answers, "If that means giving up my raise, I won't do it." The president *may* have meant exactly that, but if he didn't, the sales manager has started an unnecessary quarrel.

Equivocation

Both sides in an argument should strive to keep the meanings of key terms consistent. Using the same word in more than one sense, whether intentionally or not, is known as **equivocation.** Suppose that a young man and his fiancée are exchanging views on fidelity in marriage. "I promise that I will be faithful to you," the young woman says. "I'll always give you a faithful account of my activities, no matter what they are." Using the word *faithful* in two senses—to mean "monogamous" the first time and "accurate" the second—is an example of equivocation.

CIRCULAR REASONING

Going around in a circle is no way to make progress. Beginning with a preconceived solution to a problem and only pretending to seek evidence that supports it is like going around in a circle. Begging the question, asking loaded questions, using loaded words and phrases, and relying on question-begging definitions are all ways of reasoning in a circle.

Begging the Question

In its simplest form, an argument consists of a claim and evidence supporting that claim. But the claim should not be used as part of the evidence. **Begging the question** is taking for granted the point that is open to dispute; this often involves using the claim to support itself. Here *begging* means "evading" or "dodging." When begging the question, an arguer is evading the responsibility to support an assumption by stating it as if it has already been proven. This may occur because the arguer has no evidence to back up the claim or because it hasn't occurred to him or her that there is any need to do so.

One form of begging the question occurs in debates about the authority of the Bible. People argue that the Bible is the word of God by quoting a passage such as "All scripture is inspired by God" (2 Tim. 3:16) from the Bible itself. If evidence to support the claim that the Bible is inspired comes from the Bible itself, the argument is circular.

Loaded Questions

A **loaded question** is a question based on an assumed answer to another, unasked question. One well-known example is, "Have you stopped beating your spouse?" It is really a double question:

1. Have you beaten your spouse in the past?

2. If so, are you still doing it?

A person who answers yes to "Have you stopped beating your spouse?" is admitting having beaten a spouse in the past; an answer of no admits that the beating is still going on. Such a question is called "loaded" because, like the loaded dice used by cheating gamblers, it is unfair.

The question often asked of newlyweds, "When are you two going to have a baby?" is loaded because it assumes that the couple have already answered yes to the unasked question "Are you two planning to have children?" Should someone feel compelled to ask such a question, dividing it into two parts is a better approach; then, if the answer to the first question is no, the second question need never be asked.

If in the course of an argument someone asks a question you think is loaded, you have a right to pause and say, "Well, that's really two questions. Let me tackle them one at a time." When the answer to the first question is no, the second question becomes irrelevant.

Loaded Words and Phrases

Sometimes people word statements in a way that makes it hard to disagree with them. For example, if someone remarks, "Only a very naive person would believe that Governor Walsh will really fight to reduce the income tax," it takes courage to answer, "I think he will." Words such as *obviously* and *clearly* and expressions such as "any schoolchild knows" and "it's as plain as the nose on your face" are loaded words and phrases aimed at intimidating opponents. Like loaded questions, **loaded words and phrases** have unfair implications. Standing up to people who use loaded words and phrases can be difficult, but accepting their statements without protest gives them an unfair advantage.

Question-Begging Definitions

Because the side that controls definitions in a debate controls the debate itself, many people try to introduce arguable definitions without supporting them. A **question-begging definition** is an arguable definition presented as if it were a statement of fact. Remember that a controversial definition requires the same support as any other claim. In other words, a definition can be a thesis sentence in disguise. Suppose two friends, Harlan and Jean, have just seen the movie *The Sun Also Rises*, based on Ernest Hemingway's novel. They have both been impressed (quite differently, as it turns out) by the bullfighting scenes.

"Bullfighting is disgusting," Harlan begins. "The UN should take action against it."

"Come on," Jean replies. "It's Spain's national sport—like baseball in the U.S. It's not our business to impose our ideas of right and wrong on another culture."

"Cruelty to animals is wrong wherever it occurs," says Harlan. "You can't defend it in the name of cultural diversity."

Harlan has just defined *bullfighting* as "cruelty to animals." If Jean does not challenge his definition, she will find herself trying to justify cruelty—a losing proposition. Actually, Harlan is making the claim "Bullfighting is cruelty to animals"; he should now try to support his claim.

EXERCISE 2

Directions: The items below illustrate faulty reasoning. Identify the main flaw in reasoning in each item by writing the correct letter in the space at the left.

> **Example:** __A__ Has our state board of corrections stopped the absurd practice of asking inmates' opinions about how to run the prison system?
>
> A. loaded question
>
> B. glittering generalities
>
> C. equivocation

_____ 1. The president of the university should make sure that student morale improves because it's the president's responsibility to guarantee that the attitudes of people attending the school are good.

A. loaded question

B. glittering generalities

C. begging the question

_____ 2. Candidate Constance Hernandez is a marvel. Vote for the best! Hernandez for mayor.

A. equivocation

B. loaded question

C. glittering generalities

_____ 3. This is a free country, so access to all beaches should be free.

A. equivocation

B. question-begging definition

C. loaded question

_____ 4. Execution by lethal injection is a type of officially sanctioned murder even more barbarous than death in the electric chair.

   A. loaded question

   B. question-begging definition

   C. glittering generalities

_____ 5. Why do I think that Washington, DC, is a more livable city than New York City? Because I know it's a better place to live, that's why.

   A. loaded question

   B. begging the question

   C. loaded words and phrases

_____ 6. Is our board of directors going to grant top managers runaway salary increases again this year?

   A. loaded question

   B. equivocation

   C. glittering generalities

_____ 7. Cheating in a college course is merely simplifying the process of earning a passing grade.

   A. question-begging definition

   B. glittering generalities

   C. equivocation

_____ 8. Chemistry is the discipline you have enrolled to study. Because discipline is essential to your work as chemists, you must expect harsh penalties for lateness and sloppy work.

   A. loaded question

   B. equivocation

   C. glittering generalities

_____ 9. Public schools should be run by teachers and principals, not by overpaid, out-of-touch district officials.

   A. loaded words and phrases

   B. equivocation

   C. question-begging definitions

_____ 10. The burden of injustice that is naturally part of all heterosexual relationships must be lifted without delay.

   A. loaded question

B. begging the question

C. equivocation

PERSONAL ATTACKS

The line between an argument and a quarrel is sometimes difficult to draw. Because differences of opinion can become emotional, even bitter, when they involve people's deepest feelings, an opponent who supports what appears to be a bad cause may seem stupid or immoral. However, changing the direction of an argument from the subject under discussion to the intelligence, character, or behavior of an opponent is unfair and confuses the issue. Instead, when people listen to or read an argument, they should try to separate the facts about the issue from their feelings about the people involved.

Ad Hominem Attacks

The Latin phrase *ad hominem*, which means "to the person," refers to the practice of arguing against a claim by attacking the person who makes it. The character or reputation of a claim's advocate does not determine whether the claim itself is sound or unsound. Nevertheless, politicians frequently use *ad hominem* attacks. Suppose that a candidate for mayor proposes a comprehensive ethics code for city government. His opponent, instead of analyzing the program and attacking its provisions, replies, "This is a fine time for Mr. O'Hara to start talking about ethics! When he was a district attorney, he was suspected of being unfaithful to his wife." Not only an opponent's character, but also his or her race, ethnic group, religion, personal appearance, and other qualities have been used as the basis of *ad hominem* attacks. *Ad hominem* generally applies to a personal attack on anyone, male or female, but *ad feminam* is sometimes used to describe a personal attack on a woman.

Criticism of a person who makes a claim is not always irrelevant. Suppose a surgeon tells a patient that he needs a serious heart operation. The patient then discovers that the surgeon has been censured by a medical board for recommending unnecessary surgery. Certainly the patient should seek a second opinion about his own case. However, he may turn out to need the operation anyway. The surgeon who has been wrong so many times before may be right this time. Similarly, a hardened criminal may testify truthfully at a trial; members of the jury are right to be suspicious of his testimony but should disregard it only if they are sure he is lying about this case, not because they believe hardened criminals are incapable of telling the truth. In short, attacking people's credibility or character may cast doubt on the value of their evidence but does not prove that they are wrong.

Tu Quoque Arguments

Closely related to *ad hominem* attacks are *tu quoque* arguments. *Tu quoque*, which is Latin for "you [do it] too," refers to the practice of answering criticism by saying that one's critic is guilty of the same or equally bad behavior. For example, a teenager being lectured by her father about the evils of marijuana might answer, "You're in no position to talk. You smoke three packs of cigarettes a day, so how can you stand there and say smoking marijuana will hurt me?" The teenager may be right when she implies that her father should give up smoking, but her point is irrelevant to an argument about the dangers of smoking marijuana.

Tu quoque arguments can be deceptive because we so strongly believe that people should "practice what they preach." Doctors whose own health habits are poor, members of the clergy who commit the sins they attack in their sermons, and politicians who vote against programs to aid the needy because they are too expensive but take lavish trips at public expense can all become objects of ridicule. Nevertheless, remember that the soundness of an argument does not depend on the character of the person who makes it. A doctor's advice may be good, a preacher's sermon may be morally correct, and a politician's vote may be in the public interest whether these people act consistently in their personal lives or not.

Poisoning the Well

Poisoning the well is a type of personal attack in which someone suggests at the beginning of an argument that any evidence coming from a particular source will be tainted, like water from a poisoned well. Poisoning the well differs from other forms of *ad hominem* argument in that it occurs even before one's opponent has an opportunity to speak. In an argument about women's rights, for example, a woman may say, "Men have no idea what women go through. They have no right to participate in this debate— women's rights are women's business." If a man responds, his contributions may be ignored because his opponent has cast doubt on them before they were made.

EMOTIONAL APPEALS

Making a personal attack on an opponent is by no means the only way of appealing to an audience's emotions. Unscrupulous people can exploit the values, prejudices, hopes, and fears of readers or listeners to persuade them that one side of an argument is stronger than it really is. Although getting an audience to care deeply about an issue is one of the legitimate tasks of a speaker or writer, playing on people's emotions to confuse their thinking is unfair.

Ad Populum Appeals

Many people can be swayed by appeals to patriotism or loyalty to their own group. In Latin, this practice of making emotional appeals to a group's shared beliefs and prejudices is called *ad populum*; it means "to the people." An office-seeker using a phrase such as "Let's keep our city great" instead of suggesting specific programs to solve economic or social problems is making an *ad populum* appeal. So is a speaker who tries to stir up his listeners' prejudices against people of another race or ethnic group.

Appeals to Fear

Fear is one of people's strongest emotions. Television commercials that appeal to people's fear of being robbed while on vacation, for example, have been very effective in selling traveler's checks. They show vacationers having fun on a beach or napping by a hotel pool while nearby a thief is stealing their money. The claim "Traveler's checks are safer to carry than cash" may well be true, but a few dramatized hypothetical examples don't prove it. These appeals may succeed because people often imagine themselves as potential victims—whether the events depicted are likely ones or not. Unfortunately, frightening people is an easy way to manipulate them.

Most appeals to fear occur in the form of warnings: "Buy Atlas Homeowners' Insurance, or you may lose everything in a fire." Some warnings should be heeded, but each case must be judged on its merits: asking "How real is the danger?" and "Is this the best way to protect against it?" should help you decide whether a warning is worth paying attention to or not.

Appeals to Pity

An old joke tells of someone who kills his parents and, having been tried and convicted, begs the judge to take pity on him because he is an orphan. Arguers who use *ad misericordiam* (Latin for "to pity") try to persuade people by playing on their compassion instead of supplying evidence. A realtor who pleads for you to buy a house "because I haven't made a sale in two months, and I won't be able to pay my own mortgage if I don't sell one soon" is appealing to pity. As a prospective buyer, however, you should be more concerned about whether the house is reasonably priced than whether the realtor can pay his or her bills.

EXERCISE 3

Directions: The items below illustrate faulty reasoning. Identify the main flaw in reasoning in each item by writing the correct letter in the space at the left.

Example: __C__ When guns are outlawed, only outlaws will have guns.

A. poisoning the well

B. appeal to pity

C. appeal to fear

_____ 1. The prime minister of France is just a middle-aged hysteric.

   A. *ad hominem* attack

   B. *tu quoque* attack

   C. appeal to pity

_____ 2. My sister is hospitalized with pneumonia, and my father has recently been laid off. My family will be devastated if I get a failing grade after all the trouble we've been having.

   A. appeal to fear

   B. appeal to pity

   C. poisoning the well

_____ 3. Don't bother listening to Professor Levin's lectures. You won't hear anything more tedious and useless during the whole time you're in college.

   A. poisoning the well

   B. *tu quoque* attack

   C. appeal to fear

_____ 4. We cannot forget the terror of world war and nuclear devastation; no limitation of our defense capabilities can ever be allowed.

   A. appeal to fear

   B. *ad hominem* attack

   C. *tu quoque* attack

_____ 5. I can't believe you're telling me to stop drinking. You drink yourself.

   A. poisoning the well

   B. appeal to pity

   C. *tu quoque* attack

_____ 6. We are gathered today to celebrate the achievements of real Iowans, the wonderful people we all take so much pride in supporting.

   A. *ad populum* appeal

   B. *tu quoque* attack

   C. appeal to fear

_____ 7. The speaker I am introducing is not qualified to suggest a program for preventing sexual abuse; I'm sure you'll want to discuss your objections with her.

   A. *tu quoque* attack

    B. appeal to pity

    C. poisoning the well

_____ 8. The defendant has lost his wife, his job, and his home; surely he has suffered enough, so the drug charges against him should be dropped.

    A. poisoning the well

    B. appeal to pity

    C. *ad populum* appeal

_____ 9. The only reason Mr. McDonald opposes the reorganization of our office is that he's too lazy to make changes.

    A. *ad hominem* attack

    B. appeal to fear

    C. *tu quoque* attack

_____10. The research and development department is in no position to preach against extravagance since its expenditures were over budget again last month.

    A. poisoning the well

    B. *tu quoque* attack

    C. appeal to fear

FALSE APPEALS TO AUTHORITY

In many situations nothing could be more sensible than asking an expert for advice. A person who is unwell should ordinarily consult a doctor, and a person who is being sued would usually benefit from consulting a lawyer. Similarly, people supporting a claim often wish to introduce expert testimony in its favor. But some appeals to authority—appeals to anonymous authorities, appeals to tradition, the bandwagon appeal, transfer, and the plain folks appeal—are based on errors in reasoning.

The Appeal to Anonymous Authorities

Experts are worth listening to because they have special knowledge. When a claim is supported by authorities, we assume that they are basing their beliefs on long, careful study. In other words, we are asked to believe something not merely because experts believe it but because they have good reasons for believing it. When authorities are properly identified, we can do further research to evaluate their reasoning and their credentials.

Appealing to **anonymous authorities** is claiming that unnamed experts hold particular views. Judging an authority's reasons for an opinion is impossible if the authority is not identified. Phrases such as "Washington insiders believe . . ." or "according to a reliable source . . ." appear frequently in news stories, but the views attributed to such unnamed authorities should not be taken as seriously as those expressed by identified sources. Unfortunately, some writers and speakers fudge the facts, maintaining that experts support their opinions when no such experts exist.

The Appeal to Tradition

People occasionally argue that something should be done because it has always been done or should be done in a certain way because it has always been done that way. For example, the saying "A woman's place is in the home" has sometimes been used in arguments about women's rights. Those who quote this saying are arguing that because women have traditionally been restricted to roles as mothers and homemakers, they should always be limited to these roles.

Traditions can be valuable ways for individuals or groups to express their identity and their links with the past. However, an appeal to tradition can be used as an argument against any change whatsoever. Plainly each suggested change should be supported or attacked on its merits; if we invariably continued to behave exactly as we have always done, progress would be impossible.

The Bandwagon Appeal

"Everybody's doing it" is a familiar appeal in advertisements; this slogan implies that a person who doesn't join the crowd is missing out on a good thing. A television commercial for a political candidate may show several people in succession, each claiming that he or she will vote for Senator Waters. Such a commercial implies that the election will be a landslide and that votes for Senator Waters's opponent will be wasted. Such an appeal is based on the **bandwagon** technique: a claim that a candidate or cause merits support because others are already supporting it. Just as a wagon carrying a band attracts a crowd behind it during a circus parade, an already popular idea often attracts a larger and larger following.

The bandwagon technique can mislead in two ways. First, people using it can suggest that an idea is popular when it really isn't; for example, it can be employed to sell products nobody wants or needs or to support candidates who are far behind in the polls. Second, following a crowd isn't always the best way to arrive at a sound conclusion: large numbers of people have been wrong before. Accepting popular opinions is no substitute for thinking issues through for oneself.

Transfer

Transfer is the association of a product or an idea with an image that people already feel strongly about. Dressing a handsome actor in a cowboy outfit and showing him smoking a cigarette is an attempt to transfer people's positive feelings about cowboy life to the cigarette. A commercial featuring a car with an American flag in the background can be used to transfer people's positive feelings about the flag to the car. When the ad points out that a product is "made in the USA," it tells nothing about the product's quality or price. It may be in people's best interest to purchase goods made in their own country as often as they can, but the ad isn't supporting that claim. The advertiser is simply hoping that people's good feelings about their country will somehow rub off on the product.

The Plain Folks Appeal

Plain folks is the strategy of associating products, ideas, or candidates with seemingly ordinary people who recommend them. Imagine a television commercial that shows a man in a three-piece suit recommending a bank. Many people might find this recommendation unconvincing—of course a banker would claim his own bank was sound. But a person in a hard hat and jeans who recommends the same bank might seem just like one of them and therefore be more credible. Politicians who are photographed eating a hot dog or tossing a football with their children are making a similar effort to seem like plain folks.

EXERCISE 4

Directions: The items below illustrate faulty reasoning. Identify the main flaw in reasoning in each item by writing the correct letter in the space at the left.

Example: __B__ Unnamed sources revealed today that small firms are now more important to aerospace research than the giant electronics and aircraft companies.

    A. plain folks appeal

    B. appeal to anonymous authorities

    C. bandwagon appeal

_____ 1. Look for the red, white, and blue label of Premier American Mustard; American is our middle name.

    A. plain folks appeal

    B. transfer

    C. appeal to anonymous authorities

_____ 2. Down Home cookies are made the way your mom used to make them—nothing fancy, just down home flavor.

    A. plain folks appeal

    B. bandwagon appeal

    C. appeal to anonymous authorities

_____ 3. Experts argue that the Department of Justice should be tougher on banking scandals.

A. plain folks appeal

B. transfer

C. appeal to anonymous authorities

_____ 4. Everyone else in the eighth grade can stay out until midnight on school nights. Why can't I?

A. bandwagon appeal

B. plain folks appeal

C. transfer

_____ 5. The United States should continue playing the role it has customarily played: arbitrator of disagreements among all other nations.

A. transfer

B. appeal to tradition

C. bandwagon appeal

_____ 6. Ordinary people are rallying to the support of South Dakota senator Ross Summers as he opens his campaign for the presidency. Summers consistently opposes slippery big-city politicians and speaks out for the average working person.

A. plain folks appeal

B. appeal to tradition

C. transfer

_____ 7. More and more people are living together to test their compatibility, making sharing a home an excellent alternative to legal marriage.

A. transfer

B. appeal to tradition

C. bandwagon appeal

_____ 8. The official glue of the National Football League is Thicky Sticky Plus.

A. transfer

B. plain folks appeal

C. bandwagon appeal

_____ 9. Doctors recommend Ripplex Muscle Molder.

A. appeal to anonymous authorities

B. appeal to tradition

C. bandwagon appeal

_____10. Americans have always loved sizzling steaks, hearty beef stews, and delicious barbecued hamburgers; there's no reason to turn away from red meat now.

A. appeal to tradition

B. appeal to anonymous authorities

C. transfer

IRRELEVANCE

Sticking with the real subject of an argument can be very difficult at times. Side issues arise frequently, and it's often tempting to pursue them. Occasionally, arguers who feel they're losing try to sidetrack an argument deliberately, hoping they can do better in a discussion of some other issue. But more often, arguments go astray because both participants lose track of the original claim. A response that does not follow logically from what has previously been said or written is called a **non sequitur**. The red herring, straw man, and false analogy are types of arguments that wander off a topic.

Red Herring

When a herring is smoked, it changes color to reddish brown. During a fox hunt, drawing a red herring across the path of the hunting dogs will cause them to lose the fox's scent. Just as dogs can be drawn off the track, an argument can be diverted by a remark that causes the discussion to take off in an irrelevant direction. Such a remark is called a **red herring**.

Suppose someone suggests that the school year should be lengthened by six weeks, pointing out that "other industrialized nations have a longer school year than we do."

"So what?" an opponent replies. "Most of them also restrict college and university admissions to their top students. Should we copy that, too?" This irrelevant comment, which attempts to divert the discussion from the length of the school year to access to higher education, is a red herring.

Straw Man

In a fistfight, a scarecrow made of straw would make an extremely weak opponent. Given the choice, most people would rather battle a scarecrow than a real person. Similarly, when confronted by a strong argument, some people prefer to answer a weak one instead, even if they have to invent it. A **straw man** (or straw figure) is a weak or implausible argument attributed to an opponent and attacked as if it had really been made. The opponent's real argument is usually ignored in the process.

Suppose someone were arguing that the City Council should pass a law guaranteeing homosexuals fair housing opportunities. An opponent of the law might ask, "How would you like it if your children saw two of your gay neighbors kissing in public?" However, the issue under discussion is not whether people should indulge in public displays of affection. No one advocating the law argued that public displays of affection were desirable. Nevertheless, it's easier to argue against potentially inappropriate behavior than against people's right to live where they choose.

Another way of setting up a straw figure consists of selecting a weak but unimportant aspect of an opponent's argument and attacking it as if it were the main point. Suppose someone maintains that the federal government should institute a program of national health care. She quotes statistics to show that millions of uninsured working people face being driven into poverty by catastrophic illness and argues that the quality of health care often depends on patients' ability to pay. She also mentions that many people lack basic dental care and that small children needing fillings and braces never see a dentist because their parents can't afford one. "Aha!" shouts an opponent. "Do you really want the taxpayers of this nation paying for kids to get their teeth straightened? Ridiculous!" Pretending that a minor aspect of an opponent's case is crucial just because it is easier to attack than the rest is a way of obscuring the real issue.

False Analogy

By using an analogy, an arguer can make his or her point in an interesting way. A person using a **false analogy**, however, is trying to show that two unlike situations are similar when, in fact, any similarities are trivial or irrelevant. A woman accused of unethical business practices might defend herself by claiming, "It's a jungle out there. I just obeyed the law of the jungle. That's all." Business can be highly competitive, so comparing it to a jungle is superficially appealing. But unlike the life of a tiger in a jungle, a business person's life is subject to a code of ethical conduct. The business-woman's analogy is faulty because she suggests that the two situations are far more alike than they are.

COMBATTING FAULTY REASONING

Once you become alert to the mistakes described in this chapter, you'll be in a better position to avoid them. Not making them yourself is only part of your task; challenging other people's faulty reasoning is just as important. However, you should use your knowledge not to score debating points but to set arguments back on the right track. To achieve this aim, it's sometimes best not to use technical names for these faulty patterns. Someone accused of committing the *post hoc* fallacy, for example, will probably feel either bewildered or defensive. A far better method of returning the argument to a more reasonable path is to keep your criticisms as simple and nonthreatening as possible. Point out that two events are not necessarily related just because one came after the other. If you remember a textbook example of *post hoc* reasoning, such as the humorous supposed relationship between washing a car and "causing" a rainstorm, use it to make your point.

Replying in ordinary language is a good way to attack any kind of faulty reasoning. For example, if your opponent makes what you consider a hasty generalization, you might reply, "Well, you've given some interesting examples, but are you sure you've got enough of them to draw such a sweeping conclusion?" Or suppose your opponent is using a key term in two senses (the kind of fault known as *equivocation*). After he or she uses the term in what you consider an inappropriate sense, ask for a definition of it. Having been given the definition, you can refer to the term's original use and make the point that for an argument to reach a meaningful conclusion, key terms should be used consistently throughout.

You will sometimes find that countering other people's faulty reasoning can be very difficult, especially when emotional issues are involved. Don't be surprised if your opponents refuse to accept your criticism or accuse you of trying to trick them. In such cases, you can take some comfort from knowing that you have done your best and have at least tried to avoid faulty reasoning yourself.

EXERCISE 5

Directions: The items below contain errors in reasoning. On the lines that follow each item, use ordinary language to explain what is wrong with it.

Example: Factory workers are like mechanical extensions of the machines they operate: faceless, emotionless, totally dedicated to their duty.

<u>The comparison between workers and machines does not apply to all or even most workers. People seldom behave like machines.</u>

1. Our great country is dedicated to individual liberty, so I have taken the liberty of ruling on the applications for promotion without consulting with the promotions committee.

_____

_____

2. Racism is not our real problem; we should turn our attention to the need we all share for a reliable, affordable mass transportation system.

_____

_____

3. The supporters of the Withdraw from the Olympics Now movement are headed in the wrong direction; they're probably about to attack the Olympic logo as inartistic when it's actually a beautiful and meaningful symbol.

_____

_____

4. A mastery of college-level science is like the ability to read and write. No one can function adequately without basic scientific literacy.

_____

_____

5. Leading psychologists agree that women today are too straightforward with men. According to these experts women can get their way more often through guile and flattery.

_____

_____

6. Candidate Byler's experiences as a dishwasher, truck driver, and factory worker certainly qualify him as a spokesperson for us ordinary people.

_____

_____

7. We must meet all the workers' demands or they will go out on strike.

_____

_____

8. Of course, the other entrants in the poetry contest must come from Salem County, but my poems are so good that it doesn't matter what county I live in.

_____

_____

9. Malika Rainer wants to save the alligators in the Everglades, but I'd never pay attention to a fuzzy-minded ecologist like her.

_____

_____

10. Billy's grades in math started to go down after he began using a calculator. Buying him the calculator was obviously a mistake.

_____

_____

*F*allacies, mistakes in reasoning that often occur in arguments, have been studied since the time of Aristotle. Faulty generalizations result when people misunderstand how induction works while oversimplifications occur if they assume that problems are less complicated than they really are. When people deliberately express their beliefs in unclear ways, the result is glittering generalities or equivocation. Circular reasoning stems from taking a claim for granted rather than trying to prove it. Personal attacks and emotional appeals are attempts to substitute feelings for evidence in arguments. Relying on unidentified authorities or implying that an idea's popularity or association with tradition or with ordinary people is enough to justify it is a false appeal to authority. Irrelevancies occur when participants in an argument intentionally distract readers or listeners from the substance of their claims. One way to combat faulty reasoning is by not using technical terms for fallacies but by expressing the problems in ordinary language instead.

CHAPTER EXERCISE

I. MATCHING

Directions: Match each term on the list below with its definition by writing the correct letter in the space provided. Some of the terms on the list will not be used.

TERMS:

A. *ad hominem* attack

B. *ad misericordiam* appeal

C. *ad populum* appeal

D. appeal to anonymous authorities

E. bandwagon appeal

F. begging the question

G. either-or dilemma

H. equivocation

I. false analogy

J. hasty generalization

K. loaded words and phrases
L. plain folks appeal
M. *post hoc* fallacy
N. red herring
O. slippery slope fallacy

P. special pleading
Q. straw man
R. transfer
S. *tu quoque* argument

DEFINITIONS:

_____ 1. conclusion based on too few specific examples

_____ 2. assumption that there are only two possible solutions to a problem

_____ 3. belief that because one event happened before another, the first event caused the second one

_____ 4. presentation of only favorable information

_____ 5. treating a point that is open to dispute as if it were an established fact

_____ 6. terms chosen because of their unfair implications

_____ 7. attack on a person rather than on his or her argument

_____ 8. claim that an accuser is guilty of the same behavior he or she criticizes

_____ 9. appeal to a group's shared feelings or prejudices

_____ 10. evidence attributed to unnamed experts

_____ 11. argument that something should be done because many other people do it

_____ 12. association of products or candidates with ordinary people

_____ 13. irrelevant issue used to sidetrack an argument

_____ 14. an easily attacked argument falsely attributed to an opponent

_____ 15. comparison based on trivial or irrelevant similarities

II. MULTIPLE CHOICE

Directions: On the line at the left write the letter of the phrase that best completes each item.

_____ 16. When a person arguing a controversial issue shifts the burden of proof to his or her opponent, he or she is

A. arguing from ignorance.

B. using the best way to make a solid case for a claim.

C. appealing to pity.

_____17. Glittering generalities and equivocation are examples of

A. faulty generalizations.

B. personal attacks.

C. intentional vagueness.

_____18. "Have you stopped beating your wife?" is an example of

A. a loaded question.

B. poisoning the well.

C. an appeal to fear.

_____19. "If you offer people unemployment insurance, soon they'll expect government insurance against every conceivable misfortune" is an example of

A. a question-begging definition.

B. an _ad misericordiam_ appeal.

C. the slippery slope fallacy.

_____20. A beer commercial featuring an American flag and an eagle is apparently based on the assumption that

A. people will transfer their positive feelings about the United States to the beer.

B. viewers want to participate in the solution of complex moral issues.

C. simplifying a problem by finding only two possible solutions is the quickest way to solve it.

7

First Steps in Persuasive Writing

"*Did you finish the assignment?*" *Ellen asked Rick as they waited for their political science class to begin. Around them other students were complaining about the thousand-word essay their professor had assigned on Friday and expected them to hand in Monday morning.*

"Yeah, I finished," said Rick, "even though my whole weekend was ruined. I had tickets to the game on Saturday afternoon, but I gave them to Jeff, my roommate. I had so much trouble getting started, I knew by Friday evening I wouldn't be able to go. I must have rewritten my opening sentence a dozen times. When I couldn't get it right, I got so depressed I had to send out for pizza to cheer myself up."

"I don't work that way," said Ellen. "I spend the first couple of hours just gathering ideas. Then I get my thoughts down on paper. It doesn't matter to me how rough they are. After that, I can gradually get them into presentable shape."

"None of that scribbling down ideas for me," said Rick. "If I have to write something, I just try to write it." Ellen said nothing.

"I finished a pretty good draft by Saturday morning," she began again after a few seconds. "Then when I got back in the evening, I read it over, edited it, and typed up a clean copy. I proofread it this morning before I came to class."

"Where'd you go Saturday afternoon?" Rick asked. Ellen mumbled something. "What?" Rick demanded.

"I said I went to the game," Ellen answered. "Jeff called me and said he had two tickets . . ."

UNDERSTANDING THE WRITING PROCESS

The **writing process** is a series of mental and physical steps leading to a finished piece of writing. Because Ellen thinks of writing as a step-by-step process, she can tackle her task one part at a time, making it more manageable. If you understand the writing process, you can experiment with the steps that cause you the most difficulty, testing various techniques for accomplishing them until you discover the ones you find most useful.

Stages of Writing

One way of thinking about the writing process is to divide it into the following stages:

1. prewriting
2. drafting
3. revising
4. editing
5. proofreading

During the first stage, **prewriting**, you think about a subject and gather material. Prewriting involves recalling ideas you may already have about your topic and forming new ones before you start to write. At this stage you can begin to set general goals based on your understanding of the writing task, your potential audience, and your own reasons for writing. These goals will make it easier to begin **drafting**, that is, writing a preliminary version (a **rough draft**) of your argument. This includes composing a thesis statement and making a start on putting your ideas in the most effective order. A very rough draft intended merely to help you sort out what you really want to say is known as a **discovery draft**.

The next stage, **revising**, gives you a chance to rethink your ideas. As you revise, you add to, delete from, and reorganize your material. Often the revision stage is preceded by **incubating**, taking time away from writing to develop new ideas and solve writing problems. During this stage your subconscious mind continues to wrestle with troublesome passages, and solutions to difficulties sometimes seem to pop into your head. **Editing** is a matter of making your writing as clear and correct as possible. Finally, **proofreading** is checking to make sure no errors appear in the final form of a written argument.

Individual Approaches to the Writing Process

The picture of writing as an orderly, step-by-step activity does not necessarily correspond to the way writing is done. Rather than perform each step in turn, most writers feel free to repeat earlier steps (or jump to later ones) at any point during the process. One writer, Tamika, does enough prewriting to gather material for a few paragraphs. She then drafts those paragraphs and begins to revise them. As she rewrites, she often discovers that she doesn't have enough ideas to develop her subject properly, so she tries prewriting again. After she drafts some more, Tamika returns to prewriting for material to carry her through the next several paragraphs, and so on. Another writer, Lee, prefers to prewrite from beginning to end before writing a word of his rough draft. And he prefers to draft the whole paper before revising anything. But when Lee does revise, he often discovers that the entire project needs to be thought through some more. This sends him back to prewriting.

These two examples suggest that every writer can develop an individual approach to writing, following whatever steps are helpful in whatever order seems easiest. As you read this chapter, think of each suggestion as something you can try in order to see how well you like it. If it works, continue to use it. If not, keep trying until you find the approaches that are right for you. Below is a questionnaire that will help you evaluate your present approach to the writing process.

A WRITING QUESTIONNAIRE

What do you do when you write? To help you think about the stages in your writing, answer the questions below on the lines at the left. Use the following code:

N = never

S = sometimes

O = often

A = always

_____ 1. Do you like to write?

_____ 2. Do you have a favorite place in which to write?

_____ 3. Do you ever write when you're not required to do so?

_____ 4. Do you have a general approach to writing that works for you?

_____ 5. Do you have ways of gathering ideas before you start to write?

_____ 6. Do you plan your writing so that the material is in an effective order?

_____ 7. Do you support your main ideas with good reasons and examples?

_____ 8. Can you find and improve any parts of your writing that don't completely make sense?

_____ 9. Do you use strategies that help you prevent or cope with writer's block?

_____10. Do you produce more than one version before you are satisfied with your writing?

_____11. Does your own writing ever surprise you? In other words, do you read something you've written and say to yourself,"I didn't realize I remembered so much about . . ." or "I didn't realize I felt that way about . . ."?

_____12. Are you flexible enough to change your opinions on topics as you write about them?

_____13. Do you have effective ways to polish and correct what you have written?

_____14. When you show someone else your writing, do that person's comments help you improve what you have written?

PREWRITING

Prewriting makes starting a paper easier because it allows you to postpone concerns about mistakes in word choice, spelling, or other aspects of your writing. Instead of being distracted by these details, you can use prewriting to deepen your understanding of a topic in order to create and develop pertinent ideas.

When you put words on paper, you have two jobs, one as a writer and the other as an editor. The writer in you is responsible for finding ideas and the editor for shaping them. ("The two main skills in writing are making a mess and cleaning up the mess," as writing theorist Peter Elbow puts it.) But imagine both a writer and an editor trying to work on the same job at the same time. They would be like two cooks trying to prepare an elaborate meal in a very small kitchen. Under these conditions neither one will perform well.

As the writer in you tries to write, the editor sometimes looks over your shoulder saying, "That won't do. That's stupid. Go back and fix that before you write another word." If you listen, you'll pause to rewrite your first sentence—perhaps over and over again. Some writers can never write opening sentences well enough to satisfy their editor selves and give up in despair.

Prewriting can help you put words on paper without worrying about whether or not those words are exactly right. By prewriting, you can send the editor in you out to lunch while your writer self gets on with the job. As you prewrite, keep in mind the important rule that something is better than nothing. However bad a piece of writing is, it can be improved. On the other hand, a writer who has written nothing hasn't started yet.

Experienced writers have developed systematic strategies that help at each stage of the writing process. The following approaches emphasize exploring and discovering ideas:

keeping a journal

talking about your writing

freewriting

brainstorming

asking questions

drawing cluster diagrams

Keeping a Journal

You probably encounter interesting situations at work, at school, or even at home that suggest opportunities for persuasion. Clashes of opinion, instances of injustice, and ways of simplifying work or saving money all provide scope for constructive arguments and therefore make good starting points for journal entries. A **journal** is a place to record your thoughts, positive and negative, about events in the world around you. Your journal is a repository of source material for future writing you may want to do, such as a paper for one of your classes or a letter to a newspaper.

The word *journal* comes from the French word *jour*, meaning "day." Technically, a journal is a book written in every day although many people who keep journals write in them less frequently than that. The word *diary* comes from Latin *dies*, "day." Unlike a diary, which preserves personal experiences and feelings, a journal contains responses to events of wider interest. Like a diary, however, a journal is personal in the sense that in it you are writing for yourself. (You may also take a course in which the instructor asks you to keep a journal. If so, he or she will make clear which of your entries other people will read.)

When writing in your journal, you needn't worry about the niceties of spelling or grammar. Your approach can be conversational, informal, and experimental. The important thing is to keep a record of times when you feel strongly about issues and have something to say about them.

Your primary source of journal entries is your own power of observation. By staying alert, you can gather material on which to sharpen your critical thinking; this means looking carefully at both the strengths and weaknesses of arguments and evaluating them conscientiously and impartially. Your journal is a good place to develop the discipline of questioning what you see so that you find new points of departure for your thinking and writing. Look for contradictions and points of comparison in situations you observe, and try your hand at proposing solutions to some of the problems you encounter in your daily life.

News reports are also good sources of journal entries. If you're interested in persuasive writing, you probably already keep up with the news. Whether you watch TV, listen to the radio, or read newspapers or magazines such as *Time* and *Newsweek*, you probably encounter discussions of topics that interest you. Sometimes you may want to use your journal to congratulate the author of an article for having expressed a point of view effectively. Or you may wish you could talk back to the television set to tell a commentator how wrong you think he or she is. In situations like these you can respond to your own satisfaction by making entries such as the following:

Understanding Science   9/11

I just read an article in *Newsweek* that says scientists have discovered a tiny area of the brain that is three times larger in heterosexual men than in homosexual men. The scientists don't even know if this area causes homosexuality or if it becomes smaller because people are homosexual. But gay rights groups are already responding as if something conclusive has been proven. Some think gays will be forced to undergo brain surgery; others are glad that homosexuality has been shown to have a physical cause.

Every so often people get all excited about a so-called scientific discovery that fizzles out almost immediately. (I still remember the excitement when two scientists thought they had discovered the secret of cold fusion.) I think this proves that most Americans really don't understand how science works. Instead of making people memorize the names of the planets or look at amoebas under a microscope, science education should help people understand the scientific method. People who know how scientists test and then modify or reject hypotheses wouldn't get so excited over these very early developments. Scientists must continue to test hunches, and the press has the right to report the early results of these tests. But the general public should become more sophisticated about exactly what they do and don't mean.

You can save journal entries in whatever form you like best: a bound notebook, a loose-leaf binder, or scraps of paper in a folder. If you wish, you can write for a set amount of time each day or just now and then when you want to express an idea. A journal is a good place to experiment with different formats; for example, you can make lists of your thoughts or ask questions without feeling any need to provide answers, at least for the moment. You might even try writing an entry expressing a view opposite to one you actually hold. Below are more hints on journal writing.

HINTS FOR JOURNAL WRITING

1. Stick with your journal writing; a large number of entries is one indication of a high-quality journal.
2. Start each entry on a separate page, beginning with a title and date.
3. Write quickly without stopping.
4. Try to avoid crossing out ideas. Even incomplete or awkward expressions of your views can provide useful starting points later on.
5. Leave space at the end of each entry so you can add further comments when you reread what you've written.

The questions below should suggest good starting points for journal entries.

TOPICS FOR JOURNAL ENTRIES

1. What problems have you read or heard about lately that made you angry or uncomfortable? What solutions to the problems can you propose?
2. What has annoyed you recently? Describe the incident that annoyed you as objectively as you can and examine it from several points of view.
3. What events of national and international importance do you remember? To what current issues are these events related?
4. If you could discuss an important issue with a famous person (alive, dead, or fictional), what person would you choose? What issue? Why?
5. What are the qualities of an ideal coach or boss? What suggestions do you have for improving leadership at school or at work?
6. What experience have you had that taught you a lesson? How can this lesson be related to an issue that also affects other people?
7. Which has been more important to you, what you've learned in school or outside of school? Based on your own experiences, what improvements in education would you recommend?

8. What is the most difficult decision you ever made? How could the situation you faced be made easier for people who must make a similar decision?

9. Were you ever unfairly punished? What kinds of punishment are most effective? How could your ideas be applied to the issue of fair punishment for convicted offenders?

10. What are people your age afraid of? Are these fears justified? What could be done to diminish them?

EXERCISE 1

Directions: Read the following journal entry:

Generic Brands   6/12

Yesterday in the supermarket I overheard two people discussing generic brands. I've never bought one of those generic products myself so I was interested in what other people thought of them. The woman claimed that generic products are just as good as the name brands while the man argued that a well-known brand name guarantees a product's quality. "You get what you pay for," he said over and over.

Imagine you had written this journal entry a week ago. Add any thoughts you have after rereading it now. Answers will vary. Sample answers are given at the back of this book.

_____

_____

_____

_____

_____

_____

Now answer the following questions:

1. Which side of this argument do you think would be easier to support? Why?

_____

_____

2. If you were to write a persuasive essay based on this journal entry, what would your claim be?

_____

_____

3. What further information would you want to find in order to support your claim?

_____

_____

4. What title would you use for your essay?

_____

_____

Talking About Your Writing

Most people talk more easily than they write. They've had more experience with talking than with writing and find that the give and take of conversation stimulates their thinking. If you're one of these people, you'll probably benefit from discussing your ideas with someone before you sit down to write a persuasive paper. If you can express yourself clearly when discussing your ideas, chances are you'll also do a good job of writing about them.

Merely having another person to talk to will help focus your thinking. But a friend you respect and trust can be invaluable because he or she can draw on knowledge of your personality and interests to guide you along the right path. If you begin without a topic, a friend can remind you of issues that have interested you in the past.

When you're facing problems with your writing, putting the difficulties into words can be an important step toward solving them. For example, suppose you just can't decide whether attempts to control nuclear waste have been effective or not. Talking this over could help you understand why you can't make up your mind. Maybe you haven't yet gathered enough material on your topic.

After you have planned your paper, you can talk through each section of it, explaining how the sections support your overall claim. To make sure you're being clear, ask your partner to paraphrase each statement you make. This means that after you express an idea, the other person responds with something like "What you're saying, then, is . . ." and then restates your idea in his or her own words. If your friend's restatement seems inaccurate to you, don't argue about it. Instead, try to rephrase your original idea in a clearer way.

You can also ask a friend to take the part of someone who disagrees with your ideas. In this kind of roleplaying, your friend's objective is to challenge your claims and compel you to defend them. This relatively small investment of time spent roleplaying can inspire you to think of some points you probably wouldn't have come up with on your own.

You can also benefit from teaching your material to another person. Someone completely unfamiliar with your topic, such as a younger family member, is best because teaching this person will force you to simplify and clarify your ideas. For example, trying to teach a younger sister about the Federal Reserve's role in forming U.S. economic policy would require you to define key terms in simple ways and clearly explain the cause-effect links in your argument. The other person's questions and reactions should help you make your material interesting and comprehensible.

An additional useful approach is to find an expert who knows your subject well. For instance, a criminal justice professor might be willing to discuss penalties for convicted drug sellers with you, or a neighbor who lived through the Depression might enjoy discussing his memories. If you consult an expert, make an appointment well ahead of time, and keep your discussion short. Sending a thank-you note is also a good idea.

The people who discuss issues with you don't necessarily have to be friends, family members, or experts. By seeking out people whose ideas differ from your own, you can gain insights into opposing views and learn to express your opinions in ways that make sense to your opponents. At first you may be tempted to reject every opposing idea and jump in with a defense of your own opinions, but you'll learn more by asking questions and listening to the views of others. Your goal is to gain new insights, not merely repeat your own often-expressed ideas.

If no one is around to talk to, you can even benefit from talking to yourself. When ideas seem to evaporate before you jot them down, try using a tape recorder. Recording yourself talking about your writing as you do it can help you recapture original intentions that get lost as you wrestle with the task of expressing opinions on paper. You can even debate issues with yourself in dialogues, either orally or in writing,

TRY IT OUT

Try writing your own dialogue to help you explore both sides of a controversial issue. Choose an issue from the following list:

abortion	immigration
animal rights	legalizing drugs
capital punishment	national health insurance
euthanasia	sex education
evolution v. creationism	standardized testing in schools

Write a dialogue between two characters named Bud and Lou about the issue you have chosen, keeping the two sides as evenly matched as possible. Here is the start of a sample dialogue on the issue of abortion, written by someone who opposes abortion on demand:

Bud: I think any woman should be able to have an abortion during the first three months of her pregnancy. All she should need to do is consult with her doctor. If the abortion is medically safe, that ought to be all there is to it.

Lou: You're wrong. The woman herself may want an abortion, but she's not the only one involved. The father of the child has rights, too—and above all the unborn child has the right to life.

Bud: But the woman's rights should take priority. She's the one who must carry the child for nine months and run the medical risks of giving birth to it when the time comes. If it's born, she'll need to take care of it—don't tell me the father will take equal responsibility in raising it because few men do. She's the one who should decide whether to have the child or not.

Lou: You're right that the woman's life will be affected, perhaps drastically, but with abortion on demand, whether the child will have a life or not is up to her. No inconvenience the woman undergoes is equal to losing one's whole life, especially when it hasn't even begun yet.

Continue this dialogue, or begin one of your own. Try to write more than one page. Then underline the passages in which either person makes an effective point. Your underlined passages should be helpful if you plan an argumentative essay on the topic you choose.

Freewriting

Freewriting consists of putting words down on paper without lifting your pen or even pausing to think. By freewriting you can generate ideas in ways that would not be possible if you were using more orderly methods. To try freewriting, set a kitchen timer, alarm clock, or similar device to go off in five minutes. Then write as fast as you can on whatever subject you choose, without ever stopping. If you get stuck for something to say, write "I can't think of anything" over and over until the ideas begin to flow again. Don't worry about making mistakes or sounding stupid. Just keep writing until the timer goes off.

Freewriting helps you summon up half-forgotten incidents and ideas and make sense out of new events and unfamiliar concepts. Digressions (passages unrelated to your main subject) are welcome in freewriting since they can open up new areas to investigate. You'll probably find that freewriting reveals opinions that surprise you, helps you understand yourself, and provides fresh viewpoints on controversial issues.

The following passage is an example of unedited freewriting on political developments in the Soviet Union during late August, 1991:

An amazing couple of weeks—I still can't believe what I saw. When the TV showed those tanks rolling down the streets of Moscow, I thought we were going to witness a bloodbath. The courage of those people. They've been oppressed for seventy years. Who would have thought that they would find the courage to stand up to the military? I can't think of anything. I can't think of anything. Would I have the courage to fight for my freedom if I had to? I wonder if those demonstrators represent the Soviet people as a whole, or were they really only the Moscow intellectuals? Were most Russians just willing to accept whoever took over the country? But I remember that interview with a woman who seemed like a very ordinary person—like anyone in my neighborhood—and she spoke so well about freedom and how she was willing to die for it that I felt proud and emotional. I wonder if Americans have had it too easy over this past hundred years—minorities haven't but I mean most Americans—have we come to take our freedoms for granted? Would it do us good to have to fight for them every once in a while?

After you finish, look back to find the part of your freewriting that seems to be most interesting or important. This may be a word, phrase, single sentence, or several related sentences. It may even be a thought you have as you read what you have written; that is, it needn't appear in the original freewriting passage at all. At the top of a new page, copy the portion you selected. Then try a second piece of freewriting based on that idea.

EXERCISE 2

Directions:

1. Choosing one of the unfinished sentences below as a starting point, freewrite for five minutes. Answers will vary. Sample answers are given at the back of this book.

    a.   A topic I feel strongly about is . . .

    b.   A question I wish I could answer is . . .

    c.   An issue I have conflicting feelings about is . . .

    d.   If I could solve one of the world's problems, it would be . . . because . . .

    e.   A local issue that has interested me is . . . because . . .

    f.   I used to think . . . but now I realize . . .

2. Read over your freewriting to find the part you consider most promising. Using the phrase or sentence you select from your first freewriting as your starting point, freewrite for five more minutes.

3. Read your second freewriting, underlining your best ideas. If you were to write a persuasive paper today based on these ideas, what would your main points be?

_____

_____

Brainstorming

Brainstorming, which means jotting down a list of ideas on a particular topic, is another valuable prewriting technique. Like freewriting, it draws on the hidden resources of your mind, helping you recall thoughts and feelings you may have difficulty summoning to the surface in a more structured way. Like freewriting, brainstorming relies on working quickly, getting material down on paper, and postponing revision until a later stage.

You can use brainstorming at the very beginning of a writing project as a way of discovering a topic to write about. For example, if you were assigned a persuasive essay about an important national issue, you could brainstorm a list of issues and then review it to see which one you most want to write about.

Having chosen the subject of the homeless mentally ill, Maria, a sophomore in a college psychology class, brainstormed the following list of ideas:

mental institutions

group homes

roving mental health workers (vans)

unwillingness to enter shelters

expense

need long-term care

helped by prescription drugs

dangers of street life

too confused to get help

who pays?

need homelike setting

As you can see, brainstorming, unlike freewriting, consists of writing phrases and single words, not consecutive sentences. Maria began with this disorganized list, thought further about her topic, and then did some freewriting, using items on her list as starting points. Eventually she developed the following thesis, which became the basis for her paper: "The homeless mentally ill should be placed not in shelters but in group homes or with families that, like foster parents, would be paid to provide them with food, housing, and a supportive environment."

Brainstorming is also a useful preliminary to planning a paper. After Maria stated her claim in a thesis, she brainstormed possible supporting ideas and then chose from among them the three or four she considered most convincing. For example, Maria wanted to discuss the unwillingness of some homeless people to enter shelters. She brainstormed again, trying to understand the reasons some mentally ill people avoid the shelters provided by city governments and private agencies:

unaware that the shelters exist

afraid of being robbed

drugs

disease

violence in shelters

fear of authority

lack of privacy

These notes became the basis for one section of her paper.

Unlike freewriting, brainstorming needn't be a solitary activity. Working together in a small group in which one person acts as secretary and the others fire off contributions as they think of them can be an effective problem-solving strategy. Unlike freewriting, which encourages digression, brainstorming sessions should stick to a single topic.

EXERCISE 3

Directions:

1. On a separate sheet of paper, practice brainstorming by listing as many examples of each topic in the chart below as you can think of. Brainstorm each topic for one minute.

2. Next, count how many items you have brainstormed and fill in the totals on the chart.

Topics	Number of Items on Your Lists	Unusual Items on Your Lists
A. colors		
B. girls' names		
C. flavors of ice cream		

3. In the last column write the two most unusual items from each brainstorming list.

4. Now spend three minutes listing as many controversial issues (such as unemployment, nuclear war, dishonest politicians, and airline safety) as you can think of. How many issues did you brainstorm in three minutes? _____

5. <u>Underline</u> the issues on your list that you consider most interesting or important. Then choose three of your underlined issues and transfer them to the chart below:

Topics	Number of Items on Your Lists	Unusual Items on Your Lists
A.		
B.		
C.		

6. On a separate sheet of paper, brainstorm for three minutes on each of the issues you chose. Count the number of items in each list, and fill in your totals on the chart. In the last column write two unusual ideas or examples from your list for each topic.

Conclusions:

1. If you were going to choose an issue to write about today, which one would it be? _____

2. What claim would you make about the issue you chose?

_____

_____

_____

Questioning

Imagine you are sitting in a cafeteria quietly munching a cheese sandwich when you overhear someone behind you say, "I'll never speak to Roberta again." You begin to munch more thoughtfully as you ponder the questions "Who is Roberta?" and "Why has that person decided never to speak to her again?" Such questions are as natural as children's questions about why the sky is blue or why they have to eat broccoli. By learning to ask questions in a more systematic way, you can examine issues from a wider variety of viewpoints, focus your thinking, and become a more independent learner.

Choosing a topic for an argumentative essay is often a matter of finding a question worth answering. However, a good question is unlikely to jump into your mind without some preliminary work on your part. As you read and think about a subject and start to jot down ideas, important questions will begin to take shape.

At first, you may feel only a sense of puzzlement about things you can't explain or that seem inconsistent or contradictory. People often shy away from ideas that make them feel uneasy. But an initial sense of confusion or discomfort is precisely what provokes some of the world's most creative thinking. "If the world is really round," Christopher Columbus may once have asked himself, "wouldn't I be able to reach the Indies by sailing westward?" "If women are as intelligent and capable as men," English feminist Mary Wollstonecraft most likely asked herself, "why don't they enjoy the same rights as men?"

Once you've found a question, however, you have only begun your task. Next you should test your initial question by asking further questions. For example, ask if your question is the kind that might have been answered already. If you can look up the answer in a reference book, your question won't provide enough material for a good persuasive essay.

You might also try rephrasing your question; stating it in another form may provide a clue about how to look for an answer. Suppose you are leaving your friend Tony's house after being a guest at a huge Thanksgiving dinner. As you drive away, you ask yourself, "Why do Italian-American families seem so close-knit?" You quickly realize that conclusions about Italian-American families based on Tony's grandparents, aunts, uncles, and cousins would be hasty generalizations. But if you rephrase the question as, "Are close-knit extended families part of the Italian-American experience and, if so, why?" the answer could probably form the basis of an excellent research paper for a sociology or American studies course.

By asking "What evidence would I need to answer this question?" you not only begin to plan a research strategy but also test whether you really understand your original question. (At this early stage you need not have the evidence; you just need to imagine what it would be.) For example, you might ask "Is the earth's climate really becoming warmer because of the greenhouse effect?" The last five summers in your area have been much hotter than usual: is that good evidence for global warming? Probably not; normal temperature fluctuations could account for the recent hot summers. After all, yesterday's high, ninety-six degrees, was unpleasant but did not break the record of ninety-nine degrees set in 1912. The kind of evidence you would need is provided by long-term climate studies and computer projections of temperature trends, which you could find in scientific journals. Interpreting the evidence is another matter: you would probably also need to find expert testimony to help you evaluate it.

Even after you decide that a question will lead to a satisfactory argument and that you have the time and resources to answer it, you may still want to go on raising questions. Asking a series of questions helps you explore a topic in an orderly way. A good set of related questions will prompt you to recall what you know about your topic and concentrate on what you need to learn next. Computer programs that provide related questions can aid in gathering ideas and solving problems. A more familiar set of questions is the one reporters answer in the opening lines of news stories: Who? What? When? Where? and Why? If you are proposing to write about euthanasia, for example, you could ask the following questions:

Who should decide whether a terminally ill patient should be allowed to die?

What does euthanasia mean?

When should the decision be made about whether to allow a patient to die?

Where would such a patient be allowed to die—at home, in a hospice, or in a hospital?

Why do doctors and patients' families sometimes disagree about when euthanasia is appropriate?

Another set of questions is linked to common thinking patterns. Each question suggests an approach that could be used to answer it:

Question	Thinking Pattern
What does it mean?	definition
What is it like?	comparison and contrast, description, classification
What causes it?	cause-effect
What are its parts?	analysis
Is it good or bad?	evaluation
Should it be done?	recommendation

Still another set of questions arises from an analogy with physics. A subatomic particle can be thought of in three ways: alone, as part of a wave, and in relationship to other particles in a field. In the same way, an argumentative topic can be thought of as standing still, moving, and relating to other topics. You can think about poverty, for example, by asking the following questions:

What is poverty? (standing still)

What circumstances tend to increase or decrease poverty? (moving)

How does poverty affect public health, education, and business? (relating to other topics)

Answering questions like these can help you discover the organizing principle of your argument. A clear statement of this organizing principle serves as your claim, and answering the further question "What are some examples of this?" provides illustrations to support your claim.

Another way to use questions to deepen your understanding of a topic is to rule off columns with the following headings: 1) First Thoughts, 2) Questions, 3) Responses, 4) New Questions. In the first column write your initial ideas about your topic. Then, in the second column, form a question based on each of your first thoughts. Jot tentative answers to these questions in column three. Finally, use the last column for new questions that come to mind based on what you've written in the first three columns. This technique encourages you to discard superficial interpretations and probe more deeply into promising aspects of your topic. The following chart illustrates a student's use of this technique to develop ideas on the issue of women's exposure to toxic chemicals at work:

First Thoughts	Questions	Responses	New Questions
Women do many dangerous jobs.	What jobs do they do?	Women work with dangerous chemicals that could harm their unborn children.	Could these jobs be done by robots?
Women deserve equal pay for equal work.	Should men and women take equal risks?	No one should be compelled to take any risk without being fully informed of the danger.	Are companies advising workers properly?
Women should be protected from risk even if they don't want protection.	Why wouldn't they want protection?	They may be denied access to high-paying jobs that involve more risk.	What about the risks to unborn children? Who protects them?

You may also find it useful to question your questions. That is, you can ask, "What does that question mean?" or "Why did I ask that?" Doing so will help you become more aware of how you form your best ideas. You can also use questioning to locate and eliminate problems that arise as you write. For example, you can begin a writing session with the question "What's on my mind that could distract me from my writing?" Jotting down any potentially distracting concerns will clear your mind before you go to work. Below are some more hints on using questions during the writing process.

TIPS ON USING QUESTIONS TO PRODUCE IDEAS

1. Keep a written record of your questions and answers.

2. Leave space so you can add more ideas later.

3. As you work on your argument, continue to make lists of questions. Cross off questions as you answer them or discover that they're not relevant.

4. Show another person your opening paragraph and thesis sentence to find out what questions they suggest.

QUESTIONS FOR EXPLORING AN ARGUMENTATIVE TOPIC

1. Which aspect of this topic interests me the most? Why?

2. What key words are associated with this topic? What do they mean?

3. How can this issue be stated as a problem? What are some alternative ways of expressing this problem?

4. What events related to this topic have I read or heard about?

5. What have I heard people say about this topic?

6. How have the key issues related to this topic changed over the years? How might they change in the future?

7. What could I compare this topic to?

8. How could this topic be broken into parts?

9. What disagreements are there about this topic?

10. What do both sides agree on?

11. What values do each side's views reflect?

EXERCISE 4

Directions:

1. Choose one of the topics on the list below:

domestic violence	drug testing in the workplace
steroids	job rights of the disabled
pollution	preservation of the rain forests
racism	public use of national parks
effects of pesticides	side effects of prescription drugs

2. Choose at least six questions from the list "Questions for Exploring an Argumentative Topic" and answer them for the one you have selected.

3. Underline the parts of your responses that you think would be most helpful if you chose to write a persuasive paper on this topic.

Answers will vary. Suggested answers are given at the back of this book.

Drawing Cluster Diagrams

Diagrams are arrangements of words, lines, circles, or other shapes that simplify and clarify ideas and illustrate the relationships between them. Diagramming aids logical thinking, but, like other prewriting techniques, it can also help you discover ideas and feelings you're not consciously aware of.

When Susan was asked by her boss to draft a memo on sexism at Harrison Pharmaceutical Company, she began by drawing a cluster diagram. As she looked closely at her finished diagram, she found she had begun to explore ideas she would not otherwise have thought of. (See the diagram on the following page.)

Because drawing this kind of diagram involves forming clusters of related ideas, this technique is usually called **clustering**. It is also sometimes known as webbing or mapping since a finished diagram looks like a spider web or a road map. Unlike other ways of gathering material for an argument, a cluster can head in several different directions at once, not merely move forward in a straight line.

To start a cluster diagram, write a word or phrase in the middle of a piece of paper and circle it. Almost any word works as the nucleus of a cluster, but words likely to trigger associations, such as *family*, *happiness*, and *fear*, should help you get started quickly. If you have already found a subject, you can use it as the center of your cluster: a word or phrase such as *drugs*, *poverty*, *AIDS*, or *saving the environment* makes a good starting point.

Each time you add a new idea to your cluster, draw a line to connect it to one already on the diagram, linking one concept or example to another. Don't worry about where to add a new word: just write it wherever it seems to fit. Work quickly and smoothly. Your goal at this point is to produce as many different ideas as you can. Don't evaluate ideas as you add them; later, as you look back, you'll be in a better position to decide which of them you can use in your argument.

You may want to set a time limit, such as five or ten minutes, to work on your diagram. Or you can continue to work on it until you feel ready to write. Sometimes you'll use all the ideas on your diagram in your written argument, but more often you'll choose only some of them. The effort of listing ideas you don't use is not wasted, however; a bad idea will often trigger a good one.

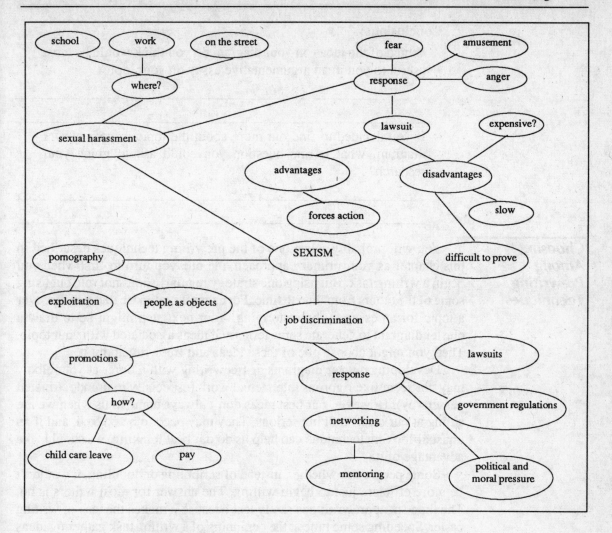

EXERCISE 5

Directions: Choose a topic of your own or one from the list below. Write your choice in the center of a sheet of paper. Add related ideas and examples, drawing lines to link them to material already on your diagram.

Possible topics:

cheating	women in the military
world hunger	prayer in public schools
divorce	cultural diversity in education
acid rain	illiteracy
date rape	preservation of historic buildings

Conclusions:

Which of the ideas on your diagram do you think would be most useful to you in an argumentative essay on your topic?

_____

_____

If you decided to find out more about the topic in your cluster diagram, what is one question you could ask to guide your research?

_____

_____

Choosing Among Prewriting Techniques

You will probably select one of the prewriting techniques described in this chapter as your primary approach, the one you turn to first when you begin a writing task. But using one strategy regularly does not rule out using some of the others from time to time. For example, suppose that you discover a topic for an essay by brainstorming. Your next step might be to draw a cluster diagram to generate some terms and ideas associated with your topic. Then you might choose one of these ideas and freewrite about it.

Developing cluster diagrams or freewriting with a timer at your elbow may not seem like rigorous intellectual work (especially to unindoctrinated passers-by). However, our best ideas don't always come to us when we are sitting at our desks looking serious. They may need to be coaxed, and if an unusual-looking technique can help us do our best thinking, we should take advantage of it.

Some people ask whether, instead of scribbling or doodling, it wouldn't be more efficient just to begin writing. The answer for most writers is no. The time spent prewriting is rarely lost because it makes the task of writing easier. Spending some time at the beginning of a writing task gathering ideas means you'll be less likely to pause in the middle to think of what to write next. If you don't believe it, try writing both ways. You will probably become a confirmed prewriter. Following the hints provided below will also help you improve your prewriting skills.

TIPS FOR PREWRITING

1. Aim to gather as many ideas as possible, regardless of quality.

2. Keep working rather than pausing to evaluate. Judging too quickly can block the flow of your ideas.

3. When you're thinking of examples, make them as specific as possible.

4. If one prewriting technique is no longer producing new ideas on a topic, switch to another approach.

5. Keep all your notes until your writing project is finished. An idea that doesn't look useful at the moment may be just what you need later on.

The writing process is a series of mental and physical steps (prewriting, drafting, revising, editing, and proofreading) that lead to a finished piece of writing. Prewriting, the first stage of the writing process, involves thinking about a subject and gathering ideas. One useful prewriting technique, keeping a journal, allows writers to record their observations and reactions and to experiment with writing. Talking about writing helps people choose topics, gather ideas, improve reasoning, and solve writing problems. Freewriting consists of writing for a set period of time in order to remember half-forgotten incidents and ideas. Brainstorming is listing as many ideas as possible on a particular topic; it enables writers to discover topics and gather specific support for general ideas. Raising questions helps locate organizing principles for arguments and identify the types of evidence needed to support claims. Clustering consists of drawing weblike diagrams that can head in several different directions at once, not merely move forward in a straight line. Writers benefit from learning a variety of these prewriting techniques and switching from one to another when necessary.

CHAPTER EXERCISE

I. MATCHING

Directions: Match each term on the list below with its definition by writing the correct letter in the space provided. Some of the terms on the list will not be used.

TERMS:

A	brainstorming	G.	journal
B.	clustering	H.	prewriting
C.	discovery draft	I.	proofreading
D.	drafting	J.	revising
E.	freewriting	K.	rough draft
F.	incubating		

DEFINITIONS:

_____ 1. the first stage of the writing process

_____ 2. writing a preliminary version of a paper

_____ 3. adding to, deleting from, and reorganizing written material

_____ 4. taking time away from writing to develop new ideas and solve writing problems

_____ 5. checking to make sure no errors appear in the final form of a written argument

_____ 6. writing whatever comes to mind without stopping

_____ 7. quickly listing whatever comes to mind on a topic

_____ 8. generating ideas by creating a weblike diagram

II. MULTIPLE CHOICE

Directions: On the line at the left write the letter of the phrase that best completes each item.

_____ 9. The main stages in the writing process are

    A. prewriting, drafting, revising, editing, and proofreading.

    B. incubating, revising, and editing.

    C. brainstorming, freewriting, questioning, and clustering.

_____ 10. Prewriting allows people to concentrate on

    A. correcting errors in word choice, spelling, and punctuation in each sentence.

    B. thinking of ideas and editing them at the same time.

    C. gathering ideas.

_____ 11. Freewriting helps people

    A. avoid digressions.

    B. remember half-forgotten events and ideas.

    C. write more correctly.

_____ 12. Both freewriting and brainstorming usually involve

    A. gathering ideas quickly.

    B. working with a small group of other people.

    C. carefully avoiding writing errors.

_____ 13. Someone who is creating a cluster diagram should

    A. add ideas wherever they seem to belong on the diagram.

    B. evaluate ideas before adding them to the diagram.

    C. both A and B.

III. TRUE OR FALSE

Directions: On each line at the left write T if an item is true or F if it is false.

_____14. The writing process is a series of mental and physical steps leading to a finished piece of writing.

_____15. Prewriting should be done only before drafting, never after starting to write a paper.

_____16. People should always proofread their journal entries to make them as clearly and correctly written as possible.

_____17. Talking over an issue can help focus a writer's thinking.

_____18. Another name for freewriting is clustering.

_____19. Answering journalist's questions such as Why? or When? can help a writer gather material for an argument.

_____20. People should avoid writing about topics that puzzle them.

8

Planning a Written Argument

*"**W**ouldn't it be a wonderful idea," thought Ellie, "if this Christmas each store owner at the mall contributed merchandise for distribution to needy families?" She was sure her church group would be willing to collect and distribute the donations. After thinking some more about her plan, she decided to write a letter to interest the merchants in helping out.*

Ellie thought first of how many families in Lincoln Township were living below the poverty line, so she wrote a detailed description of people who made do with too little food and lacked warm clothing and decent places to live. She added a short history of the township during the past fifteen years, reminding her readers of the better times before the steel mill closed and stressing how many jobs had been lost. Rereading her letter, she was proud of how well she had described conditions in the area.

But when Ellie's friend Ruth read the letter she asked, "What's your point? I know times are bad, and people want to help, but what exactly do you expect them to do?"

CREATING A THESIS SENTENCE

Ellie had forgotten that the two indispensable elements of every argument are a claim and data to support that claim. Without a **thesis**, a clear statement of her argument's claim, her letter lacked focus. A thesis sentence serves two purposes: it tells readers or listeners what an argument is about, and it helps the arguer choose relevant evidence. If Ellie includes a thesis in her letter, such as "All local merchants should give generously to a Christmas drive for the needy," her readers will understand exactly what she's driving at. And if Ellie uses her thesis to control her argument, she'll omit the economic history of the area since it is only marginally related to her main point.

In many debates a thesis is imposed; the participants are told to argue for or against a particular claim. Some kinds of persuasive writing are also based on an assigned thesis; for example, an instructor in U. S. history might require a class to "write an essay showing how the election of Abraham Lincoln to the presidency in 1860 made the Civil War inevitable." The thesis of the students' essays must be based on the assigned claim. Their task is to support the claim by providing the best evidence they can find in its favor.

Most of the time, however, people compose their own thesis sentences. Someone might write a letter or memo to support a claim he or she already believes, such as "Capital gains taxes inhibit investment and should be repealed." Opportunities for persuasive writing may also arise out of an interest in a general topic—higher education, for example. By freewriting, brainstorming, or applying some other prewriting technique to this topic, the writer may discover a thesis, such as "Access to higher education should be determined strictly by intellectual ability, never by athletic skill."

An essay's success can be measured by whether or not it convinces readers to share the opinion expressed in its thesis. A thesis statement that leaves readers in doubt about what the writer means will never change their views on an issue. For instance, the thesis that "The federal government's farm policy must guarantee that economic aid to farmers will achieve desirable results" will hardly change anyone's mind about farm subsidies since it is so vague that few people would disagree with it. A thesis such as "The federal government must subsidize small farmers to keep family farms from disappearing" is clear, precisely worded, and memorable.

Avoiding Common Errors in Writing a Thesis

Many persuasive essays go wrong at the start because their writers lose sight of what a good thesis statement should be. The following guidelines should help keep you on the right track:

1. A thesis should be a complete sentence, not just a sentence fragment stating a topic. "Recent immigration to the United States" is only a sentence fragment. "Our school board should modify elementary and high school curricula to reflect the ethnic backgrounds of recent immigrants" expresses both a topic and an opinion about it and is therefore a thesis statement.

2. A thesis should take a stand on an arguable point, not state an undisputed fact. A factual statement such as "Several African countries have achieved independence in the last fifty years" does not provide much scope for argument. In contrast, "In the last fifty years the United States could have done more to foster democracy in emerging African nations" can be supported by evidence and provides a basis for informed discussion.

3. A thesis should not merely announce a writer's general intentions. An essay that begins "In this paper I am going to discuss the disposal of industrial solid wastes and sludge" fails to express the writer's opinion. Instead, "Industrial solid wastes and sludge can be disposed of safely" states an arguable claim.

4. A thesis should be a statement, not a question. Asking "Should teenagers be required to obtain parental consent to receive free condoms in high schools?" implies that the writer has no opinion on the subject. On the other hand, the statement that "Teenagers should be required to obtain parental consent to receive free condoms in high schools" states an opinion and is therefore an acceptable thesis sentence.

5. A thesis should not be too broad. The thesis "Governments should make the environment a higher priority" covers too much ground for an essay. It suggests that the writer will discuss many environmental problems, such as global warming, the thinning of the ozone layer, and the destruction of the rain forests, and it fails to specify whether local, state, or national governments should be responsible for solving these problems. The risk of tackling such a broad topic is that the writer will have time only to skim its surface, mentioning ideas but never developing and supporting them. When you first start to think about an issue, your choice of a topic is likely to be too broad. You can test a thesis sentence by asking yourself whether an entire book could be written on your topic. If the answer to this question is yes, then you need to focus the topic.

6. A thesis should not be too narrow. "Grown children should not ask their parents to store their belongings" is too limited; it does not provide enough scope for a meaningful, well-reasoned argument. If your reaction to your own thesis sentence is "So what?" or "Who cares?" you've probably chosen too narrow a topic.

Formulating a Counterclaim

A **counterclaim** is an expression of opinion that directly contradicts a claim. For example, the claim that "The United States should destroy all its nuclear weapons as an example to other nations" has as its counterclaim

"The United States should *not* destroy all its nuclear weapons as an example to other nations."

After you formulate a thesis for an argumentative essay, write a counterclaim and ask yourself, "Could an honest, well-informed person believe this?" If the answer is yes, your original thesis is probably a good one. If the answer is no, you should rewrite your thesis to make it more genuinely argumentative.

To understand how a counterclaim can help you test your thesis, consider the fallacy called straw man described in chapter 6. A straw man is a weak argument attributed to an opponent and then attacked as if he or she had actually argued it. Attacking a straw man requires no particular strength or skill, and defeating one proves nothing worthwhile. You should make sure that the counterclaim for your own argument is not a straw man but something people might really support. For example, the claim "Steroid use should be discouraged among college athletes" is not a strong thesis because few people would argue its opposite: "Steroid use should be encouraged among college athletes." Changed to "College coaches should be held responsible for steroid use by their players," the thesis becomes arguable because many people would maintain that college coaches should not be held responsible.

Using a Thesis to Help Readers Follow an Argument

The usual position for a thesis is toward the beginning of an essay, most often at the end of the opening paragraph. Including the thesis near the beginning is a courtesy to your readers. If you attempt to build suspense by providing your evidence first and your thesis statement afterwards, readers must plow through the evidence, find the thesis, and perhaps reread your essay to see how your support relates to it. Stating your thesis near the beginning allows readers to understand more quickly how each item of support is related to your main point.

Some authors do not include a thesis at all. They want to make readers formulate it for themselves, involving them more fully in following and interpreting the evidence. In such essays, the thesis is implicit—that is, suggested but not stated directly. However, inexperienced readers prefer explicit thesis statements, and inexperienced writers need them to keep their essays on track. Many experienced writers do include clear thesis statements; they've learned that relying on readers to make the right inferences can be risky.

To help readers along even further, many writers provide a thesis statement that is also a mini-outline of the essay. Instead of "The training of prison guards must be improved," the thesis "The training of prison guards must be improved to ensure greater discipline, provide better role models for prisoners, and inspire greater respect from the public" helps readers grasp not only the writer's main point but also the plan of the entire essay.

Such elaborate thesis statements are not required but can provide valuable help with both reading and writing a complicated argument.

EXERCISE 1

Directions: Some of the items below are good thesis statements, but most are not. Identify them by using the following code:

OK   an acceptable thesis statement

SF   a sentence fragment

F   a fact, not an opinion

A   an announcement, not a thesis

Q   a question, not a statement

B   a statement that is too broad

N   a statement that is too narrow

Example: __SF__ How higher state taxes will result in lost jobs as businesses move elsewhere.

_____ 1. Are big corporations attempting to create the impression that workman's compensation programs have been abused?

_____ 2. Mikhail Gorbachev visited Beijing in 1989.

_____ 3. Career success leads to prosperity and emotional gratification.

_____ 4. In this paper I will discuss my beliefs about free societies and whether or not they should be able to regulate their citizens' rights to buy and sell products abroad.

_____ 5. Doctors should not have a financial stake in the laboratories and other health-care businesses to which they refer patients.

_____ 6. My family has found that cooling only our living room is less wasteful than using central air conditioning.

_____ 7. Illnesses have many consequences for sick people and for their families.

_____ 8. Brokers warning investors about the changing values of limited partnerships.

_____ 9. Women who give birth to drug-addicted infants should be jailed, and their babies should be placed in foster homes.

_____ 10. In the United States there are about 40 million grandparents, many with several grandchildren.

ORGANIZING A PAPER

Once you've settled (at least tentatively) on a thesis, you're ready to tackle the problem of arranging your ideas effectively. Devising a plan can be as interesting as solving a puzzle. But unlike a puzzle, a writing problem usually has many possible solutions. It's up to you to select the one that presents your material most convincingly.

Some writers prefer to jot down a few words on a notepad or the back of an envelope. Others rely on a formal outline, complete with roman and arabic numerals and uppercase and lowercase letters. The size of your writing task partly determines how much planning you do (with a longer project requiring more detailed planning), but your individual preferences are just as important. Whatever style you choose, try to remain flexible; a plan that can't be changed can be as bad as no plan at all.

Putting Ideas in Order

When you prewrite, reasons, examples, and possible objections tumble out of your brain almost at random. If you've previously thought a great deal about a topic, you may be able to begin writing based on only a sketchy plan. But however familiar the subject matter, resist the temptation to plunge ahead with drafting before doing at least a little planning. Without a plan, you're likely to find yourself laboriously rewriting a disorganized draft later on.

Efficient readers bring a set of expectations to what they read. If an argument meets these expectations, they can grasp it quickly and easily. Readers dislike being compelled to struggle; the more difficult your argument is to follow, the less likely they are to accept it. Therefore, following a customary pattern will usually be more persuasive than choosing an unpredictable one. A common pattern is the following:

1. a brief introduction leading to a thesis
2. support for the thesis
3. refutation of opposing views
4. a conclusion restating key points

CHRONOLOGICAL ORDER

Arranging ideas in **chronological order** means following the time sequence in which events occurred. For example, the claim "High unemployment in Germany contributed to the growing power of the Nazi party in the early 1930s" suggests a chronological organization that begins with the increase of unemployment and traces the growth of the Nazi party that resulted from it.

SPATIAL ORDER

You can also arrange some arguments in **spatial order,** which means moving from one location to the next in a logical sequence. Just as chronological order moves through time, spatial order moves through space. The thesis "Many children with Down's syndrome can be brought up at home and trained to function in the community" suggests a plan based on location, beginning with the children's home environment and then discussing their role in the community.

EMPHATIC ORDER

One of the most useful ways to present an argument is to arrange material in **emphatic order,** which means organizing main points according to their importance. If, for example, you are trying to persuade readers that young people will benefit by participating in a summer theater program, you might bring up the participants' chances to improve their acting skills, make friends, and gain self-confidence. Since self-confidence is a quality young people will find useful no matter what careers they choose, readers are likely to consider it the most important. Because they encounter it last, they will perceive your case as growing progressively stronger. Also, they'll remember your last point best at that crucial stage when they must evaluate your argument as a whole.

OTHER ORGANIZATIONAL PATTERNS

If you believe your audience is uninterested in or even hostile to your argument, starting with the most important idea might be more effective. Suppose, for example, that the theater program charges each participant $1,000. Given the expense, convincing parents to pay for a teenager's month of acting in summer stock may require a powerful argument. Therefore, beginning a letter to parents by emphasizing the self-confidence young people will gain from the program is probably best. Once you've gotten them interested, they will probably be more receptive to your less compelling points as well.

Another good way to organize ideas is according to how familiar the material will seem to your audience. Suppose you are arguing the claim "Public confidence in large-scale, expensive scientific projects has decreased dramatically in the last thirty years." Beginning with the most familiar subject, the tragic crash of the *Challenger* space shuttle, before covering ideas that your audience may not know as much about, such as the partial failure of the Hubble telescope, will make it easier for them to follow your case.

Other organizational plans are also useful on occasion. Starting with the least controversial points and gradually moving to more debatable ones could appeal to readers who otherwise might not be won over. Or if you are discussing a situation with several possible outcomes, you might want to organize them by how likely they are to happen.

Often you'll be able to bring two or more of these organizing principles to bear on the same argument. To show that your club must take steps to increase its membership, for example, you might want to give an account of declining attendance over the years, using a chronological arrangement, and then discuss your suggestions for gaining new members in emphatic order. If you have difficulty forming a good plan, try noting each point you want to make on a separate index card and rearranging the cards until you find an order that appeals to you. You may find that you hit on a good arrangement even without being able to label the principle behind the organization you have chosen.

TRY IT OUT

Are you good at arranging the key points in an argument? Each of the informal plans below contains three main ideas. Try your skill by numbering the items in the order you would choose if you were writing about each topic. Invent an organizing principle of your own or use one from the list below:

chronological

spatial

least important to most important

most important to least important

easiest to understand to most difficult to understand

least controversial to most controversial

most familiar to least familiar

most likely to happen to least likely to happen

others

PART I

Number the items in each plan in the order you would use. On the line below the plan, write the principle of organization you followed. Answers will vary. Sample answers are given at the back of this book.

Example: Ways to improve the well-being of children:

__2__ immunize more children against dangerous diseases

__1__ reduce malnutrition

__3__ provide better primary education

principle of organization: <u>most important to least important</u>

1. Ways that saving the earth can become a year-round effort:

_____ buy living Christmas trees that can be planted after the holiday

_____ start the academic year by working with school staff to organize a recycling program

_____ set mower blades higher and leave grass clippings as a natural mulch

principle of organization:_____

2. Reasons job seekers who can relocate should consider moving to other parts of the country:

_____ increased demand for educators in Nebraska

_____ expanded business services jobs in Colorado

_____ growth in construction jobs in Oregon

principle of organization:_____

3. Past mistakes in public housing that should not be repeated:

_____ constructing high-rise buildings

_____ constructing buildings so different from others in their neighbor-hoods that they stigmatize residents

_____ using shoddy building materials

principle of organization:_____

4. Ways to increase sales of automobiles made in the United States:

_____ improve safety features

_____ decrease environmental impact

_____ improve styling

principle of organization:_____

5. Ways airlines can become more competitive:

_____ reduce the number of employees

_____ cut services

_____ lower prices

principle of organization:_____

6. Ways to make reading a habit for children:

_____ surround them with books

_____ encourage them to select their own reading materials

_____ read aloud to them

principle of organization:_____

PART II

Now brainstorm two plans of your own and choose a principle of organization to use as the basis for putting your ideas in order.

1. _____

    ____ _____

    ____ _____

    ____ _____

principle of organization:_____

2. _____

    ____ _____

    ____ _____

    ____ _____

principle of organization:_____

Making an Informal Plan

The simplest kind of plan begins as a list of ideas, often the result of brainstorming. Suppose, for example, that you are taking a ten-minute history quiz in which your instructor asks you to show that ancient China had already achieved a high level of culture by the time of Marco Polo's visit. You might begin by brainstorming the following list of Chinese accomplishments:

    printing

    city planning

    gunpowder

    decorative arts—bronze, jade

    poetry

    landscape painting

    architecture—pagodas

Looking at the list, you feel pleased that you remembered so much of last night's reading assignment. Then you realize that you're not quite ready to write. For one thing, gunpowder doesn't seem to suggest high culture in the same way the other items do, so you cross it out. You want to treat city planning and architecture together. Similarly, printing seems to belong with poetry, and the decorative arts and landscape painting also make a good pair. A few numbers jotted down next to the items make this plan clear:

    2   printing

    1   city planning

         ~~gunpowder~~

3   decorative arts—bronze, jade
2   poetry
3   landscape painting
1   architecture—pagodas

Now you're ready to start writing, having taken perhaps three minutes to recall information and put it in the right order. Businesspeople answer letters and compose short memos, and lawyers and politicians prepare brief speeches by this simple and useful method.

Making a Tree Diagram

Tree diagrams are drawings in which words and branching lines illustrate the relationships between ideas. These diagrams resemble drawings of trees, so they're also known as issue trees or topic trees. Drawing a tree diagram compels a writer to develop and label ideas and envision the overall structure of an argument. Unlike a cluster diagram (discussed in the previous chapter), a tree diagram is hierarchical. In other words, the diagram shows which ideas are most important and most general (those at the top) and which are less important and less general (those at lower levels). Following is a tree diagram for an argument about violence in movies:

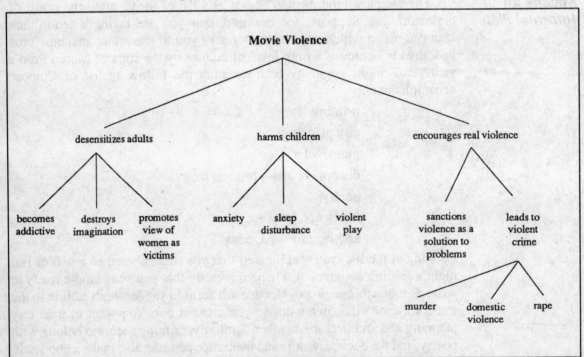

Preliminary thesis: The trend toward increasingly graphic violence in Hollywood movies must be reversed because it desensitizes adults, harms children, and encourages real violence.

Tree diagramming helps organize the wealth of material gathered during the prewriting stage. To make a tree diagram of your own, study your notes to determine your most important general points and write them at the top of a sheet of paper. Next, search for important subpoints to back up these main ideas. When you've found some, write them at the ends of branching lines leading down from the appropriate main points. Add supporting details and illustrations at the ends of additional branching lines.

Outlining

Like tree diagrams, informal outlines illustrate relationships between ideas. **Informal outlines** are indented lists of main ideas and key supporting details arranged in the order in which they will appear in an argument. These informal outlines are strictly planning tools; therefore, they need not be labeled with letters and numbers, and they can contain complete sentences as well as phrases and single words. Since informal outlines often contain scratched-out entries and scribbled additions, they're sometimes called scratch outlines.

MAKING FORMAL OUTLINES

A **formal outline** is a balanced, carefully written plan consisting of progressively indented elements labeled with a standard sequence of letters and numbers. The most important and most general elements in a formal outline are not indented and are numbered with roman numerals. The more specific levels are each further indented and labeled with capital letters, arabic numbers, and lowercase letters. Each letter or number is followed by a period, and each entry in the outline begins with a capital letter:

   I. Main idea
       A. Subpoint
           1. Supporting idea
           2. Supporting idea
               a. Detail
               b. Detail
       B. Subpoint
           1. Supporting idea
           2. Supporting idea
           3. Supporting idea
   II. Main idea
       (and so on)

CHOOSING BETWEEN TOPIC OUTLINES AND SENTENCE OUTLINES

Formal outlines are classified according to whether their elements are expressed as words and phrases or as complete sentences. A **topic outline,** consisting of words or phrases, provides a condensed overview, making it easy to use as a guide for writing. A **sentence outline** is exactly like a topic outline except that all of its elements are sentences. Making a sentence outline requires you to express complete ideas, not merely mention topics as you might in a topic outline. Such definite statements would provide more detailed guidance than the items in topic outlines, and some of the sentences would probably survive unchanged in successive drafts of your argument. Sentence outlines are harder to write and harder to modify than topic outlines. However, they're especially useful if a project is unusually complex or technical.

The amount of detail included in an outline depends on its purpose. For example, a formal outline can be used to introduce readers to the structure of your argument. When an outline is intended to give only a general overview, it can be brief. On the other hand, if someone will be evaluating your argument chiefly in terms of the outline, it should include more detail. For example, your boss may ask to see an outline of a proposal you make and judge from that whether or not your idea looks promising.

IMPROVING FORMAL OUTLINES

In a formal outline, at least two items must be included under each heading. The justification for this rule is that an outline should break material into parts, and a whole cannot be divided into only one part.

NOT: I. Main idea

        A. Subpoint

            1. Supporting idea

        II. Main idea

Additional subdivisions are needed:

        I. Main idea

            A. Subpoint

                1. Supporting idea

                2. Supporting idea

            B. Subpoint

        II. Main idea

It's always permissible to leave a section undivided, but a good formal outline contains no A without a B, no 1 without a 2, and so on.

Overlapping categories always weaken an outline. The following segment of an outline illustrates subpoints that don't divide the main idea adequately:

NOT: I. Minimizing the risks of blood transfusions

        A. Transfusions before 1990

   B. Use of blood donated by patients themselves before surgery

   C. Efforts to reduce the number of transfusions

   D. Possible future production of blood substitutes

   E. Transfusions after 1990

Following this outline would result in a confusing argument because the first and last categories cover the same time periods that the middle categories do. One way to improve it would be to eliminate subheads A and E.

USING PARALLELISM

Parallel items are in the same grammatical form. The items in the following outline are not parallel:

NOT: I. Training for senior management positions

   A. Informal training

   B. Need to attend formal training sessions

To correct the lack of parallelism, change subhead B to "Formal training":

   I. Training for senior management positions

   A. Informal training

   B. Formal training

Using parallel form makes these ideas easier to understand and remember.

UNDERSTANDING THE ADVANTAGES AND DISADVANTAGES OF OUTLINING

Careful outlining compels clear thinking and orderly argument. Making an outline involves testing the relationships between main ideas and subpoints, determining precisely where supporting details belong, and eliminating inconsistent and irrelevant material.

Although outlining has many advantages, it can also create problems. Because a formal outline looks impressive, making one can give you a false sense of control over a large body of information when you have not yet grasped its full significance. Such an outline can commit you to an apparently orderly approach that fails to address essential questions. You also risk getting caught up with formal requirements (struggling to provide a second subhead, for example, when you have only one good subpoint) and distorting material to fit the outline.

The way to avoid these pitfalls is not to jump to the outlining stage too quickly. Including vague entries (such as "B. Additional evidence") is a sign that you should return to prewriting before outlining further.

Outlines are most helpful when they're used as guidelines, not plans that must be followed rigidly. Many successful writers don't use formal outlines, and you may not necessarily want to make one unless it helps you get organized, serves as an introduction for your readers, or fulfills your instructor's or employer's requirements.

EXERCISE 2

Directions: Complete the formal outline below by selecting items from the following list and writing them in the spaces provided.

Misdiagnosis due to low academic expectations for ghetto children

Use of qualified contractors to remove lead paint

Middle-class and upper-class children

Exposure to lead more widespread than previously thought

Lowered IQs

Thesis: Parents should be aware of the risk of lead poisoning to young children.

I. Lead much more dangerous to young children than previously thought

    A. Effects of lead poisoning

        1. Hyperactivity

        2. Memory loss

        3. Reading disabilities

        4. _____

    B. Effects probably irreversible

II. _____

    A. One in nine children at risk

    B. Lead present in 78 percent of houses built before 1980

III. All economic levels exposed

    A. Poor children

        1. Danger from peeling paint

        2. _____

    B. _____

        1. Danger from lead dust during housing renovation

        2. Misdiagnosis due to mistaken belief that lead poisoning affects only poor children

IV. Precautions against lead poisoning

    A. Tests for lead in homes

    B. _____

    C. Removal of lead dust wherever possible

DRAFTING AN ARGUMENT

A person who complains "I know what I want to say, but I don't know how to say it" may be trying to envision an entire argument before starting to write. But most arguments are so complicated that they can't be mapped out word for word beforehand. Often, starting to write provides the momentum to think of ideas that a person wouldn't have come up with otherwise.

If you're having trouble getting started, you may need to put yourself on a writing schedule. Beginning long before a project is due will give you a chance to work on your argument awhile and then set it aside until your next writing session, when you'll have a fresh perspective on it. And don't wait for the right mood to strike before you begin; instead, set a specific time to start and do so, even if you're not feeling particularly creative.

It helps to remind yourself that your draft is just that—a draft, something to respond to and refine later. Rather than perfect each sentence as you go along, write down your general ideas in a rough form, avoiding the temptation to focus on trivial revisions (such as changing *however* to *on the other hand*). Leave wide margins and double or triple space to provide room for revisions. Writing on only one side of a page will keep you from flipping repeatedly through your draft to find specific passages.

If you hit a snag, reread all or part of your argument to remind yourself of the general direction you have taken. Then if sections of the paper still seem especially difficult to write, skip them temporarily and come back to them later when you're fresh. Leave a note to yourself when you stop writing; jotting down "Find information on the causes of cheating" or "Refute opposing views here" will make it easier to get started next time.

At one time or another, even professionals experience **writer's block**, a temporary inability to put words on paper. Below are some tips for preventing and overcoming writer's block.

CONQUERING WRITER'S BLOCK

1. Schedule regular writing sessions for the time of day when you're at your best.

2. Limit distractions. Turn off the TV and let friends and family members know that you don't want to be disturbed.

3. Jog your thinking by using some of the prewriting techniques discussed in chapter 7 such as freewriting, brainstorming, asking questions, and drawing diagrams.

4. Highlight everything you like in a copy of what you've already written and delete the rest. Make a new start based on what's left.

5. Post a list of the steps in your writing task and check off each step as you complete it.

6. Jot down on a calendar how much time you spend writing each day. A row of zeroes should motivate you to get back to work.

7. Know when to stop. Don't keep reworking material when you should be moving on to something new.

Drafting Good Paragraphs

When writing a draft, you needn't begin at the beginning. Since introductions and conclusions are among the most difficult parts of an essay to write, try beginning in the middle, on the body of the paper. Once you finish drafting the main part of your paper, you'll find it easier to see how it should begin and end.

Plan your drafts paragraph by paragraph, not sentence by sentence. Good readers expect each paragraph to discuss a single aspect of a subject and anticipate that a new paragraph will signal a change of direction, however slight. Therefore, develop one, and only one, main idea in each paragraph, discussing it as fully as you think necessary before moving on. Paragraphs in academic and business writing are usually between six and twelve sentences long (although introductions and conclusions are often shorter).

If you're not sure whether or not to start a new paragraph, keep your readers' needs in mind. For example, a long, undivided block of text (such as two full pages) is uninviting. Sometimes a long passage contains logical places to divide the material into units readers can assimilate easily, but even arbitrary breaks are better than no breaks at all.

Often the decision to start a new paragraph is obvious. When you know you're about to discuss a new point, write a **topic sentence**, a general sentence that limits and controls the material in a paragraph. Usually, a topic sentence begins a paragraph, but one can also appear in the middle or at the end. Good writers sometimes omit topic sentences altogether, implying the main ideas that unify their paragraphs rather than stating them directly. However, you'll probably find that including topic sentences helps you keep the main idea of each paragraph constantly in mind.

A topic sentence should be the most general sentence in its paragraph. The other sentences in the paragraph discuss aspects of the idea expressed in the topic sentence or provide specific examples to clarify and illustrate it. One way to develop a paragraph is to write sentences at three levels of generality:

Topic sentence (most general)

Main support for topic sentence (general)

Detail (specific)

Detail (specific)

Main support for topic sentence (general)

Detail (specific)

Detail (specific)

(and so on)

Paragraphs consisting mostly of general sentences may seem a little hollow. Consider the following example from an essay arguing that the hunt for Nazi war criminals should continue:

Among the nations that once harbored Nazi war criminals, Argentina continues to conceal the most important information. If the Argentine government could be convinced to open police files and other information sources, several enduring mysteries could probably be solved. Its failure to do so continues to frustrate both historians and people who want to track down the last living Nazi war criminals and bring them to justice. By refusing to cooperate, the government is signaling that Argentina is still not prepared to scrutinize and come to terms with its pro-Nazi past. Opening official files could clarify the fates of several key Nazi leaders and might also reveal the location of plunder worth billions of dollars.

By remaining at the first two levels of generality, the writer has failed to make this paragraph as convincing and memorable as it could be. The following fully developed paragraph is more interesting and persuasive because it includes specific details:

Among the nations that once harbored Nazi war criminals, Argentina continues to conceal the most important information [*topic sentence*]. Opening Argentine files could clarify the fates of several key Nazi leaders [*main support*]. Martin Bormann, Hitler's deputy, may have died in Berlin during the last days of the war, but some historians, including Gerald Posner, an authority on Nazi war crimes, suspect that he escaped to Argentina [*detail*]. According to Posner, the Argentine police have a file on Bormann nearly a foot thick, which they refuse to open for public inspection [*detail*]. Argentine records might also reveal the location of plunder worth billions of dollars [*main support*]. In 1945, six German U-boats landed in Argentina, carrying a reported 550,000 ounces of gold, 3,500 ounces of platinum, and 4,638 carats in diamonds as well as currency and artworks [*detail*]. The Argentine police interrogated crew members of these submarines, but the files recording these interrogations are still sealed [*detail*].

Ensuring Unity and Coherence

A paragraph is unified when the ideas and details it contains fit comfortably within the limits established by its topic sentence. Material that does not support the topic sentence is irrelevant and should be eliminated or moved to a different paragraph. The following paragraph from an essay on environmental problems in the former Soviet Union contains an irrelevant sentence:

> Another environmentally unsound project from the 1960s was a plan to divert water from the Aral Sea to irrigate cotton fields in central Asia. Schemes to irrigate desert land in the western United States have also caused environmental problems. As a result of the Soviet irrigation project, the amount of water in the Aral Sea has decreased by two thirds. Former port cities have been stranded, and local weather has changed for the worse. Sandstorms now blow salt from the former sea bottom across the cotton fields, killing the crops.

The second sentence, "Schemes to irrigate desert land in the western United States have also caused environmental problems," destroys the unity of this paragraph.

Readers find arguments more persuasive when they are **coherent**, that is, when the connections between ideas are clear. To ensure coherence, a writer can provide indications roughly equivalent to signposts along a highway. Transitional words and phrases, repetition of key words, and parallel sentence structure all keep readers on the right road as they follow an argument from claim to conclusion.

USING TRANSITIONAL WORDS AND PHRASES

The clearest signposts are **transitional words and phrases** (such as *however, for example,* and *on the other hand*), which explicitly point out the relationships between ideas. Suppose readers of an essay on animal rights encounter the following thesis statement:

> Experimentation on animals should be halted because it is cruel, immoral, and unnecessary.

They now know not only the writer's claim but also the three main ideas she will present to support it. The second paragraph begins as follows:

> *First,* animal experimentation is unnecessarily cruel.

After a section describing various scientific experiments, the author moves on to her next point, introducing it in the following topic sentence:

> *Second,* animal experimentation is immoral because it involves speciesism, the belief that human beings are more important than other animals and therefore entitled to exploit them.

After arguing that speciesism cannot be justified, she concl
a third point, again introducing it with a transitional word:

Last, all this cruelty and arrogance is unnecessary.

She goes on to show that a large number of animal experiments are performed by cosmetics manufacturers. She maintains that animals are tortured and killed for trivial purposes, such as to develop a new line of mascara, and that companies could make the cosmetics safe for humans by using tissue cultures and computer simulations instead of testing them on animals. At this point, whether her readers agree with her or not, they have understood her because she has clearly shown how the three sections of her essay relate to her thesis.

The following chart lists words and phrases that can mark a transition from one point in an essay to the next.

TRANSITIONAL WORDS AND PHRASES

Exemplification

for example	for instance	specifically

Addition

also	besides	furthermore
in addition	moreover	

Comparison and Contrast

conversely	even so	however
in contrast	instead	in the same way
likewise	nevertheless	nonetheless
on the contrary	on the other hand	otherwise
similarly	still	

Emphasis

certainly	indeed	in fact
surely	surprisingly	

Time

finally	first	last
later	meanwhile	next
second	subsequently	then
third		

Result

accordingly   as a result   consequently

hence

Conclusion

in brief   in conclusion   therefore

thus

EXERCISE 3

Directions: Identify the better transitional word or phrase in each of the
sentences below by writing the correct letter on the line provided.

Example: __B__ The economy has been worsening. (A. On the contrary, B. As a result,) layoffs are up and consumer confidence
is down.

_____ 1. The proposed cuts in Defense Department contracts affect
Missouri the most. (A. In addition, B. Therefore,) Texas and
Arizona will be badly hurt if the cuts are made.

_____ 2. The federal government seems indifferent to charges of mis-
management in high places. (A. For example, B. Converse-
ly,) federal officials have repeatedly ignored accusations by
CIA analysts of distortions in key intelligence reports.

_____ 3. Academic qualifications are not always the basis for admission to the most selective colleges. (A. Nevertheless, B. In
fact,) major donors to these colleges are often motivated by
the desire to ensure places for their children and
grandchildren in future classes.

_____ 4. Users of computer bulletin boards have a right to freedom of
speech. (A. Nevertheless, B. In the same way,) efforts have
been made to censor computer-based discussion services.

_____ 5. The Polite Society claims that buying and selling a bus ticket
in England requires people to say "thank you" to each other
six times. (A. Surely, B. Surprisingly,) the British have no
standard reply to "thank you" comparable to "you're welcome" in the United States.

_____ 6. About 75 cents of every dollar collected by organized
charities is devoted to the charities' programs and the remaining 25 cents to fund raising and administrative costs. The
American Red Cross devotes 92 cents of every dollar to its

programs; (A. even so, B. hence,) it has not entirely escaped criticism.

_____ 7. The suffering of catastrophically injured accident victims is often increased by long delays in bringing their cases to court. (A. On the other hand, B. For instance,) delays of four to five years are not uncommon.

_____ 8. Bats, long the objects of superstition and misinformation, do pose some real dangers to humans. (A. Specifically, B. Besides,) humans can contract rabies and histoplasmosis, a fungus affecting the lungs, from infected bats.

_____ 9. The Moscow Brain Institute was founded in 1924 partly to preserve and study the brains of public figures such as Lenin and Stalin. (A. In brief, B. Similarly,) the Kaiser Wilhelm Institute for Brain Research in Berlin attempted to collect brain specimens of famous people for analysis.

_____10. The budget of Washington, D.C., must be approved by the U.S. Congress. (A. As a result, B. In contrast,) the city cannot even alter garbage collection schedules without congressional approval.

Using Your Own Wording to Signal Transitions

Movement from one section of an argument to the next is often indicated through phrasing such as "Another complaint about the Secretary of State is . . ." or "Perhaps most disturbing is . . ." For example, the following excerpt is taken from the part of the essay described above dealing with cruelty to animals:

> In an experiment conducted at the University of Pittsburgh, two scientists applied electric shocks to over a thousand mice, first through their feet and later through clips attached to their ears and eyes. The scientists wanted to find out if the mice could gradually grow accustomed to the shocks, but not surprisingly, many of the mice died between the first day of testing and the second.
>
> *Even more cruel* was an experiment done on cats at the National Institute for Medical Research in London. There, scientists injected a substance called tubocurarine into the cats' brains. . . .

The words "Even more cruel" not only introduce the description of a second experiment but also link the two paragraphs together, leaving readers in no doubt about how the writer's argument is progressing. This kind of explicit transition makes her essay easier to read.

Repeating Key Words

Repetition of important words or phrases helps readers follow an argument and provides a satisfying sense of coherence. The following paragraph, taken from an essay on the mass media and family values, relies on repetition to make its point:

> The people who control television in the United States support traditional family *values* far less than do the people who watch their shows. According to a recent survey of over one hundred highly placed television executives and writers taken by the Center for Media and Public Affairs, only 45 percent of them place a high *value* on monogamy in marriage, compared to 85 percent of the general public. Eighty percent of those surveyed do not believe homosexual acts are wrong, compared to 24 percent of the public at large, and fully 97 percent support a woman's right to abortion, compared to only 59 percent of average Americans. This *value* gap between the makers of TV shows and their audience is also reflected in attitudes toward religion: 45 percent of those in the television industry have no religious affiliation (the figure for the country is 4 percent). The average Americans who make up the vast majority of television viewers support family *values*, even if these *values* are not always reflected in their lives. In contrast, those who rule our country's most popular medium of entertainment appear to *value* individual freedom far more highly than the principles that sustain the traditional family.

Repetition of the word *value* provides coherence for this paragraph.

The next paragraph of the essay begins with the following sentence:

> The people who control newspapers and news magazines also lag behind the general public in their support of traditional family values.

The parallel structures of the two topic sentences also help ensure coherence for the essay as a whole. Readers can see at a glance that the ideas expressed in parallel form have something in common; they can compare them easily and understand how they contribute to the argument.

Drafting Effective Introductions and Conclusions

Arguments with dull beginnings are seldom read while those with weak endings are seldom remembered. A good introduction sets the tone for an argument, and an effective conclusion leaves readers with a clear, memorable restatement of the writer's message.

DRAFTING INTRODUCTIONS

The most important goal of an introduction is to capture readers' attention. Every day America's mailboxes are crammed with letters advertising everything from magazine subscriptions to Hawaiian vacations. Many people throw these advertisements away without even opening them. Direct mail advertisers know this and try to counter by making the envelopes as intriguing as possible. Messages on envelopes such as "Urgent—Open Immediately" and "You May Already Have Won $20,000,000" are the junk mail equivalents of introductions to essays. If they don't induce people to read on, the real message never gets through.

To grasp the importance of writing effective introductions, imagine a stranger finding your essay on the floor of a classroom or office. As he strolls to the wastepaper basket, he glances at the first few lines, just to make sure he hasn't found anything important. What can you do in your opening paragraph to keep that person from throwing your paper into the trash? Consider using one or more of the following techniques to interest prospective readers in your argument:

a brief narrative of an incident or anecdote

an interesting quotation

one or more questions (as long as the essay goes on to answer them)

an intriguing statistic

the definition of a key term

necessary background or an explanation of the topic's importance

Of these opening ideas, the most likely to interest readers is the anecdote. People are curious about other people; their natural curiosity is one of a writer's strongest allies. Consider the following introduction to an essay about companies that supply inaccurate credit reports:

> Betty Fermi thought she had done very well for herself in the five years since she graduated from college. She had a good job as an actuary for an insurance company and a pleasant three-room apartment overlooking a park. She had always paid her rent and other bills on time. However, when she decided to buy a new Chevrolet sedan and applied for a car loan, she discovered that at least one credit-checking service considered her a deadbeat. The service had confused her with another Betty Fermi, who had just declared bankruptcy after running up $30,000 in credit-card debt. Moreover, when Fermi called the mistake to the company's attention, officials refused to correct it.

At this point many readers will have begun to identify with Fermi and want to find out how to prevent the same thing from happening to them.

A second function of an introductory paragraph is to lead plausibly into the writer's thesis. If an opening paragraph is interesting and informative, readers are more likely to accept the claim made in the thesis. The opening paragraph of the essay on credit checking agencies concludes with the following thesis:

> Companies that provide businesses with consumer credit ratings must respond to complaints by correcting mistakes promptly.

Often you can improve an introduction by condensing it. There's no need to put your readers through the discomfort of watching you fumble for ideas. Instead, cut any part of your introduction that does not serve your readers' purposes.

DRAFTING CONCLUSIONS

Your conclusion should provide a satisfying sense of an ending rather than lead readers to wonder if a final page has been mislaid. The most common feature of a conclusion is a summary of an argument's main ideas. A concluding paragraph can also contain the same elements as an introduction along with one or more of the following:

predictions for the future

recommendations for changes

judgments based on key points

Since you're probably not a world expert on your topic, you may feel like apologizing in your conclusion, admitting that other views may be equally valid and backing away from your claim. Avoid this temptation. Readers feel betrayed if you back down from the stand you've taken. At the opposite extreme, try not to overstate your main points since claiming too much undermines your credibility. Be sure your conclusion follows logically from the rest of your paper and avoid adding anything new that will catch your readers off guard.

EXERCISE 4

Directions: Listed below are the opening lines of ten introductions and conclusions. In each space at the left, write the letter identifying the technique it illustrates. Use the following code:

A   anecdote or incident

B   quotation

C   question

D   interesting statistic

E   definition of a key term

F   prediction

G   recommendation

Example: __F__ Further study is likely to verify the identification of the archeological site where the Dead Sea Scrolls were found and the accuracy of the scrolls' radiocarbon dating.

_____ 1. If married career women have the best of both worlds—happy families and challenging jobs—why are so many of them complaining?

_____ 2. "I saw mud spattering all over, so I ran for my life," said Mindy Brandenburg, a survivor of the deadly volcano that recently devastated the Philippine island of Luzon.

_____ 3. In conclusion, considerable evidence suggests that televised warnings about the risks of beer drinking are a scare tactic that will not work.

_____ 4. An engraved wedding invitation addressed to me arrived recently, an invitation pointedly stating that I could not bring a guest. After an initial burst of pleasure at my friends' decision to marry, I felt troubled.

_____ 5. Thus, men must work together to change divorce and custody laws that currently favor women, to win the right to paternity leave, and to resolve the psychic crises that have incapacitated them.

_____ 6. Nearly 90 percent of deaf children are born to hearing parents.

_____ 7. In his day Henry Ford received an avalanche of mail from people interested in Ford cars, including the offer of six mounted moose heads to be traded for a new Model T.

_____ 8. "There is nothing—absolutely nothing—half so much worth doing as simply messing about in boats," says Toad in *The Wind in the Willows*.

_____ 9. The Congressional franking privilege is the right of members of Congress to send mail free to the people they represent.

_____10. Therefore, city buildings should conform to the same local fire codes that govern privately owned buildings.

After prewriting, the next stage in the writing process is drafting, which includes composing a thesis (a statement of an argument's claim) and planning the argument as a whole. An argument usually begins with a brief introduction leading to a thesis, followed by support for the thesis, refutation of opposing views, and a conclusion restating key points. Arguments are often organized in chronological order, spatial order, and emphatic order although other organizational schemes are also possible. Informal plans, tree diagrams, and outlines enable writers to arrange their material. Clear topic sentences help unify paragraphs while transitional words and phrases, repeated key words, and parallel sentence structure improve coherence.

CHAPTER EXERCISE

I. MATCHING

Directions: Match each term on the list below with its definition by writing the correct letter in the space provided. Some of the terms on the list will not be used.

TERMS:

A. chronological order   H. sentence outline

B. coherence   I. spatial order

C. counterclaim   J. thesis statement

D. emphatic order   K. topic sentence

E. formal outline   L. transitional words and phrases

F. informal outline   M. tree diagram

G. parallelism   N. writer's block

DEFINITIONS:

_____ 1. clear statement of an argument's claim

_____ 2. expression of opinion that directly contradicts a claim

_____ 3. organization in the order in which events occurred

_____ 4. organization in terms of location

_____ 5. organization according to importance

_____ 6. drawing in which words and branching lines illustrate relationships between ideas

_____ 7. balanced, carefully written plan consisting of progressively indented elements labeled with a standard sequence of letters and numbers

_____ 8. use of the same grammatical form

_____ 9. general sentence that limits and controls the material in a paragraph

_____10. indication of clear connections between ideas

II. MULTIPLE CHOICE

Directions: On the line at the left write the letter of the phrase that best completes each item.

_____11. A thesis sentence should be

    A. a question.

    B. an undisputed fact.

    C. a statement of an opinion.

_____12. A thesis usually

    A. appears at the end of an essay's opening paragraph.

    B. is the first line of an essay.

    C. is the last line of an essay.

_____13. The purpose of writing a counterclaim is to

    A. test a thesis to see if it is arguable.

    B. organize ideas in the most effective way.

    C. avoid overlapping elements in an outline.

_____14. A common organizational pattern for an argument is

    A. introduction, supporting details, thesis, conclusion.

    B. introduction, opposing views, refutation of opposing views, key points, thesis, conclusion.

    C. introduction, thesis, support for the thesis, refutation of opposing views, conclusion.

_____15. When there is little time for planning, a recommended approach is to

    A. brainstorm a list and number the items on it.

    B. start writing quickly without a plan.

    C. prepare a formal outline.

_____16. Unlike informal outlines, formal outlines

    A. are indented.

    B. can never include single subpoints.

    C. contain main ideas and details arranged in the order in which they will appear in an essay.

_____17. A topic outline contains

    A. only words and phrases.

    B. only sentences.

    C. words, phrases, and sentences.

_____18. A good way to cope with writer's block is to

A. write only when in the mood for it.

B. try to perfect each sentence before going on to the next one.

C. schedule regular writing sessions for the time of day when one is at one's best.

_____19. An effective approach to writing paragraphs is to

A. make most paragraphs three or four sentences long.

B. unify and clarify each paragraph by repeating the main idea in a large number of general sentences.

C. begin paragraphs with topic sentences.

_____20. Introductions and conclusions

A. are usually longer than the other paragraphs in essays.

B. should make a strong first and last impression.

C. never contain transitional words and phrases.

9

Choosing an Effective Style

*"**I** think Ms. Warshaw is brilliant," said Sandra. "Whenever I get one of her memos, I have to read it five or six times to understand what she's talking about."*

"That may not be a sign of brilliance, exactly," Meredith replied.

"Her writing is so deep," Sandra went on. "Who else would have thought to call reorganizing the office 'priority locational resources reallocation' or buying rest room supplies from a cheaper distributor 'enhanced sanitational assets acquisition' ?"

"Who indeed?"

"And look at this one," said Sandra, waving Ms. Warshaw's latest effort under Meredith's nose. "It's got a sentence nearly two pages long!"

UNDERSTANDING STYLE

Have you ever seen a sweater in a department store display and thought "That looks like something my brother would wear"? Just as some people have such recognizable styles of dress that you can almost pick out the clothing they would choose for themselves, writers have individual styles based on particular preferences. Characteristic decisions about what words to use and how to combine them in sentences comprise a writer's **style**. Some people's writing styles reveal them as intelligent, clear thinking, and careful. A style such as Ms. Warshaw's communicates other qualities, not very pleasant ones from Meredith's point of view.

A good style is readable and interesting, not necessarily eye-catching or elaborate. Your writing style should be as representative of you as your thumbprint. Your own voice should come through in your writing, the voice that results from knowing and accepting yourself and saying as clearly as possible what you have to say.

Reading widely is the best way to develop an effective style. When you study the work of skillful writers, you will notice, for example, that they rely on strong, specific nouns and verbs to convey their meaning rather than on weak or trite adjectives and adverbs. Habitual sentence patterns, such as the use of an occasional short sentence to change the pace after a series of long ones, are also a matter of style.

Achieving a natural style is sometimes easier if you picture a specific reader, perhaps a friend you respect and for whom you would like to express your views clearly. But keeping a potential reader constantly in mind can also be inhibiting. As a result, some writers think only now and then of how a reader would respond and mainly aim to please themselves.

In a college course your professor is your main audience, but you should write *for* the professor, not *to* him or her. If you write directly to the professor, you're likely to write more informally than you should, omitting information you're sure he or she already knows but that is essential to your argument. Instead, keep in mind the needs of a more general audience: educated people who expect clear, well-organized prose but who lack the specific information you can provide.

SELECTING THE RIGHT REGISTER AND TONE

If you wear a sweat suit to a wedding where all the other guests are in evening dress, people will certainly notice and disapprove. On the other hand, wearing a tuxedo or a formal gown to play tennis will provoke amusement and head shaking. Just as people have clear ideas about the kind of dress appropriate for different occasions, they have definite expectations for different kinds of writing.

Choosing Among the Formal, Middle, and Informal Registers

The term **register** refers to the variety of language that fits a particular occasion or subject. Different registers require different kinds of vocabulary, punctuation, and sentence and paragraph length. Eulogies, legal briefs, and scholarly papers are written in the formal register. Letters to friends, diary entries, and memos to long-time colleagues are written in the informal register. In between, in the middle register, falls a great deal of academic writing, such as short papers for English classes and answers to essay exams, as well as much of the writing published in newspapers and popular magazines.

THE FORMAL REGISTER

A writer submitting a proposal to a company's board of directors or an article to a scientific journal must follow accepted conventions if he or she expects to be taken seriously. Polysyllabic words (*employer* instead of *boss*, for example) and difficult technical terms are appropriate in formal writing so long as they are vital to the writer's meaning and not included merely to impress people. Formal word choice is required (such as *much* or *a great many* rather than *a lot*), and the pronoun *one* is sometimes used. Many sentences and paragraphs in the formal register are lengthy because the complex ideas typical of formal writing require amplification.

Some kinds of language appropriate to the other registers seem out of place in formal writing. The following list gives suggestions that will help you make appropriate choices.

WHAT TO AVOID IN THE FORMAL REGISTER

1. Informal wording: guys, kids, mad (for *angry*), too (for *very*)
2. Almost all abbreviations and shortened forms: TV, ad, dorm, prof
3. Contractions: don't, he'll, let's
4. Vague phrasing: kind of, sort of
5. Exclamation points

THE MIDDLE REGISTER

Although college research papers are usually written in the formal register, most college writing is in the middle register, part way between formal and informal. Like the formal register, the middle register requires vocabulary suited to an educated audience. On the whole, the conventions for sentence and paragraph length in the formal register apply in the middle register as well.

On rare occasions a **colloquialism** (a word or phrase appropriate to casual speech, such as *giveaway*) or **slang** (a very informal colloquialism such as *humongous* or *freaked out*) is used in the middle register for its vigor or humor. However, because informal language changes quickly, it often makes writing seem dated or hard to interpret. For instance, slang popular in the 1960s, such as "the fuzz" for police officers, is unfamiliar to many people today. To determine whether a word is appropriate to a particular register, check its usage label in a dictionary. (A **usage label** is a term or abbreviation indicating that a word or a particular use of a word is not standard.) The word *slang* and the abbreviation *obs.* (for *obsolete*) are examples of usage labels. Unlabeled words are considered part of the standard English vocabulary. However, you should keep in mind that many standard words can be used as slang. For example, *hit* is standard in most of its usages but slang in "hit the sack."

Abbreviations, contractions, and other shortened word forms that are inappropriate in the formal register may be used in the middle register, but sparingly.

THE INFORMAL REGISTER

Writing in the informal register is freer than writing in the formal and middle registers, but it still follows certain conventions. Vulgar expressions and swear words are not appropriate even in informal writing, nor are nonstandard terms (words such as *ain't* that are not generally used by educated native speakers). Certain uses of standard words are considered nonstandard. For instance, *like* is used as an interjection ("It was, like, awesome") only in nonstandard speech. **Regionalisms** (terms common only to limited geographical areas) are standard in the speech of particular regions but not in the writing. Regionalisms such as *goober* ("peanut") and *tonic* ("soft drink") may not be understood outside the areas where they are common.

Informal writing is often characterized by imprecise word use, such as *pretty* to mean "somewhat" (as in "He's pretty funny") rather than "attractive" (as in "The flowers are pretty"). Pronouns may have vague antecedents in informal writing ("Margo started talking to *this* man she had met") and *like* may be used as a subordinating conjunction in place of *as* ("Charlie flunked the exam *like* I knew he would"). Short sentences and paragraphs are acceptable in the informal register. Small numbers (1 through 10) can appear as numerals in informal writing but should be spelled out (one through ten) in college essays and most business writing. If you are unsure about whether or not to use a long form (*telephone* for "phone," *cannot* for "can't"), follow the general rule "If in doubt, write it out."

A sense of what to avoid in the formal and middle registers will develop gradually as you gain experience in academic and business settings. Good writers differ on which specific words and constructions belong in which register, so if you are writing for an employer or a college professor, follow the instructions you are given.

TRY IT OUT

Can you adapt your writing to the demands of different registers? Experiment with writing formally and informally by describing a change you would like to make at school or at work. Select a topic such as a new college major, a semester of independent study, or an innovative way to reorganize the files in your office.

First, use the informal register to write a letter to a friend explaining the proposed change. Such a letter might begin "Dear Kathy, Believe it or not, I've finally found a truly fantastic major!" Then use the formal register in a letter on the same subject to your academic advisor, a department chairperson, or a top executive in your company. Such an account might begin, "Dear Dr. Bartlett: I would like to change my major from forestry to accounting."

EXERCISE 1

Directions: The items below illustrate informal speech. Rephrase them so that they are appropriate to writing in the formal or middle register. Write your versions on the lines provided. Answers will vary, but sample answers are given at the back of this book.

Example: People with asthma freak out when the air quality stinks.

<u>Asthma sufferers are distressed by poor air quality.</u>

1. Move your stuff out of here before Mr. Leithauser flips out on you!

2. The whole office can't forget the fun bash my boss threw over at his place.

3. Lots of people get so bombed they drive like idiots, so who needs it, right?

4. Some guys like working overtime, but they're pretty out of it!

5. When you're in jail, you can watch TV and yack on the phone a lot.

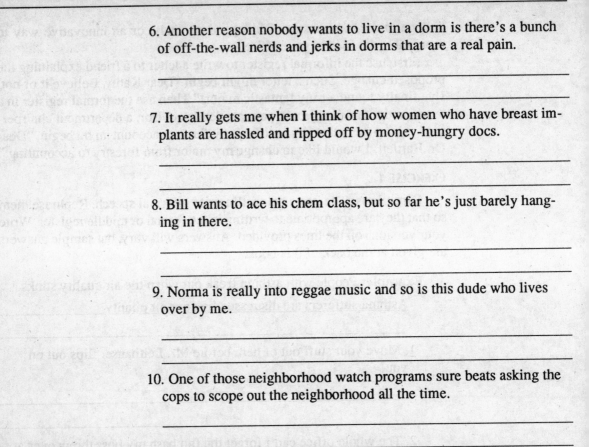

6. Another reason nobody wants to live in a dorm is there's a bunch of off-the-wall nerds and jerks in dorms that are a real pain.

_____

_____

7. It really gets me when I think of how women who have breast implants are hassled and ripped off by money-hungry docs.

_____

_____

8. Bill wants to ace his chem class, but so far he's just barely hanging in there.

_____

_____

9. Norma is really into reggae music and so is this dude who lives over by me.

_____

_____

10. One of those neighborhood watch programs sure beats asking the cops to scope out the neighborhood all the time.

_____

_____

Deciding Between a Personal and an Impersonal Tone

Just as choosing the correct register for a particular piece of writing can make its intended audience more receptive to it, choosing the correct tone can increase its effectiveness.

TONE

Tone is the quality of speech and writing that reveals people's attitudes toward their subjects, their audiences, and themselves. A tone of voice can vary from affable and kindly to arrogant and defensive; similarly, tone in writing can reveal a wide range of emotions and perspectives. In argument, writers must choose between a personal and an impersonal tone—that is, they need to decide how close a relationship to establish between themselves and their audiences. Generally, a personal tone is appropriate to the informal register while an impersonal tone is appropriate to the formal and middle registers.

Using pronouns precisely will help you set the correct tone in all your writing. The first sentence of this paragraph, which is typical of this book, uses the words *you* and *your* to establish a personal relationship between us, the authors, and you, the reader. A less personal version of the sentence

would be "Using pronouns precisely will help writers set t̶̶
all their writing." Sentences of this type also appear in this
the pronoun *one* would be still more impersonal: "Using pron̶
will help one set the correct tone in all one's writing."

PERSON

Choosing pronouns is easier if you understand the grammatical term
person, which refers to the distinction between a person speaking (first
person), a person being spoken to (second person), and a person or people
being spoken about (third person). Third person pronouns (such as *she*, *one*,
and *they*) are used in the formal register almost to the exclusion of first-person pronouns (such as *I* and *we*) and second-person pronouns (such as *you*
and *your*), both of which are mostly characteristic of the informal register.

Using *I* (or *we* if more than one author is involved) is acceptable in the
formal and middle registers so long as the first-person pronoun is both
accurate and necessary. When recounting a personal experience or opinion,
substituting such expressions as "In the experience of the author . . ." or
"This writer thinks . . ." for the straightforward *I* can seem pompous. However, using *I* excessively calls too much attention to a writer. Consider the
speaker's self-important attitude in the following passage:

NOT: *I* have carefully considered the question of whether pilots should
or should not be allowed to fly double shifts, and after six months
of study *I* have concluded that *I* cannot support such a proposal.

Readers of this report want to know whether pilots should or should not
be allowed to fly double shifts, not how much the writer struggled to reach
his conclusion. The rephrased version, "Pilots should not be allowed to fly
double shifts," still leaves no doubt that this is the writer's opinion since it
appears in his report and is not attributed to anyone else. The version below,
in which the writer includes a personal reference, is also acceptable since it
keeps his role in proportion to its importance:

Six months' study has convinced me that pilots should not be
allowed to fly double shifts.

Sometimes writers use *we* to refer to themselves and their readers, taken
together. For example, in the sentence "We must work together to ensure
that a patient's poverty no longer results in delayed treatment for cancer"
the writer uses *we* to refer both to herself and to readers who agree with her
view.

The pronoun *you* can be used in the formal and middle registers only
when writers address readers directly. In a business letter, the sentence "I
expect to hear from you by the fifteenth of next month" is acceptable because
the pronoun *you* clearly refers to the person receiving the letter. However,
you is also an informal way of referring to people in general, as in the

sentence "If you park illegally anywhere downtown, your car might be towed away." This use of *you* to mean "anyone" is too casual for the formal or middle register. Fortunately, an idea expressed by this general use of *you* can always be recast in the third person: "Drivers who park illegally anywhere downtown might have their cars towed away."

WRITING CLEARLY AND CONCISELY

A written argument is intended to convert readers to its author's viewpoint. But people won't budge an inch from their original convictions if what they read is repetitive or garbled. To be convincing, writers must produce straightforward, readable prose.

Writing Clearly

Most written arguments require complex thinking but not necessarily complicated expression. In fact, the more involved your ideas, the more you need to write simply and clearly. Most readers will not tolerate fuzzy thinking, so you should scrutinize each word you write to avoid antagonizing people. Work to produce clear, orderly sentences; group related ideas together and emphasize essential points.

As the American novelist Ernest Hemingway (1899–1961) pointed out, "Writing plain English is hard work." When people neglect to do that hard work, arguments are likely to be muddled. Writers need to grasp their own viewpoints fully and make them clear to readers who are not necessarily familiar with key terms.

JARGON

Jargon is specialized vocabulary understood by people who have studied a particular discipline but obscure to outsiders. *Myocardial infarction* is medical jargon for heart attack; *dog* and *blitz* are football jargon for different kinds of defensive maneuvers. People who understand these terms prefer them because they're precise. But those who know their meanings sometimes forget that others don't. A doctor telling a worried family that a loved one has suffered a myocardial infarction and a lifetime football fan telling a novice to watch a dogging linebacker and a blitzing safety are ignoring the needs of their audiences.

Sometimes in writing an argument you will need to unravel baffling material for your readers. For instance, to understand why you oppose building a new nuclear power plant in your area, your readers might need to know exactly what caused the accident at Three Mile Island in Pennsylvania in 1979. To succeed, your explanation must be clear. This may mean substituting ordinary language for jargon or adding everyday definitions for the jargon you do use.

Writing Concisely

Some people write as if they're being paid by the word—they seem to think the longer a piece of writing is, the better. The opposite is true. **Concise** (brief and clear) writing conveys information as succinctly as possible. Using too many words is known as being wordy; the unnecessary words are called padding or deadwood. Like dead branches that must be cut before a tree can grow properly, deadwood should be pruned to reveal the essential meaning of each sentence. Deleting needless words is like cleaning up clutter in a messy room or weeding a flower garden. Once it's done, everything that remains looks better.

A certain amount of repetition is built into the standard organizational pattern of an argument: main ideas are stated in the thesis, the topic sentences, and again in the conclusion. Within a paragraph, key words are repeated to keep main points in readers' minds. However, **redundancy** (needless repetition) merely weighs readers down:

> Campers are not required to bring optional equipment such as battery-operated reading lamps.

The word *optional* means "not required" and is therefore redundant.

Often writers include phrases such as "The point I am trying to make is . . ." and "It should be pointed out that . . ." Such expressions can be dropped entirely. The following list suggests additional ways to replace deadwood with concise wording.

CONCISE REPLACEMENTS FOR WORDY PHRASES

Wordy Expressions	Concise Replacements
at this point in time	now
due to the fact that	because
each and every	each
for the purpose of	for
in order to	to
in the event that	if
in today's society	today
in view of the fact that	because
the reason is because	the reason is
until such time as	until

EXERCISE 2

Directions: On the lines provided, write a concise version of each wordy sentence below. The number at the end of each item indicates how many words are in the revised version of the sentence at the back of this book. See if you can do as well or better at eliminating unneeded words. (Answers will vary.)

Example: Those programs that at the present time require welfare recipients to attend classes should be ended and instead replaced by the provision by the government of publicly funded jobs for people on welfare (14).

Programs requiring welfare recipients to attend classes should be
replaced by publicly funded jobs.

_____

1. In Maine, by the year 2000 tourism and the tourist industry should take the place of and supersede in importance the position currently held in Maine by the industry devoted to lumber (15).

_____

_____

2. It should be pointed out that the best way to stabilize and maintain the faltering economies of countries in Latin America is to ease the process whereby loans are made available to enterprises that are small and that thereby do not now qualify for loans intended for the purpose of business (18).

_____

_____

3. William Ewart Gladstone was one of the most illustrious, famous, and celebrated prime ministers Great Britain ever had, but it is said that he was also one of the prime ministers around whom many and numerous controversies developed (16).

_____

_____

4. The reason that at the beginning of the twentieth century Italian intellectuals planned and dreamed of starting the 1900s with a new national culture is because they hoped such a culture would include and embrace all Italians (17).

_____

_____

_____

5. The point I'm trying to make is that pigs are reputed to have high intelligence and by reputation at least are known to have greater intellectual capacities and potentialities compared to what is known about the basic mental capabilities of dogs (9).

_____

_____

_____

6. At this point in time in our society today a key element in congressional campaigns is the sum total of the amount of money disbursed and paid out by each and every candidate in order to participate in a race for a seat in Congress (14).

_____

_____

_____

7. The refurbishment and restoration of the ceiling of the Sistine Chapel authentically reflects and manifests the intentions Michelangelo had in mind for the original chapel ceiling (10).

_____

_____

_____

8. The right to express one's views, by which I mean freedom of speech, a freedom guaranteed to all, is currently being menaced and today faces many threats on the college campuses of our country (10).

_____

_____

_____

9. In view of the fact that hospitals devoted to making a profit wrongly and unfairly monopolize patients who have a great deal of wealth of their own, it comes as no surprise that, indeed, hospitals not intended to make a profit are inequitably burdened with the care of the poverty-stricken indigent and also find that they are unjustly responsible in addition for those patients who lack medical insurance (18).

_____

_____

_____

10. Children should be given allowances, and each year they should be given yearly increases, but at the same time they should be required to spend the money they get through the larger allowances on increasing numbers of the things they need and want to purchase (19).

_____

_____

_____

AVOIDING INAPPROPRIATE LANGUAGE

Of the crimes perpetrated by writers, boring their readers and insulting them are among the worst. Timid, outworn wording will make readers yawn; abuse and ridicule can anger them. Shun both extremes by learning to detect the following categories of wrong words in the wrong places: clichés, emotional and offensive language, euphemisms, and doublespeak.

Clichés

Sometimes the first words that come into writers' minds are precisely the ones they need to make their points clearly and forcefully. But most of the time people think first of expressions they've heard over and over again—"I cried my eyes out"; "This is the last straw"; "She's always there for me." Such phrases are **clichés**, expressions that have been used so often they've lost all of their freshness and much of their power to communicate precisely. One sign of a cliché is that given the first part of it, almost anyone can provide the rest. For example, given "The sweet smell of," most people can supply the word _success_ almost without thinking.

Many clichés are comparisons that were once clever and illuminating but are now so familiar that they no longer make much of an impression.

The comparison "pretty as a picture" once had the power to suggest a beautiful painting of an exotic scene. If something was as pretty as a picture on a wall, it must have been truly appealing. Now, however, the phrase "pretty as a picture" has been used so often that it means no more than "pretty." Besides being trite, a cliché is sometimes inaccurate. To say a coat has undergone a lot of wear and tear, for example, is imprecise if the coat is worn but not torn.

A fresh comparison that surprises people is far more effective and memorable than a cliché would be. For example, the expression "pretty as a peach tree" can bring into people's minds an image of a flowering tree in full bloom. The comparison between the object being described and a peach tree has the power to communicate because it is new. However, if it became popular and were repeated often enough, it would become a cliché and be no better than "pretty as a picture" is now.

Using clichés as substitutes for precise observations leads to tired, uninteresting writing. Eliminating clichés is indispensable if you want to avoid sounding (and thinking) like everyone else. It's not a satisfactory solution to enclose clichés in quotation marks to show that you know you shouldn't really be using them. Instead, substitute a plain statement for the cliché; instead of "worth its weight in gold," write "very valuable."

In clichéd writing, commonplace ideas and worn out wording take the place of careful observation and original thinking. When the only support you provide for a claim is one cliché after another, your argument becomes slack and lifeless, and your credibility drains away. The basic rule when evaluating phrasing such as "It meant the world to her," "wise as an owl," or "last but not least" is "If you've heard it before, don't rely on it in your paper."

EXERCISE 3

Directions: Show your familiarity with the clichés below by filling in the blanks.

Example: Keep your __nose__ to the grindstone.

1. He's as blind as a _____.

2. My car is as old as the _____.

3. It's just the tip of the _____.

4. Do it slowly but _____.

5. She's as busy as a _____.

6. Let's take the _____ by the horns.

7. He's as dead as a _____.

8. My friend Joe is as sick as a _____.

9. It's time for you to face the _____.

10. Sink or _____.

Now choose two of the items from the list above and complete them with interesting, original wording of your own.

_____

_____

Emotional Language

Readers want to detect some emotional commitment on a writer's part. Few people would continue reading an essay that begins "I don't suppose anybody really cares, but . . ." If a writer doesn't care, readers won't either.

People who are fiercely committed to their beliefs can be persuasive, but most readers distrust authors who allow biases to distort their reasoning. Such writers are often suspected of misrepresenting facts or even lying. An objective reader compensates for suspected bias by shifting a little to the other side, working extra hard to detect an essay's factual errors and flaws in reasoning.

Suppose, for example, you are reading an essay on the psychology of child molesters by a writer who appears at first to be well informed and reasonable. After describing a particularly brutal case history, he continues with a sentence about the molester that begins, "This disgusting pervert . . ." You may have been horrified by the example yourself, but once the writer displays his emotions, your attitude toward his argument changes. You realize that he is expressing his own loathing, not trying to understand what makes molesters act as they do. Whether you share the writer's feelings or not, you can no longer entirely trust his recommendations about effective treatment for convicted molesters.

Fortunately, there are usually several ways to express the same idea, so you can choose one that reveals strong feelings without the prejudices that sometimes accompany them. Think of potential readers as fair-minded people who are not yet on your side. Your task is to persuade them by presenting yourself as fair minded too. If you call your opponents unpleasant names or poke fun at their positions on issues, you're likely to offend readers rather than win them over. When you have convincing material to offer as evidence, present it as vividly as you can and let your readers draw their own conclusions. If your argument has flaws, you are better off strengthening it by reasoning more carefully or collecting better evidence than trying to mask its weaknesses by name calling and overdramatizing your position.

Offensive Language

Some emotional language is objectionable because it is offensive. Calling an opponent "stupid" or "dishonest" not only does nothing to improve a writer's argument but is also likely to alienate both the target of the abuse and the audience. However, some writers use offensive language because they are unaware that their choice of words could insult people or hurt their feelings.

A writer who attempts to inject humor into the discussion of a serious issue must always be alert to the possibility of offending others. While an occasional quip may be welcome in an otherwise earnest debate, many people see no humor whatsoever in topics such as abortion or capital punishment. Remember also that many jokes derive their humor from an underlying hostility toward people the joke teller would like to feel superior to, such as those with other ethnic backgrounds or a different sexual orientation. Before including any joke in an argument, a speaker or writer must be certain both that the joke is funny and that its humor does not stem from cruelty or bigotry.

Swear words can also offend. Using *damn* or *hell* is not only too informal but also risks the loss of readers' respect and good will. Remarks springing from intolerance of other people's beliefs and practices can have the same effect. This does not mean that you should never tackle controversial issues, but that you should be careful not to give needless offense.

Unfortunately, speakers and writers can be unaware of the stereotypes that underlie some common words and phrases. A few of these stereotypes seem harmless. For example, the term *Welsh rabbit*, which describes melted cheese poured over toast, is probably based on an ethnic slur: Welsh hunters are supposedly so incompetent that their families end up eating cheese and bread instead of rabbit. Welsh people might not object to being stereotyped as incompetent hunters; however, stereotyping is usually more obviously hurtful. A person of Dutch descent might be offended by the term *Dutch treat* because it unfairly implies that the Dutch are less generous than other nationalities. And a person of Gypsy origin might well object to the word *gypped*, pointing out that Gypsies are no more inherently dishonest than other ethnic groups.

In choosing terms for ethnic groups, you will avoid giving offense if you select the designations favored by the groups themselves. For example, do they prefer Indian or Native American; black or African American; Eskimo or Inuit; Hispanic, Latino, or Chicano? You may find that mentioning ethnicity is not even required. Referring to a "Native American doctor" is usually unnecessary; just say "doctor." Always beware of any wording that denigrates groups of people by referring to their gender, race, ethnicity, religion, social class, sexual orientation, or physical ability.

SEXIST LANGUAGE

Sexist language (wording that reveals a bias against one sex, usually females) implies that only men or women ought to fill certain roles or possess certain characteristics; it can also cause offense and should be avoided. The use of a term such as *mankind* to mean "men and women" or *he* to mean "he or she" is no longer acceptable. The word *his* in "When a lawyer is appointed to a judgeship, *his* law firm often gains prestige and influence" implies that only male lawyers can be appointed as judges. Terms such as *businessman* (instead of *executive* or *businessperson*), *stewardess* (instead of *flight attendant*), and *congressman* (instead of *member of Congress*) are based on stereotypes about the roles suitable to men and women.

Adding the term *lady*, *woman*, or *male* to a title such as *doctor*, *lawyer*, or *secretary* is also inappropriate. The designations "woman doctor" and "male secretary," for example, suggest that women who become doctors or men who become secretaries are somehow exceptional. The growing number of people who work at jobs once thought appropriate only to the other sex makes such usages old fashioned and inaccurate.

The following list contains common sexist terms and their more accurate equivalents:

<u>Sexist Terms</u>	<u>Nonsexist Equivalents</u>
chairman	chairperson (or chair)
mailman	mail carrier
male nurse	nurse
mankind	humanity (or men and women)
old wives' tale	superstition
policeman	police officer

There are several ways to avoid sexist use of pronouns. In place of *he*, *him*, and so on you can use "he or she" and its equivalents: "When a lawyer is appointed to a judgeship, *his or her* law firm often gains prestige and influence." But several of these pronoun pairs in the same sentence or in several sentences in a row can seem awkward. A smoother alternative is to recast the sentence or entire passage in the plural since plural pronouns do not indicate gender: "When lawyers are appointed to judgeships, *their* law firms often gain prestige and influence." Another option is dropping pronouns entirely: "The law firm of a lawyer appointed to a judgeship often gains prestige and influence." In addition, when you use hypothetical examples, assign roles to males and females on an equal basis to avoid giving an impression of sexism.

Euphemisms

A **euphemism** (derived from the Greek words *eu*, meaning "pleasant," and *phēmē*, meaning "speech") is a word or phrase that takes the place of a term with unpleasant or offensive connotations. Euphemisms are substitutes for more forthright terms referring to sex, disease, death, and other natural bodily functions.

People today occasionally use euphemisms to avoid mentioning unpleasant subjects directly, but the practice was far more prevalent during the Victorian era (1837–1901). Victorian euphemisms still used today include calling the breast and leg of a chicken light and dark meat (because Victorians considered the words *breast* and *leg* sexually suggestive) and referring to a toilet as a *lavatory* (a room for washing one's hands). The word *toilet* illustrates the tendency of euphemisms to take on the unpleasant meanings they were intended to avoid; it originally meant "lady's dressing room." Now it is usually replaced by a term such as *bathroom* or *rest room*.

It's easy to laugh at Victorian squeamishness, but some euphemisms still have their place. For example, rather than saying of a beloved old pet, "I'm going to have the dog killed," using a euphemism such as "put to sleep" might well spare your family's feelings somewhat. However, in argument, euphemisms lead to pompous, boring writing. Referring to a person as having "gone to his rest" when you mean he's dead or writing that a woman is "expecting" when you mean she's pregnant seems unnecessarily timid. Worse, some euphemisms are too imprecise to be useful: "making love," for example, can mean anything from engaging in flirtatious conversation to having sexual intercourse. If you require a direct term to make your point, do not hesitate to use it.

Doublespeak

Related to euphemisms, but often more sinister, is **doublespeak**, language intended to mislead people or conceal information. In his novel *1984*, published in 1949, George Orwell (1903–1950) portrayed a world in which totalitarian governments try to alter people's perception of reality by altering their language, constantly repeating slogans such as "WAR IS PEACE" and "FREEDOM IS SLAVERY." Orwell modeled the terrifying details of *1984* on the propaganda techniques developed by real governments during the twentieth century. Since Orwell's novel was published, the use of language to conceal unpleasant realities has spread from government officials to corporate policy makers, public relations experts, and advertisers. Therefore, detecting intentionally misleading language is becoming increasingly important. The following examples are adapted from William Lutz's book *Doublespeak*, published in 1989:

During the Vietnam War, Pentagon officials were keenly aware of the need to keep public opinion on their side. They waged frequent battles with journalists over language, as when Colonel David Opfer, Air Attaché in Cambodia, lost his temper with a group of reporters over their accounts of U.S. air attacks: "You always write it's bombing, bombing, bombing. It's *not* bombing! It's air support!" In the same spirit, the military preferred to use "friendly casualties" caused by "accidental delivery of ordnance equipment" to refer to American soldiers mistakenly killed by U.S. bombs or shells.

When the Sun Oil Company fired 500 people from its corporate headquarters staff some years ago, its spokesperson remarked, "We don't characterize it as a layoff. We're managing our staff resources. Sometimes you manage them up, and sometimes you manage them down." Corporations have also referred to firings as "workforce adjustments," "headcount reduction," and "negative employee retention."

In 1985 the Texas state legislature passed a law prohibiting a student who received an F in any subject from playing high school sports. Coaches who lost some of their best players due to the new law protested vigorously. Ed Joseph, president of the Texas High School Coaches' Association, defended the rights of such students to participate: "They're not failing," he pointed out. "They're deficient at a grading period."

After you become alert to doublespeak, you'll find that it is all too common in many walks of life. An effective defense against it in argument is to rephrase your opponent's doublespeak in simple, straightforward language. Suppose, for example, someone claims that your town is "in a period of negative economic growth." If you respond, "You mean that local businesses are losing money, right?" your opponent may squirm, but she will probably admit that you have paraphrased her comment accurately enough.

EXERCISE 4

Directions: The numbered phrases below illustrate emotional and offensive language, doublespeak, and euphemisms. Match each item to the more desirable wording that should replace it by writing the correct letter in the space at the left. Some of the lettered items will not be used.

A. businessperson	H. mail carrier
B. dentist	I. member of the clergy
C. died	J. murder
D. getting fired	K. my opponents
E. humanity	L. seat belt
F. is pregnant	M. superstition
G. jail	

Example: __H__ mailman

_____ 1. my witless opponents

_____ 2. clergyman

_____ 3. long-term structured environment

_____ 4. passed on to his reward

_____ 5. unlawful deprivation of life

_____ 6. expects a little bundle of joy from heaven

_____ 7. being presented with a career change opportunity

_____ 8. lady dentist

_____ 9. mankind

_____10. passive passenger restraint device

W_riters express their individual styles through the words they use and the way they combine them in sentences. Two important aspects of style are register, the varieties of language that fit particular occasions and subjects, and tone, the qualities of speech and writing that reveal writers' attitudes. Clear and concise writing requires the avoidance or definition of jargon and the elimination of redundancy. Clichés, emotional and offensive language, euphemisms, and doublespeak are inappropriate in arguments._

CHAPTER EXERCISE

I. MATCHING

Directions: Match each term on the list below with its definition by writing the correct letter in the space provided.

TERMS:

A. cliché

B. colloquialism

C. concise

D. doublespeak

E. euphemism

F. jargon

G. person

H. regionalism

I. register

J. sexist language

K. slang

L. style

M. tone

N. usage label

DEFINITIONS:

_____ 1. characteristic decisions about what words to use and how to combine them in sentences

_____ 2. the variety of language that fits a particular occasion or subject

_____ 3. word or phrase appropriate to casual speech

_____ 4. very informal colloquialism

_____ 5. term or abbreviation indicating that a word is not standard

_____ 6. term common only in a limited geographical area

_____ 7. the quality of speech or writing that reveals writers' attitudes toward their subjects, their audiences, and themselves

_____ 8. the grammatical distinction between a person speaking, a person being spoken to, and a person or people being spoken about

_____ 9. specialized vocabulary understood only by people who have studied a particular discipline

_____10. brief and clear

_____11. wording that reveals a bias against one sex

_____12. expression used so often it has lost its freshness

_____13. word or phrase that replaces wording considered unpleasant or offensive

_____14. intentionally misleading language

II. MULTIPLE CHOICE

Directions: On the line at the left write the letter of the phrase that best completes each item.

_____15. Writing in the formal register is often characterized by

A. long words, long sentences, and long paragraphs.

B. abbreviations and shortened forms of words (such as *phone*).

C. a personal, emotional tone.

_____16. Nonstandard terms are words

A. common only in certain regions.

B. not generally used by educated native writers.

C. containing several syllables.

_____17. The word *you* is

A. appropriate in the formal register only when referring directly to the reader.

B. never used in the middle register or the informal register.

C. never used in writing at all.

_____18. Redundant writing

A. effectively communicates key points.

B. contains no deadwood.

C. is unnecessarily repetitive.

_____19. In the formal and middle registers the language most likely to convince readers is

A. as emotional as possible.

B. euphemistic.

C. clear and concise.

_____20. Language intentionally used to mislead readers is

A. impossible to respond to in a written argument.

B. justified if it helps a writer prove a claim.

C. common in government and business.

10

Polishing a Persuasive Paper

"**D**amon!" snapped Tasha. "Don't you want a film festival in Millburn anymore?"

"Of course I do," Damon answered, without opening his eyes. "Please, Tash, watch it. You're blocking my sun."

"But that proposal absolutely must reach the mayor's office by Tuesday. Why aren't you upstairs working on it?"

"I am working on it," said Damon, "even as we speak. I wrote a draft of it last night. It has some problems, sure—that's why I'm letting it incubate."

"You're letting it what?"

"I'm letting my subconscious mind take over," said Damon. "When I come back to it, I'll fix the glitches and make it the most convincing proposal the City Council's ever read. I haven't ever let you down, have I? Want some lemonade?"

DRAWING ON YOUR SUBCONSCIOUS TO SOLVE WRITING PROBLEMS

Can Damon really be making progress on his proposal while he's lying in the sun? It's possible. Haven't you ever had a good idea pop into your head as you were driving or found a simple solution to a baffling writing problem only after you set a draft aside? As Damon knows, these apparently spontaneous ideas and insights result from **incubating**, taking time away from writing so that new ideas and solutions to writing problems can evolve.

Incubating usually refers to the process of hatching eggs by keeping them at a favorable temperature. Like eggs, writing needs time and the right conditions to develop. As you're resting your conscious mind, new ideas about your work are probably forming beneath the surface. Skipping the incubation step means never moving beyond your first impressions of a topic. No matter how good those initial thoughts may be, your later ideas, seen from a fresh perspective, are almost always better.

Merely procrastinating will not provide the benefits of incubation. However, because Damon has already done some concentrated work on his proposal, relaxing in the sun should yield some new insights. Most people find that the more work they've done on an argument already, the more beneficial incubation can be. Once they've gotten a good start, even an hour or two off can yield additional perceptions.

How does incubation work? According to one theory, a new combination of ideas—a new synthesis—somehow takes shape in the back of your mind while you're not consciously thinking about writing at all. An alternative explanation is that time away from writing gives you a chance to forget ways of conceptualizing material that aren't working. This may be what happens when you apparently stumble onto a simple solution to a problem that seems unsolvable while you're concentrating on it. Before you take a break, each time you try to rework your material, the same ineffective ways of thinking about it lead to the same dead ends. Later, after a period of incubating, you forget the old formulations and can move ahead with better ones. On the other hand, incubation may merely provide a chance to mull over ideas in an unpressured way. Whichever explanation you prefer, incubation requires two time-consuming stages: a period of preparation and a period of rest. Therefore, starting a writing project long before it's due is obviously a good idea.

Prepare yourself to benefit from incubation by answering the following questions at the end of each writing session:

What problems must I solve to improve what I've written so far?

What problems will I face in the section of my paper I'll be writing next?

When you're ready to quit for the day, it's natural to brush off difficulties with the vague idea of tackling them later. But training yourself to identify problems as they develop will make your writing easier in the long run.

Many people are so busy they don't have the luxury of wondering what to do while they're not writing. They have to go to work or do the laundry or check their children's homework. However, if you have the time, you may find that exercising, listening to music, or consciously trying to clear your mind is especially helpful for triggering new insights.

Ideas can melt away as quickly as snowflakes, so if inspiration strikes, jot down your thoughts. When you return to your writing, rather than move ahead with a preset plan, take the time to look over your notes and to let fresh insights reshape your material.

REEVALUATING YOUR ENTIRE ARGUMENT

Some writers think of **revising** (rewriting based on an overall analysis of an essay's effectiveness) as the stage of the writing process that follows drafting. However, most people do at least some revising as they draft, reworking earlier material at the same time that they're pondering what to put next. Arguments can be carefully revised one small section at a time, but this approach tempts writers to concentrate on trivial spelling corrections or comma changes that they could make more efficiently at the editing stage. Both revising and editing are a matter of adding, deleting, changing, and reorganizing material. However, revising involves making changes that affect an argument's content while editing concerns particulars such as sentence completeness and correct spelling.

Revising for Clarity and Power

Revising is normally the hardest part of writing, but it's also the most important: it can create outstanding prose even from unpromising odds and ends. Many professional writers continue to revise until deadlines compel them to stop. Even then, most of them acknowledge that further rewriting would have helped. If you're willing to put the same kind of effort into your own revisions, you'll be impressed by the clarity and power that result. On the other hand, repeated revision can be frustrating; after a while you may feel like crumpling your draft into a ball and tossing it into the nearest wastepaper basket. You'll be much better off resisting this impulse. A last-minute effort on a whole new topic is bound to be less convincing than a revised version of an essay on which you've already worked hard.

Approaches to revising vary. Mostly, revising involves painstakingly rephrasing and reorganizing, but there are a few revision tricks that can make the task easier. For example, highlighting your thesis and topic sentences helps you evaluate them in relationship to each other. This strategy focuses your attention on the elements of your argument your readers will probably pay most attention to and remember longest. Another approach is to cut a draft apart and tape it back together in a more effective order; this can be less confusing than covering sheets of paper with a tangled mass of circles and arrows. Still another revision tactic is outlining a draft to check for missing evidence and faulty reasoning. If you're working at a computer, you can also try printing several different versions of an argument to see whether condensing, expanding, or reorganizing it would be helpful.

The following checklist provides questions that will help you reconsider your paper as a whole.

A GUIDE TO REWRITING

The Entire Paper

1. Have I explored my topic deeply enough, or are there signs that my thinking is superficial?

2. Is my thesis clear?

3. Are the points I use to support my thesis convincing? Do I believe them?

4. Are my generalizations supported by specific details?

5. Are my facts correct?

6. Are there contradictions or inconsistencies in my paper?

7. Have I included any material that is irrelevant to my argument?

8. Have I organized my essay effectively?

9. Is the tone of my argument reasonable, appropriate, and consistent? Do I sound like myself?

10. Have I avoided faulty reasoning?

11. Have I presented my opponents' views fairly and shown what is wrong with them?

12. Do I have an interesting title?

Individual Paragraphs

1. Does my opening paragraph effectively introduce my thesis?

2. Is each paragraph unified?

3. Is the main idea of each paragraph either expressed in a topic sentence or clearly implied?

4. Should the ideas and details within any of the paragraphs be rearranged?

5. Does my concluding paragraph provide a satisfactory sense of an ending?

TRY IT OUT

Which of the questions on the list above refer to specific problems you sometimes have with your writing? Check off the five questions you think will be most helpful to you. Then choose a draft of an argument you've written (ideally one you've set aside for a while) and evaluate it in terms of the questions you chose. Jot down your answers and use them to guide your revision.

To make your rewriting more productive, consider highlighting your thesis and topic sentences to evaluate the relationships between them, outlining your argument to probe it for weaknesses, and cutting your paper apart and taping it back together to improve its organization.

After you've rewritten your argument, answer the following questions:

1. What is the most important improvement you made?

   _____

2. What type of change (deleting, adding, substituting, or rearranging) did you make most often?

   _____
   _____

3. Which question(s) on the rewriting guide did you find most helpful?

   _____
   _____
   _____

4. How do you usually revise? What improvements in the way you revise would you like to make in the future?

   _____
   _____
   _____
   _____

**Following
Ethical
Standards**

People engaged in argument have two objectives. The first is to win—that is, to show that their claims are more convincing than their opponents' claims. The second is to pursue truth, wherever it leads. The second objective is the more important.

In a way, revising an argument means arguing against yourself to test the truthfulness of your claims. Seeing what you've written through an opponent's eyes means searching carefully for weaknesses, improving your reasoning, and finding better evidence. If you can't support your claim with convincing evidence, the ethics of argument require you to modify it, even if that means conceding some points to the other side. (Ethics are standards of conduct that apply in a particular kind of activity.) According to the ethics of argument, winning through dishonesty is worse than losing because the real victim of an unsound argument is truth itself.

As you revise an argument, hold yourself to high standards by insisting that the evidence you use is relevant. For example, suppose you claim in a letter to a newspaper that the Pinnacle Company pollutes your town's water supply. It would be relevant to show that Pinnacle discharges untreated industrial waste into the stream from which your town gets its drinking water. Pointing out that Pinnacle's trucks cause frequent traffic jams on local roads may help rouse feelings against the company. However, it is irrelevant to your claim about the water supply and therefore should not be included in your letter.

Ethical argument also requires that support for a claim be typical of all the evidence that might be used. For example, suppose a political opponent claims that a member of Congress is antifamily because she voted against proposed child-care legislation. If her record during six previous years in Congress shows that she strongly supports family values, this single vote is unrepresentative of her record as a whole. Perhaps she thought the legislation she voted against was too costly, or she was planning to vote in favor of a better bill later in the session.

While your job as an arguer is to provide evidence favoring your case, to present material you know is misleading or omit facts and ideas you know would destroy your argument is unethical. Even exaggerating (knowingly making evidence seem stronger than it really is) should be avoided.

If you've quoted an expert to support your claim, carefully examine both the language you've reproduced and the way you've introduced it. Quoted words must represent a person's views fairly. Quoting out of context is sometimes tempting, but it violates ethical standards. A poster advertising a movie, for example, might quote a reviewer as follows:

"Colossal!"—Marvin Radwinski, *New York Globe*

If the reviewer actually wrote "This movie is a colossal waste of time," he's been misquoted, even though the word used on the poster does appear in his review.

Scholars in all fields have entered into an unspoken agreement to advance knowledge. This means building on other people's work but also distinguishing carefully between their own ideas and the contributions of others. Presenting another person's words or ideas as one's own is known as **plagiarism**. The term comes from the Latin word *plagium*, which means "kidnapping." Deliberate plagiarism is highly unethical and can lead to penalties ranging from loss of respect to loss of credit for a course and loss of a job. How to avoid unintentional plagiarism is discussed in chapter 12.

EDITING FOR CORRECTNESS AND PRECISION

Good editing requires thoughtful inspection of every sentence and even every word to make writing clear and correct. Grouping related ideas together improves sentences in which subjects are too far from their verbs and modifiers are awkwardly separated from the words they describe. Editing also entails cutting needless words, varying sentences to avoid monotony, and substituting vivid, specific nouns and verbs for tired, vague wording. This kind of line-by-line editing usually results in pages containing so many cross-outs and corrections that mistakes can no longer be located easily. When this happens, retyping a paper or running off a fresh computer printout makes it possible to continue editing effectively.

To become a better editor, attack one kind of error at a time, referring for explanations to a college English handbook or a manual such as William Strunk and E. B. White's *The Elements of Style*. If you are taking a class, analyze papers returned by your instructor to avoid making the same types of mistakes more than once.

Run-on Sentences and Fragments

One of your tasks as an editor is to check for wrongly combined or incomplete sentences. In the example below, two separate sentences (independent clauses), each with its own subject and verb, are incorrectly linked, creating a **run-on sentence**:

> *Unedited version*: The period between 1781 and 1930 is considered the golden age of astronomy during this time the substructure of modern astrophysics was laid.

One way to correct a run-on sentence is to use a semicolon:

> *Edited version*: The period between 1781 and 1930 is considered the golden age of astronomy; during this time the substructure of modern astrophysics was laid.

A run-on sentence can also be corrected by adding a period and a capital letter or a conjunction such as *and* or *because*. However, a comma alone can never correct a run-on sentence; using a comma instead of a semicolon in the example above would still leave the error uncorrected.

Also be alert for **sentence fragments** (incomplete sentences):

> *Unedited version*: Nurses serving during the Vietnam War who suffered from post-traumatic stress disorder.

One way to correct a fragment is to add the missing words:

> *Edited version*: Nurses serving during the Vietnam War *were among those* who suffered from post-traumatic stress disorder.

You can also correct a sentence fragment by combining it with another sentence.

Shifts in Person and Tense

Inexplicable shifts from one person or tense to another confuse and annoy readers. The following sentence is jarring because it contains an unnecessary switch from the third person (*parents*) to the second person (*your*):

> *Unedited version*: Parents of toddlers must install window guards properly, or your children risk falling from an upper-story window.

Changing the pronoun from the second person (*your*) to the third person (*their*) eliminates the awkward shift:

> *Edited version*: Parents of toddlers must install window guards properly, or *their* children risk falling from an upper-story window.

Verb tenses should also be consistent. (**Tenses** are verb forms that indicate when actions take place.) Once you've started writing in the past tense, for example, you should continue to do so unless you have a clear reason for shifting to the present or the future tense. In the following sentence *were* is in the past tense and *starts* is in the present tense:

> *Unedited version*: Women were better off economically before the feminist movement starts in the 1960s.

Because the entire sentence refers to the past, both verbs belong in the past tense:

> *Edited version*: Women were better off economically before the feminist movement *started* in the 1960s.

Subject-Verb Agreement

Agreement is correspondence in person, number, and gender. A subject and verb agree when they are both singular or both plural. Choosing the correct form of a verb is relatively easy when it immediately follows its subject but is more difficult when they are separated:

> *Unedited version*: A monthly bus pass entitling riders to unlimited trips attract new passengers.

In the edited version the verb form *attract* has been changed to agree with the singular subject of the sentence:

Edited version: A monthly bus pass entitling riders to unlimited trips *attracts* new passengers.

Pronoun-Antecedent Agreement

Like subjects and verbs, pronouns and their **antecedents** (the words to which pronouns refer) must agree. In the sentence below, the singular pronoun *it* does not agree with its plural antecedent (*developments*):

Unedited version: Recent technological developments have not had as much influence on education as it should have.

In the edited version the plural pronoun *they* correctly refers to *developments*:

Edited version: Recent technological developments have not had as much influence on education as *they* should have.

Spelling

Even people who are not especially alert to more subtle distinctions may be quick to notice spelling mistakes. Spelling errors give readers the impression that a writer is careless; if the spelling is poor, readers may feel that other details (such as the facts used to support the thesis) are also untrustworthy.

To improve your spelling, make a habit of using the dictionary, and learn standard spelling rules, such as the one governing *ie* and *ei* ("*I* before *e* except after *c* or when sounded like *a* as in *neighbor* and *weigh*"). Be especially alert to easily confused words such as *then/than* and *there/their/they're*. Keep a list of your own spelling demons to help you diagnose habitual errors and avoid them in the future. Learn to use a computerized spelling checker, but don't rely on it too much. It won't identify incorrectly used words (such as *one* for *on* or *to* for *too*). Use your computer's search function to find words you often confuse.

Answering the following questions at the editing stage will help you make your writing more effective.

A GUIDE TO EDITING

Sentences

1. Do I move smoothly from one idea to the next?

2. Are my sentences sufficiently varied to avoid monotony?

3. Have I kept related words together within sentences?

4. Have I avoided run-on sentences and sentence fragments?

5. Have I avoided awkward shifts from one person or tense to another?

Words

1. Does my wording seem natural?

2. Would my intended audience understand the vocabulary I've used?

3. Do I repeat key words enough to make my main ideas clear?

4. Have I avoided awkward or unnecessary repetition?

5. Is my word choice accurate and specific?

6. Do my subjects and verbs agree?

7. Have I used pronouns correctly?

8. Is my spelling free of errors?

EXERCISE 1

Directions: Edit the sentences below to eliminate run-ons and fragments, verb and pronoun errors, and spelling mistakes. Some answers may vary. Suggested answers are given at the back of this book.

Example: The framers of the Constitution anticipated some of the results of allowing slavery in the new nation but fail$_\wedge^{ed}$ to predict its most significant consequences.

1. Commercial radio broadcasting benefits advertisers and station owners more then it serves the public.

2. The efforts to discredit myths about the origins of AIDS.

3. Too often, cases of suspected scientific fraud is not dealt with promptly and openly.

4. Persistent understaffing of urban police forces increases the chance of police brutality, a tradition of using overly aggressive tactics is also a factor.

5. All bicyclists ought to wear helmets, and you also need headlights, reflectors, and a rearview mirror.

6. Computer simulations should be used to test the impact of zoning laws before their enacted.

7. Teenagers with part-time jobs gain maturity from taking on new responsibilities, and he also benefits from working alongside adults.

8. The poets and promoters who publicized the Beat Generation too often destroy themselves in the process.

9. The need to simplify fare structures of U.S. airlines.

10. Ranking schools in terms of reading test scores fail to take into account the many factors that indicate a school's success.

COLLABORATING WITH OTHERS

Some people dislike showing other people their writing. If their work is praised, they think their readers are only being kind. If it's attacked, they feel hurt. Either way, they learn nothing that helps them improve their current project or do better on the next one.

Benefiting from Peer Criticism

If you are among the writers who are reluctant to share your work with others, perhaps you haven't yet found good peer critics. **Peer critics**—people who read or listen to what you have written and (usually) respond to it—can suggest fresh ideas that improve your work dramatically. They can contribute additional support for your thesis, provide leads to evidence you didn't know existed, and point up weaknesses in your reasoning that you overlooked. Working with peer critics in college is also good preparation for the business world, where a great many writing tasks require close collaboration among colleagues.

You can ask peer critics for a particular kind of response. On some occasions you may just want to share your paper with others; by reading your work aloud to a small group, you may see it in a new light. Most of the time, however, you will want your peer critics to read your essay and respond in some way. You might ask them to restate your key points; if they can do so, you've probably expressed your main ideas clearly. On the other hand, if they misunderstand your argument, try to follow the most important rule of working with others to improve your writing: learn from your readers—don't quarrel with them. Instead of pointing out how your partners could have read more carefully, ask yourself how you can revise to make your points in a fuller or more forceful way.

Peer critics can also respond to your work by role playing. They might begin by pretending to agree with everything you wrote, repeating and expanding on your most convincing points. As members of your group suggest additional lines of reasoning and further ways to support your thesis, jot them down. Then your critics can pretend to disagree with your entire paper. By listening carefully, you'll almost surely discover opposing views you should mention and refute.

A more direct way of receiving feedback is asking peer critics to evaluate your work in both general and specific terms. What seem to be the most important points in your essay? Which parts don't completely make sense? What needs to be explained more fully? These and similar questions can furnish you with valuable information, provided you listen to the answers rather than leap to your own defense. Afterwards you can reject any or all of your peer critics' comments, but at this stage your goal is to find out what a few readers think about your essay.

Toward the end of a peer-criticism session, you can ask your peers to read your paper again to look for errors. You can accept or reject any suggestion for a specific change; the most tactful way of going about this is to circle each questionable item and move on. For example, if one of your critics expresses doubt about the way a word is spelled, it's a good idea to check it later rather than argue about it.

Peer criticism can have many advantages, but it has some drawbacks, too. Because it's natural to resist making changes, the process can lead to conflicts and hurt feelings, despite the best intentions of all participants. On the other hand, some writers are too open to advice—they make whatever changes others suggest, whether they understand them or not. Maintaining a balance between resisting suggestions and succumbing to them too quickly is part of the challenge of working with peer critics.

Becoming a Peer Critic

When you are acting as a peer critic for someone else, remembering some simple rules will make the process more productive and less threatening:

1. Evaluate the writing, not the writer. Remarks that begin "You can't be serious . . ." or "You always take such a pessimistic view . . ." would make anyone defensive.

2. Offer only the kind of response the writer has requested. If you are asked to evaluate an argument as a whole, wait until later to raise relatively minor issues such as how to spell a particular word or whether a date is correct.

3. Be as specific as you can about what you like and dislike. The vaguest remarks are usually the least helpful. "I was bored at first, but it got better later" is less useful than "Your opening paragraph isn't as dynamic as the rest of your paper. Do you think you can move the story about the bear into your introduction?"

4. Find something to praise. Even in the worst writing, there is usually a well-phrased sentence, an intelligent insight, or a convincing piece of evidence you can mention.

EXERCISE 2

Directions: The remarks below were all made by peer critics. Indicate your evaluations of them by writing the appropriate letters on the lines at the left. Use the following code:

H = helpful to the writer

NH = not helpful (or not as helpful as it could have been)

Example: __H__ Isn't your second reason the most important of all? Maybe you should put it first—or even last, if you want to build to a climax.

_____ 1. This is really good. I can't exactly put into words what I like about it, but I think you're an excellent writer.

_____ 2. I think this essay starts a little slowly. The part about the riots is where I began to get interested. What about moving that up into your introduction?

_____ 3. Before I tell you what I think about the whole essay, just let me show you a really careless spelling error you made. You'll want to slit your throat when you see it.

_____ 4. I enjoyed the way you compared managing a shipping department to coaching a football team, but don't you think there are some important differences that you should discuss?

_____ 5. I've read this same stupid argument a thousand times. Can't you think of anything original to say about capital punishment?

_____ 6. I'm sorry, but I don't understand the third reason you give about why foreign aid is against our country's best interests. Maybe if I read it again . . .

_____ 7. Your essay is fine, as far as it goes, but I've got to admit that the whole topic turns me off.

_____ 8. Now that we've discussed the essay as a whole, I think I spotted a few agreement errors when I read it the first time. Do you want me to read through it again to see if I can find them?

_____ 9. You say here that art museums should be government supported, but you don't mention that people who never look at art might resent seeing their tax dollars spent that way.

_____10. I read an article in *Newsweek* a few weeks ago on this topic. If you can trace it down in the library, I think you'll find it's worth looking at.

CHOOSING AN EFFECTIVE TITLE

Suppose you're sitting in your dentist's waiting room, trying to take your mind off the pain in your tooth. You open a magazine to an article entitled "Some Thoughts on a Current Issue." Desperate as you are for reading material, the chances are excellent that you'll now turn the page without a second glance. While the article itself might be fascinating, its title is neither interesting nor informative. After all, the "current issue" could be almost anything, from searching public school students for weapons to finding safe ways to dispose of used batteries.

Think of your title—the first thing people notice about your paper—as an advertisement. Although an effective ad can't sell a product all by itself, it can at least coax people into a receptive mood. A poor ad, however, can cause prospective buyers to ignore an otherwise excellent product. Similarly, a poor title can turn readers away literally before they begin, while a good one can get them hooked so they can't resist exploring further. Successful titles are interesting or informative or both. For example, the title "A Life and Death Puzzle" might at least pique readers' interest, and "Deadly Birth Defects in Brownsville, Texas" alerts them to an argument's general topic.

Using a Working Title

You need not make a final choice of a title until your paper is almost finished. However, you'll probably want to choose a **working title**, a preliminary designation that establishes the boundaries of the subject you plan to cover, as soon as possible. While you draft, referring to a descriptive working title ("America Needs a Balanced-Budget Amendment," for example) should keep you from digressing. When you've finished your paper, you can reconsider the working title. You may want to keep it. But perhaps as you worked, you changed your emphasis a bit. Or now that the whole paper is written, you may be able to devise a title that is more catchy than your original one.

Be careful not to be too clever or enigmatic, however, since a trick title can confuse or annoy readers. Using a play on words may be a good way to capture attention (as in the essay title "Sympathy for the Devil's Foes," based on the rock song title "Sympathy for the Devil"); however, a feeble joke or obscure reference can provoke the suspicion that the essay itself is burdened by adolescent humor or cryptic allusions. Instead, try to match the tone of your title to that of your paper. A straightforward descriptive title, such as "Anti-Americanism in Brazil" or "The Survival of Ethical Banking in an Age of Default," usually works best. But descriptive titles don't have to be predictable or dull; for example, the title of journalist William L. Shirer's book *The Rise and Fall of the Third Reich* (1960) is both descriptive and dynamic.

Understanding Title Format

Always capitalize the first and last words of a title and all nouns, verbs, adjectives, adverbs, pronouns, and subordinating conjunctions. Except when they begin or end a title, do not capitalize articles (*a, an, the*), coordinating conjunctions (*and, but, or, nor, for, so, yet*), prepositions (*at, by, in, into, over, on, to,* and so on), and *to* when it combines with a verb to form an infinitive (such as "to study"). The following titles provide examples of correct capitalization:

How to Live Longer

Clearing the Air on Fossil Fuel Emissions

The Mood Turns Darker in Israel

On Delusions of World Order

Titles are not followed by periods even when they're complete sentences:

Immigrants Do Not Deprive Poor Americans of Jobs

However, titles that are questions are followed by question marks:

Are Consumers Ready for the Foods of the Future?

Many academic titles have **subtitles** (secondary, explanatory titles) that limit or expand upon the titles themselves. In academic writing, a subtitle follows a colon (:), not a semicolon or dash. The first word in a subtitle is always capitalized:

Rural Crime: A Conspiracy of Silence

Beware of making a title too long. "The Measure of Misery: A Ranking of Five Countries Across the Globe in Terms of Life Expectancy, Access to Pure Food and Water, Education, and Civil Rights" contains more information than most people can absorb in a first reading. Here, eliminating the subtitle, even at the slight risk of leaving the title obscure, would be better. A good title hints at an argument's claim but does not state its entire thesis. To understand a thesis, readers usually need the introduction that the opening paragraph provides.

When you're writing an analysis of a movie, book, article, or similar work, don't use the work's title as your own. You can, however, orient readers to your topic by using it as part of your title:

Innocents at Home: Penelope Fitzgerald's *The Gate of Angels*

When you include the titles of other works within your own title or essay, underline or italicize names of entire publications such as books, magazines, and newspapers. Use quotation marks to set off the titles of works included within larger publications: chapters, essays, and short stories, for example. Do not underline or put quotation marks around your own title.

FOLLOWING MANUSCRIPT CONVENTIONS

When a business executive looks through a pile of proposals or a professor sorts through a briefcase crammed with essays, some of them stand out—the proposal printed illegibly on orange paper, for example, or the single-spaced essay without a title. If the professor must search for students' names in ten different places as he records the grades, he'll understandably feel a bit annoyed. And the executive who must try to decipher one barely readable page after another knows she's wasting time and money. Not surprisingly, the rest of the manuscripts they must deal with, the ones that follow the conventions, are a welcome relief. Such manuscripts suggest at a glance that their authors know what they're doing and respect their readers.

The following instructions assume that you are using a word processor or typewriter to prepare a paper for a college course. Other situations may require certain adjustments. If you submit an essay to a magazine, adapt the suggestions below to the magazine's requirements for manuscripts (available from the editor). If you write a memo or a report for an employer, follow the style guidelines of your office or company. In all situations, giving your readers exactly the format they expect will increase your chances of success.

PREPARING YOUR MANUSCRIPT

1. Print or type your work on $8\frac{1}{2} \times 11$-inch white paper. Avoid erasable paper, which tends to smudge.

2. Use only one side of each page.

3. Double space everything.

4. Leave one-inch margins at the top, the bottom, and each side. If you are word processing, justify the left margin but not the right. (To **justify** text is to space it so that the ends of the lines are even.)

5. Indent five spaces at the beginning of each paragraph. Do not skip lines between paragraphs.

6. Type your name, your instructor's name, your course name and section number, and the date you submit the paper in the top left corner of the first page.

7. Your title should appear next, typed in uppercase and lowercase letters and centered.

8. Number each page, including page one, in the upper right corner, half an inch from the top. Type just the number (not "p. 1"). The top of a typical first page is illustrated on the following page:

1

Michael Wilson

Professor Elizabeth Austin

English Composition II, section 7

March 12, 1993

The Politics of Poverty

9. From page two on, type your last name before each page number: Wilson 2.

10. If you've printed your paper on continuous sheets, remove the perforated edges and separate the pages.

11. Keep your pages together with a paper clip or in a file folder; do not staple them.

12. Make a duplicate print copy or photocopy of any paper you submit.

The suggestions above apply to papers following the Modern Language Association (MLA) style. If your paper is for a class in the social sciences, you may be asked to follow American Psychological Association (APA) style. When following APA style, make your margins an inch and a half wide on all sides and use a short version of your paper title rather than your last name with each page number. APA style also forbids hyphenating words at the ends of lines.

PREPARING A FLAWLESS FINAL COPY

Some writers expend a great deal of energy devising a strong argument, organizing it, finding good specific examples to support their main points, and making sure their writing is clear and concise. Then in their haste to finish, they submit a final copy marred by careless errors. You can avoid making their mistake if you think back to the last time you read a piece of sloppy writing. After being distracted by one or two errors such as a misspelled name or missing punctuation mark, you were probably more intent on finding the next blunder than following the writer's argument. Despite the good ideas the author may have expressed, you most likely concluded that someone so negligent was not completely credible.

Writers who want their work to be taken seriously learn to proofread with care. They aim to submit letter-perfect papers, free of mistakes and inconsistencies. While proofreading, they make no distinction between typing mistakes and other kinds of errors. If other people have word processed or typed their papers for them, they proofread even harder, knowing that any errors in work they submit become their own. They have learned that making legible, last-minute corrections by hand is better than turning in a neatly typed paper containing mistakes.

Following the hints in the list below should make you a better proofreader.

PROOFREADING TIPS

1. Leave time to proofread more than once. If possible, set your paper aside for a while so you can look at it from a fresh viewpoint; otherwise, you'll miss errors because your mind will fill in what you intended to write.

2. Slow down. Ordinary reading is much quicker than proofreading.

3. To focus your attention, try touching each syllable with a pen or pencil tip. Use a blank sheet of paper to cover the lines below the one you're proofreading.

4. Read your paper aloud to listen for omitted words and misplaced punctuation.

5. Read backwards (the last sentence first, then the second to the last, and so on) to catch sentence fragments.

6. Be alert for patterns of errors that have given you trouble in the past.

7. Ask someone to help you find errors (if your instructor allows it). For complex material, have your partner read one copy aloud while you check a second copy for mistakes. Remember that you, not the person kind enough to help you, are responsible for any errors that remain.

8. Make corrections as unobtrusive as possible by using correction tape or fluid; if you're using a computer, reprint individual pages.

9. Proofread all your corrections to make sure you haven't added any mistakes.

Use the proofreading symbols illustrated on the following page to make corrections when necessary.

PROOFREADING SYMBOLS

Symbol	Use	Example
or	deleting unwanted material	err*o*r *or* an extra ~~extra~~ word
∧	inserting additional material	missing a∧word
or	transposing material	*or*∩*re* misplaced word a
⌒	closing a space	an ex⌒tra space
|	adding a space	|missing space
(stet)	restoring material deleted by mistake	(stet) ~~necessary~~ word
≡	turning a small letter into a capital	c̲apital letter needed
/	turning a capital letter into a small one	A /small letter needed
⊙	adding an omitted period	This sentence needs a period⊙
¶	starting a new paragraph	This sentence ends one paragraph.¶This sentence starts a new one.

EXERCISE 3

Directions: Find and correct thirteen errors in the paragraph below. Use the proofreading symbols given in the chart above to make your corrections. A correction has been made in line four as an example.

1   The Business Of Nature

2   Nature programs on tele vision have become increasingly

3   candid in recent years, a trend that reflects the battle for survival

4   amoung competing network and cable channels. Until recently,

5   sex and violence were considered largely unsuitable for TV nature

6   shows; now footage off moose during the mating season or killer

7   whales devouring seal pups has become almost commonplace.

8   Some critics praise this material as reflecting the lives of animals

9   more accuratly than past nature shows did. However, a stronger

10   motive then accuracy scientific seems to be at work, Attracting

11   viewers accustomed to sex and violence in other kind of program-

12   ing requires moregraphic material in nature shows as well. Dennis

13   Kane, executive producer fo *ABC World of Discovery*, has said

14   bluntly, We're looking to make films as dramatic as possible

15   without going over the top. You've got to make sure that your

16   audiences are entertained." Commercial objectives may lead to

17   greater authenticity in portraying the natural world, but they are

18   also turning nature programing into yet another source of the the

19   disturbing images already far to numerous on television.

Incubating is taking time away from writing so that new ideas and solutions to writing problems can evolve. Revising focuses attention on problems with inadequate support for main points, disorganization, and ineffective paragraphing. Revision also requires an honest appraisal of an argument to ensure that evidence is relevant and representative, quotations are not taken out of context, and plagiarism is avoided. Editing involves inspecting every sentence for clear, correct, and interesting wording. Run-on sentences, sentence fragments, shifts in person and tense, subject-verb and pronoun-antecedent agreement errors, and spelling mistakes should also be corrected. Collaborating with peer critics to revise and edit an argument requires tact and cooperation. A working title, which guides the initial stages of the writing process, can be replaced by a more catchy or informative title after an argument is completed. Manuscripts should be typed or word processed, double-spaced, on one side of a sheet of 8½ x 11-inch white paper. Proofreading an argument slowly, conscientiously, and repeatedly is essential to eliminate errors from a final copy.

CHAPTER EXERCISE

I. MATCHING

Directions: Match each term on the list below with its definition by writing the correct letter in the space provided.

TERMS:

A.	agreement	H.	revising
B.	antecedent	I.	run-on sentence
C.	ethics	J.	sentence fragment
D.	incubating	K.	subtitle
E.	justify	L.	tense
F.	peer critic	M.	working title
G.	plagiarism		

DEFINITIONS:

_____ 1. taking time away from writing so that new ideas and solutions to writing problems can evolve

_____ 2. rewriting based on an overall analysis of an essay's effectiveness

_____ 3. standards of conduct that apply in a particular kind of activity

_____ 4. presenting another person's words or ideas as one's own

_____ 5. two independent clauses wrongly punctuated as a single sentence

_____ 6. incomplete sentence

_____ 7. verb form indicating when an action takes place

_____ 8. correspondence in person, number, and gender

_____ 9. word to which a pronoun refers

_____10. person who reads or listens to writing and offers suggestions for improvement

_____11. preliminary designation that establishes the boundaries of a topic for writing

_____12. a secondary explanatory title that expands or limits a title

_____13. line up text so that it is even along a margin

II. MULTIPLE CHOICE

Directions: On the line at the left write the letter of the phrase that best completes each item.

_____14. Incubation is most effective when a writer

    A. starts working on an entirely new subject immediately after taking time off from writing.

    B. is facing a deadline requiring the work to be finished quickly.

    C. has gotten a good start on a subject before taking a break.

_____15. Revision should be mainly concerned with

    A. overall considerations such as organization, paragraphing, and support for main ideas.

    B. specific corrections such as spelling errors, shifts in tense and person, run-on sentences, and sentence fragments.

    C. changes that make an argument conform to accepted standards for manuscript form, such as printing or typing on one side of a page.

_____16. A plural antecedent in the third person should be referred to by

    A. a plural pronoun in the third person.

    B. two singular pronouns in the second person.

C. either a singular pronoun or a plural pronoun, so long as it is in the third person.

_____17. Peer critics are most effective when they

A. make their comments as broad and far-reaching as possible.

B. provide only the types of responses a writer requests.

C. concentrate on catching and correcting every error in an argument.

_____18. An argument's title should

A. puzzle readers in order to attract their interest.

B. state the argument's thesis as fully as possible.

C. be informative or interesting.

_____19. Proofreading is most effective when

A. done more than once.

B. done as rapidly as possible.

C. done entirely by a computer.

_____20. The proofreading symbol stet means

A. insert additional material here.

B. restore material deleted by mistake.

C. start a new paragraph here.

11

Doing Research

"Hey, Cal, buddy, what are you *doing* here?" said Randall, recognizing the intercollegiate wrestling champion by his huge back and enormous neck.

"Hi, Randall," said Cal, turning around. "I'm doing research, that's what."

"At the orchestra?"

"I'm writing a paper on how the budget cuts will affect the quality of life in this city," Cal replied. "I've been interviewing concertgoers, asking how they would feel if the orchestra closed. And you know, I never realized before how much this highbrow music means to ordinary working people. By the way, how would you feel?"

"Me?" said Randall. "Devastated. But then, unlike you I don't have rock and roll to fall back on."

"Nothing wrong with rock and roll," said Cal. "But you know, this guy Mozart isn't too bad either."

As Cal knows, research, while often conducted in libraries, can involve firsthand observation. When you write a research paper, you'll undertake an extensive search for answers to questions that interest you. In the process you'll become an expert on your chosen topic and gain the confidence and skill you need to master a complex subject on your own.

BEGINNING A RESEARCH PAPER

A research paper is a long formal essay supporting a thesis and based on a variety of sources. To cope with the complex process of doing research and reporting on it, you'll find it worthwhile to keep a research log, choose a topic that interests you, and formulate a preliminary thesis.

Keeping a Research Log

A **research log** is a notebook containing a cumulative record of work done on a research project. Merely jotting down how much time you spend on a project each day can motivate you to work steadily. Your research log also contains an account of your thinking about the paper as it evolves. Finding a feasible topic for a research paper always takes time; a record of the false starts and blind alleys as well as the breakthroughs can help you sort out this jumble of competing interpretations and flashes of insight. With a research log you'll save time because you won't need to retrace lines of reasoning or make the same decisions more than once.

You shouldn't use a research log for notes on your sources; putting those on index cards will give you much greater flexibility. In your log, record ideas about your paper. Begin by stating the precise requirements of your research assignment and blocking out a preliminary schedule for your work. Then keep a faithful record of the steps you follow. If you don't toss out your research log when the project is finished, looking back at it will enable you to work on your next research paper more systematically.

Choosing Your Topic

A subject that will continue to interest you during the weeks you'll devote to your paper may not be easy to find. To give yourself a range of choices, try completing the following sentences:

Some issues I've recently learned about by reading, watching movies or TV, and listening to the radio are . . .

Some issues I've studied in the past that continue to intrigue me are . . .

Some issues related to my hobbies and interests are . . .

If I could solve the problems of the world (or of this country), the situations I would want to deal with are . . .

Now select several topics from the list you've compiled and use your favorite prewriting techniques (freewriting, brainstorming, and so on) to gather your thoughts on the topics you've chosen. The topic you find easiest or most interesting to prewrite about will probably be the one you want to investigate further.

One way to focus your attention on a manageable aspect of a promising general topic is to devise a research question that you hope your paper will answer. For example, if you're concerned about the possibility of dangerous toxic wastes at federal defense installations, your initial research question might be "How serious is the problem of toxic wastes at defense installations?" Trying to answer this question would get you started reading about leaking underground storage tanks and inactive uranium tailings at federally owned sites. Based on this preliminary research, you could eventually formulate a **hypothesis** (a tentative assumption to be tested by collecting evidence) concerning the hidden costs of stopgap solutions to the military's toxic waste problems. Gradually, as you took notes and drew your own conclusions, you would transform the hypothesis into a thesis sentence expressing the views you developed.

Some research questions lead to dead ends because not enough material on them is available in the library or because they offer too little scope for argument. However, you might be able to incorporate these questions as part of a larger topic. On the other hand, you can focus a topic that seems too broad by continuing to read and think about it until you find a single aspect of the subject that especially appeals to you.

EXERCISE 1

Directions: For each topic below, write a question that could guide preliminary research for a ten-page argumentative research paper.

Example: a voucher system to give parents a choice of public schools for their children

research question: Would using a voucher system giving parents a choice of public schools for their children improve public education?

1. the safety of urban mass transit systems
research question:_____

_____

2. the effects of estrogen on postmenopausal women
research question:_____

_____

3. testing health care workers for AIDS
research question:_____

_____

4. nomination of U.S. Supreme Court justices

research question:_____

_____

_____

5. racial bias in the granting of home mortgages

research question:_____

_____

_____

6. seizing the property of suspected drug dealers

research question:_____

_____

_____

7. plastic pollution in oceans

research question:_____

_____

_____

8. sudden infant death syndrome

research question:_____

_____

_____

9. revitalizing city parks

research question:_____

_____

_____

10. term limits for elected officials

research question:_____

_____

_____

Writing a Preliminary Thesis Sentence

Your ideas are the most important part of your research paper, so you should work hardest on forming and expressing the best thoughts you can on the topic you choose. The most interesting and worthwhile papers reflect serious efforts to wrestle with important concepts.

Constructing the best possible argument becomes easier as you go through the process of devising a research question, answering it with a hypothesis, and, finally, turning the hypothesis into a preliminary thesis sentence that states the claim you expect your research paper to support. As you continue to learn about your topic and take sides in the controversies surrounding it, the wording of your preliminary thesis will probably change. Remember the following guidelines for thesis statements as you develop a preliminary thesis:

1. Express your thesis in a single declarative sentence, not a question. (Your research question is not a preliminary thesis.)

2. Focus your thesis. If an entire book could be written to support it, it is too broad for a research paper.

3. Write a thesis that states your opinion. Avoid one that is too factual.

4. Choose a thesis you can support with library research. (If little or no evidence can be found to support your hypothesis, revise it.)

5. Write a counterclaim (an expression of opinion that directly contradicts a claim) to test whether your thesis is arguable.

FINDING THE INFORMATION YOU NEED

Working on your research paper will teach you a whole battery of skills, from developing a search strategy and using the library to taking notes and organizing them.

Designing a Search Strategy

Research projects can absorb many hours, not all of them productive. To avoid aimless browsing and haphazard note taking, use a **search strategy**, a systematic approach to selecting and using sources. Search strategies vary from one researcher to another, but a good first step is to gain a broad overview of your topic. If you already know that you will need to send away for some of your research materials by writing to a government or private agency, do so as soon as possible. Using the interlibrary loan system, through which your library can borrow books on your behalf from other libraries, can also take time, so the earlier you start, the better.

As you find materials, keep track of them on **source cards**, index cards on which you record the data you'll need for the works cited section of your paper. The **works cited (references) section** is the concluding part of your research paper in which you provide information about your sources. On a source card for a book, write down the author's name, the title, the city where the book was published, the publisher, and the date of publication. For a magazine article, include the author's name, the title of the article, the name of the magazine, the date, and the pages on which the article appears.

Sample Source Card for a Book

Gordon, Mary. <u>**Good Boys and Dead**</u>
<u>**Girls**</u>. New York: Viking, 1991.

Sample Source Card for a Magazine Article

Levy, David H.   "A Sky Watchman Discovers
Comets and Immortality." <u>Smithsonian</u>
June 1992: 74–83.

Carefully made source cards will simplify the task of preparing the works cited section or references list when you finish drafting your paper. Another way to make your project easier is to add call numbers to help you find materials in the library the next time you need them. You can also include brief evaluations of your sources.

The list below provides steps to consider when you plan your own search strategy.

A STEP-BY-STEP SEARCH STRATEGY

1. Begin a research log.

2. Brainstorm, freewrite, or use other prewriting techniques to gather thoughts about possible topics.

3. Devise a research question that a paper on your topic could answer.

4. See if there is enough research material in the library.

5. Get an overview of your topic by reading an article in an encyclopedia or other reference book.

6. Make a list of key words and phrases under which the topic is found in card catalogs, computer data bases, and periodical indexes. (For definitions of these terms, see the section on using the library later in this chapter.)

7. Begin to make source cards.

8. Focus your topic if library research indicates that there will be too much material to deal with in the time you have.

9. Send away for needed material.

Using Different Types of Sources

Researchers divide the material they use into two broad categories, primary sources and secondary sources. A **primary source** is a record of a person's own experiences or observations. For example, the diary of a Civil War soldier and an interview with a police officer are primary sources. A physical object such as an archeological artifact or a creative work such as a painting or a poem can also be a primary source.

A **secondary source** is the work of a researcher who has analyzed and evaluated primary sources or other secondary sources. A historian's book about the Civil War, a criminal justice textbook, and an essay on the Mona Lisa are secondary sources.

You will probably encounter both primary and secondary sources as you do research. Primary sources are often vivid but can be difficult to interpret. Secondary sources are likely to be clearer and more readily available than primary sources, but their authors may have misunderstood or misrepresented the sources on which they are based.

Another way to categorize research materials is to distinguish between books and periodicals (works published at regular intervals, such as magazines and newspapers). Because most books take at least a year to write and publish, the information even a new book contains is often a little behind the times, especially in constantly changing fields such as politics and medicine. On the other hand, periodicals often report events before they are fully understood; one month's article announcing a scientific breakthrough may be followed the next month by a second article contradicting the first.

Increasingly, valuable sources come in forms other than print, such as television shows and sound recordings. A library was once little more than a storehouse for books. However, because libraries today are constantly acquiring new kinds of nonprint media, the following broad outline of how libraries work cannot substitute for frequent exploration of your own library.

Using Libraries

Effective researchers feel comfortable in a library. Believing that the information they need is in the library somewhere, they're confident of their ability to find it. They make no effort to memorize lists of encyclopedias, bibliographies, or indexes, but they do know that reference tools they have never heard of are available to help them; when they need to, they'll add them to their repertory of research aids.

CARD CATALOGS

Somewhere on the main floor of a library, usually near the circulation desk, are the card catalogs. A typical **card catalog** is a file containing at least one index card for every book and periodical the library owns. Most books are listed under three or more widely separated cards: one under the author's name (or one under each author if more than one person wrote it), one under the title, and one or more under the appropriate subject headings.

Some libraries have separate card catalogs for authors, titles, and subjects while others combine the author and title catalogs in one file. You can find a specific book quickly if you know the author's name or the title, but in a research project's early stages, the subject catalog is often the most helpful one. To use it efficiently, however, you must know how the subject you are looking for is filed—and some subjects appear in the catalog in unexpected ways. For example, if you want books on illegal drug use among athletes, you need to look under "Doping in Sports." To find out how to look up your subject, refer to the large volumes kept near the catalogs, the *Library of Congress Subject Headings*. A few minutes spent finding the proper headings for your research project may save you a great deal of guesswork.

While some libraries will continue to list their older books in card catalogs well into the twenty-first century, most libraries catalog newer materials on computers. In order to conduct a thorough search, you will probably need to familiarize yourself with both the card catalogs and a computerized system.

When you've found a book you want in a card catalog or through a computer search, jot down its **call number**, the combination of letters and numbers that indicates its location in the library. Unfortunately, some libraries still keep books under two separate filing systems, the older Dewey decimal classification system (organized numerically) and the Library of Congress system (organized alphabetically). To avoid frustration, ask for directions or look for a wall chart listing the locations of books filed under specific call numbers.

STACKS

In most libraries you can walk to the appropriate location and find the books you need. Shelves you can look through yourself are known as **open stacks**. They enable you to browse in books on your subject that you haven't yet discovered in the card catalog. When you browse, you can skim a book's table of contents, read a few pages, and decide whether or not it pertains to your topic.

In a library with **closed stacks**, on the other hand, you're required to fill out a call slip, a piece of paper on which you list your book by author, title, and call number. You then bring the call slip to a library employee behind a desk who sends it to the stacks where someone finds your book and brings it to you. Some of the largest and best libraries in the country operate on the closed-stack system.

Reference Books

Reference books are publications containing facts or brief summaries of information. They are always available because they can't be checked out. Before you begin to locate specialized material on your topic, use your library's reference section to get an overview of the whole subject.

General encyclopedias such as the *Americana* and the *Britannica* contain articles on thousands of topics, organized alphabetically. Encyclopedias differ in the depth of their coverage and the technical level of their vocabulary, so look up your topic in several to find the one you're most comfortable with. In addition to general encyclopedias, reference collections contain many specialized encyclopedias such as the *Encyclopedia of Drug Abuse* or the *Encyclopedia of World Literature in the 20th Century*. A specialized reference work probably exists on your subject; referring to it is a good way to follow up your search in a general encyclopedia. Don't overlook the lists of suggested readings that follow many encyclopedia entries; they are often excellent starting points for further research.

A library's reference section also includes dictionaries, not only of the English language but of many foreign languages as well. Some works called dictionaries are really mini-encyclopedias; for example, *Dorland's Illustrated Medical Dictionary* contains thousands of brief articles relating to medicine. Biographical dictionaries provide information on prominent people; works such as the *Dictionary of American Biography* and *Contemporary Artists* can expand your knowledge of men and women whose names you encounter in general or specialized encyclopedias.

Other valuable tools, such as atlases, yearbooks, handbooks, and collections of quotations, are also kept in the reference section. Two publications that are particularly useful for gaining overviews of argumentative topics are the *CQ (Congressional Quarterly) Researcher* and *Taking Sides*. The *CQ Researcher*, formerly *Editorial Research Reports*, provides summaries of opposing views on current issues. *Taking Sides* is a collection of essays on both sides of approximately three hundred currently controversial topics, with useful introductions by the editors. Both works are updated frequently.

BIBLIOGRAPHIES AND INDEXES

The single biggest obstacle to finding information on any topic is that there is far too much of it. If an individual scholar had to begin by sorting though thousands of possible sources, the simplest research project would be overwhelming. Fortunately, many tools exist to simplify this task.

A **bibliography** is a list of books, articles, and other materials on a particular subject. It can range in size from a few items at the end of an encyclopedia entry to a large volume. Check the card catalog to see if your library has a full-length bibliography on your topic; the card you're looking for will be headed by the subject itself followed by the word *bibliography* (for example, WORLD WAR II, 1939–1945, BIBLIOGRAPHY).

Closely related to bibliographies are **indexes,** lists of articles that have appeared in a particular range of periodicals or in a particular field over a specific period of time. For example, the *Readers' Guide to Periodical Literature* regularly publishes listings of articles that have appeared in more than two hundred popular magazines. The *Humanities Index* does the same for articles in more specialized publications on literature, history, philosophy, and related subjects.

Increasingly, **data bases,** collections of information stored by computer and organized to make searching for and retrieving information as rapid as possible, are used for bibliographies and indexes. For example, *ERIC* (which stands for Educational Resources Information Center), an index of recent publications in education, and the *Business Periodicals Index,* a listing of materials on business and industry, are available in most college libraries on compact disks.

This account offers only the barest sketch of what is available in a typical library. Check to see if your library offers an orientation program. And bear in mind that the most reliable guide to your library's resources is the person behind the information desk—the librarian.

TRY IT OUT

How well do you know your library? Spending some time familiarizing yourself with it before you're deeply involved in a project will ease you into the research process. Use the questions below to guide your exploration.

1. How do I check out materials? _____

_____

2. For how long can materials be borrowed? _____

_____

3. Where are the card catalogs?_____

_____

4. How are books classified (by the Library of Congress system or Dewey decimal system or both)? _____

_____

5. Are the books in closed stacks or open stacks? _____

_____

6. Where is the reference section? _____

_____

7. Where is the information desk? _____

_____

8. What materials can be accessed by computer? _____

_____

9. Where are the indexes to periodicals? _____

_____

10. In what forms (such as bound volumes and microfilm) are periodicals stored? _____

_____

11. Where are the periodicals located? _____

_____

12. What nonprint materials (such as video and audio tapes) are available? _____

_____

13. Where are nonprint materials located? _____

_____

14. What procedure is used to borrow materials through the interlibrary loan system? _____

_____

15. Which part of the library seems to be the quietest place to work?

_____

Evaluating Sources

One of your first tasks as a researcher is to determine which of your potential sources suit your purposes. In only a few minutes you can get an initial impression of whether the books and articles you're considering are up to date, reliable, and usable.

Some sources are classics that are never out of date, but for many topics, such as safety in day-care centers or the impact of acid rain, you'll want to limit yourself to material published in the last few years. Also, try to find sources from a variety of publishers. Using too many works from the same publisher, especially one promoting a specific political or religious viewpoint, makes readers suspect that you're taking a one-sided approach to your topic. Be especially wary of materials that organizations give away to promote their positions on particular issues. You can use such materials in your research paper, but be sure to balance them with material from less biased sources.

If an author is a spokesperson for a group such as an association of building contractors or an organization that supports automobile insurance reform, a book's preface or the introductory note to an article may mention this fact. It may also provide other clues to an author's possible bias. Look too for evidence that the author is well qualified to write on the subject he or she has chosen.

If a source passes your quick inspection, open it partway through and read a few lines to be sure you're comfortable with its tone and approach. This keeps you from discovering after you get home that books you've taken out are worthless to you or that you've photocopied many pages you can't use. Some sources may prove too difficult to deal with in the time you have. Others, such as a popularized account of someone's experiences as a foster child, might be easy to read but unlikely to contain material you can use in a scholarly research paper.

EXERCISE 2

Directions: Evaluate the sources described below by using the following code:

    A = probably valuable

    B = possibly valuable but must be used with caution

    C = probably not valuable

Example:

Topic: the likelihood of life on other planets

Source: a book by Charlie Sleagle (no qualifications listed on the book jacket or in the preface) called *The Aliens among Us*, published by The Far Out Press in 1971

Evaluation: __C__

1. Topic: combatting imported counterfeit products

Source: an article by Mary Evers, former deputy chief inspector for the U. S. Customs Service, called "Shoddy Fakes Pose Hidden Threats to Consumers," published in the magazine *Consumer Safety* in June 1992

Evaluation: _____

2. Topic: soybean substitutes for meat

Source: an essay by J. F. Ostermeyer, Ph.D., a nutritionist at Fairmount Hospital in Philadelphia, entitled "Soybeans: Protein without Fat," appearing in the book *Studies in Health*, published by Crest University Press in 1992

Evaluation: _____

3. Topic: the cultural value of zoos

Source: the tape of a network television interview with Joseph Zabrisky, president of the World Wildlife Rights League, an organization opposed to zoos, broadcast on January 5, 1991

Evaluation: _____

4. Topic: fighting new types of organized crime

Source: a book by Roy McMann, a former U. S. district attorney, called *The Changing Face of the Mafia*, published by Burlington Theroux and Company in 1952

Evaluation: _____

5. Topic: strikes by public school teachers

Source: an editorial in the National Coalition of Educators' journal *Teachers and Teaching* for May 1989, entitled "Protecting Our Right to Strike"

Evaluation: _____

6. Topic: choosing the right college

Source: a new brochure published by the Phipps College Office of Information Services called "Why Phipps College Is Right for You"

Evaluation: _____

7. Topic: putting parental advisory warnings on record labels

Source: an interview with Manny Lindow, lead singer of the rock group The Bogs, published in the magazine *Very Heavy Metal* in July 1990

Evaluation: _____

8. Topic: long-term effects of incest

Source: an essay by Carla Sanchez, M.D., a practicing psychiatrist, entitled "Diagnosing Adult Victims of Childhood Sexual Abuse," published in *National Psychiatric Review* in May 1992

Evaluation: _____

9. Topic: flexible work schedules

Source: an article by Myron Weiss, a free-lance journalist, entitled "Flex Time: Wave of the Future," published in the *Dallas Examiner Sunday Magazine* on April 3, 1977

Evaluation: _____

10. Topic: reforming the welfare system

Source: an undated pamphlet published by the Taxpayers' Committee to Abolish Welfare entitled "How Welfare Cheats Pick Your Pocket"

Evaluation: _____

**Conducting
Interviews**

An interview with a college faculty member, a military recruitment officer, or a teenage runaway may be just what you need to ferret out valuable, up-to-date information for your research paper. Conducting a good interview requires laying careful groundwork. Wandering into a government office and asking "Can you help me with my research paper?" is unlikely to elicit useful material from an overworked bureaucrat. However, if you've carefully prepared well-thought-out questions, you may gather worthwhile information not readily available in published sources.

If you're unfamiliar with interviewing, try practicing ahead of time by asking a friend to take the role of the person you're going to interview. You can then replace questions that seem vague or that lead to dead-end yes or no answers, along with any that might alienate an interviewee by revealing a preconception or prejudice.

When you set up an interview by a preliminary telephone call or letter, indicate how long you expect the interview to take. Get permission before tape recording, and if you tape an interview, take notes as well, making an accurate record of any comments you expect to quote in your paper. Be flexible enough to ask follow-up questions if the interview heads in a helpful but unexpected direction. And don't forget to make a record of the date and type of interview (personal or telephone) and the correct spelling of your interviewee's full name.

No one owes you an interview, so show your appreciation by writing a thank you letter promptly. Before your memory fades, go over your notes, transferring them to index cards (one idea per card) and filling in gaps. No matter how persuasive an interviewee may have been, don't let that person's ideas dominate your thinking. Remember that even an expert's memory can be fallible, so check his or her facts against other sources.

TAKING AND ORGANIZING NOTES

A research paper covers so much ground and takes such a long time to complete that it's impossible to keep track of in your head. The most efficient way to manage the abundance of material you collect is to use **note cards**, 3 x 5-inch or 4 x 6-inch index cards, each devoted to a single idea.

You may be tempted to make notes on a yellow pad or just take information directly from books and articles as you need it. However, a college research paper requires a complex synthesis of materials; a typical paragraph in a research paper contains an original topic sentence supported by data from two or more sources. Working from note cards makes this synthesis possible. Using note cards not only improves organization but also helps researchers avoid plagiarism, remain flexible, and save time in the long run.

Reorganizing material is far easier with note cards than it would be if you were continually flipping the pages of a legal pad or turning through books and articles. To make the cards easy to use, head each one with a word or phrase that describes its subject. Then reshuffle your cards, grouping them in different ways as you change your mind about how to organize your paper. Be sure to include on each note card the last name of the author of the source you're using and the number of the page on which you found the information.

Making notes on cards is a first step in writing your paper. The majority of your cards should contain **paraphrases**, restatements in your own words of ideas from source materials. Paraphrases differ from quotations in that quotations reproduce the exact language of a source and are enclosed within quotation marks. Because paraphrases of source material will appear much more often than quotations in your final paper, it's more efficient to paraphrase on the note cards than to copy quotations in order to paraphrase them later. Writing paraphrases forces you to digest and absorb source material. Later, when you start drafting, many of the paraphrases (with the addition of transitions and explanatory sections) will go directly into your paper. Some of your cards will probably also contain **summaries**, very condensed statements of main ideas from sources. Later, you'll use these summaries in your finished paper to provide needed background.

Use the following model for your note cards:

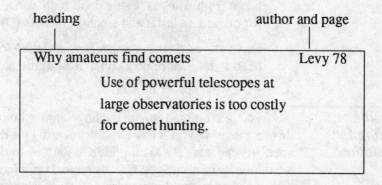

The lack of quotation marks on the card above indicates that the note is a paraphrase in the student's own words, not a direct quotation.

The suggestions below will guide you as you begin to make note cards for your research paper.

TIPS ON MAKING NOTE CARDS

1. Be selective. Take notes only on material directly relevant to your topic.

2. Make your notes precise, accurate, and complete enough to be clear when you use them to draft your paper days or weeks later.

3. Write in ink on one side of 3 x 5-inch or 4 x 6-inch cards.

4. Put only one idea from a single source on each card. If you must continue a note onto a second card, staple the cards together and label them "card 1 of 2" and "card 2 of 2."

5. On every card write the last name of the author from whose work you have taken the note and the page number. If you're using more than one source by the same author, include a shortened form of the title as well.

6. Add a subject heading at the top of every card. (Writing subject headings in pencil will make them easier to change as your research project evolves.)

7. Write paraphrases and summaries entirely in your own words.

8. Distinguish clearly between your own ideas and those you have taken from sources. Use a code such as oversized quotation marks for quoted material and square brackets ([]) for your own words.

9. Sort your cards into groups now and then to determine what you need to take more notes on and what the best way of organizing your paper will probably be.

Skimming and Scanning for Information

If you get bogged down reading large amounts of interesting but irrelevant material, you'll have trouble meeting the deadline for your research paper. Instead, rapidly skim possible sources to determine whether or not they duplicate material you already have. Don't feel guilty about not reading every word of every source you look at; that's not possible. Fast, selective skimming will enable you to eliminate material that isn't especially useful and to narrow your search to a smaller number of sources that you'll read thoroughly later.

Relying on **abstracts**, brief summaries of articles and books, can save a great deal of time. Skimming an abstract in a computer data base or printed source such as *Biological Abstracts* will help you decide whether to locate a particular article or book. Many scholarly articles are preceded by abstracts; look through them to see if you should read the articles themselves.

Scanning, glancing over printed material to find specific items of information, is another kind of rapid reading. Adjust your scanning to the type of material you're trying to locate. For example, make your eyes jump ahead to capital letters or numbers when you're searching for names or dates. Familiarize yourself with the words and phrases under which your topic is indexed so you can scan indexes and tables of contents quickly.

Annotating Copies of Your Sources

After you've discovered a source that you can definitely use in your paper, your next step may be to **annotate** it (underline its key passages and jot down notes in the margins). Photocopy library material you want to annotate and write only on your own copy. However, be wary of photocopying a great deal of material with the vague idea of annotating it later. It's better to deal with one source at a time rather than accumulate a mass of photocopies and perhaps never find time to sort through them. And don't get carried away annotating any one source too heavily; use only the codes and strategies you need to understand what you read and prepare good note cards. Below are some hints that can help you become a more efficient annotator.

TIPS ON ANNOTATING

1. Review "Becoming a Critical Reader" in chapter 1 of this book.
2. Use labeled brackets to indicate the main divisions of your source material.
3. Underline material important enough to paraphrase on note cards later.
4. Draw boxes around quotations you'd like to include in your paper.
5. Draw stars in the margins to indicate especially important ideas.
6. Label specific material you could use to support your thesis, such as facts, examples, and statistics.
7. Put question marks in the margins next to material you don't understand.
8. Add more annotations during second and third readings.

Writing Paraphrases

Paraphrasing means expressing someone else's ideas in your own words. Unlike a summary, which is much shorter than its source, a paraphrase is about the same length as the original passage or a little shorter. Most of the information you use in your paper to support your thesis will be paraphrased from sources.

The difference between paraphrasing and quoting is that when paraphrasing you reproduce ideas, not language. To paraphrase a passage successfully, you must fully understand it. Your first step should therefore be to reread it several times if necessary. One way to avoid unintentionally borrowing the language of your source is to write your own version without looking back at the text. Then, when you finish, compare your paraphrase with the original, making sure you've accurately reproduced the meaning of the passage without copying its wording or sentence structure. You shouldn't worry about repeating proper names and dates or using ordinary words such as *city* (the only common word for a large urban area) in your paraphrase, even if such wording also occurs in the original.

Assume that the following passage is taken from an article on the abuses of academic freedom:

> Professors are not merely machines for disseminating information; textbooks can provide students with all the facts they need. Scholars are not only entitled but morally obligated to express their points of view on controversial issues. However, when expressing debatable opinions, they are obliged to explain that other responsible authorities differ from them, sometimes drastically.

One student's first attempt at paraphrasing this passage was unsatisfactory:

NOT: Professors are not merely machines for providing students with information; textbooks can relate facts. Scholars are entitled—and morally obligated—to tell students their viewpoints on debatable topics. However, professors must also make clear that other responsible authorities hold different views, sometimes the opposite of theirs.

This passage is heavily indebted to its source not only for ideas but also for specific language and sentence structure. In the following version the wording and sentence structure are different enough from the original to make it an acceptable paraphrase:

> Professors can and should offer their students not only facts but opinions. However, when these opinions are controversial, they must tell their students that other well-informed people hold very different views.

Even though paraphrased material appears in your paper in your own words, you must credit the person whose ideas you have borrowed. How to do so is explained in chapter 12.

EXERCISE 3

Directions: Paraphrase the following passages as accurately as you can, taking care not to reproduce the language of the original. Answers will vary. Sample paraphrases are given at the back of this book.

Example: The murder of Francisco (Chico) Mendes on December 22, 1988, struck a blow at worldwide efforts to save the Amazon rain forest. Mendes, who lived by tapping wild rubber trees, organized his fellow tappers (called *seringuerios*) in peaceful protests against widespread destruction of the forest. A rancher whom Mendes had tried to persuade not to clear his land has been convicted of his murder.

Paraphrase: Francisco (Chico) Mendes was killed on December 22, 1988, while leading rubber tappers in peaceful efforts to save the Amazon rain forest. His murder by a local landowner seriously set back international attempts to save the forest.

1. In the great Oklahoma land rush of 1889, the U.S. government offered 160 acres of free land to people over twenty-one with enterprise enough to claim it. Pioneers demonstrated their strength and determination by making their way from the East Coast to Oklahoma by train, by wagon, or even on foot. However, the land rush also had a negative side: blacks and women were largely excluded from the right to claim land, and some of the territory the government gave away had already been granted to native Americans driven from lands elsewhere.

2. With the end of the Cold War, vast amounts of data collected by the Central Intelligence Agency and various branches of the military became available to environmentalists. Over decades spy satellites have gathered information that has proven invaluable to scientists studying global warming. Critics warn, however, that intelligence-gathering agencies will try to maintain their budgets at unjustifiably high Cold War levels by arguing that their efforts are vital to the analysis of ecological issues.

3. In the early 1970s the American divorce rate began to increase rapidly, a trend that has continued. In 1990 alone over a million children were separated from a parent by divorce. Since statistics indicate that children of divorced parents are more likely to get divorces themselves than children of two-parent families, the divorce rate in this country is likely to increase during the foreseeable future.

4. Did President Franklin Delano Roosevelt know beforehand that the Japanese would attack the U.S. naval base at Pearl Harbor, Hawaii? Conspiracy theorists argue that because Roosevelt wished to enter the war on the British side, he allowed the surprise attack to proceed without alerting the base. Critics of this theory point out that the intelligence information available to Roosevelt was incon-

clusive. Besides, no one has ever explained how alerting the base to the coming assault would have kept the United States out of the war.

5. Finding the genome, a blueprint of the genes that determine our biological heritage, will someday enable scientists to identify infants who will develop genetically determined diseases later in life. However, the ethics of gene exploration are still largely unsettled. For example, is it ethical to inform people that in a few years they will definitely contract fatal diseases for which there are no cures?

Organizing Your Notes

After you've accumulated notes from a variety of sources, the next step is to organize them. One sign that it's time to move from the note-taking to the organizing stage is that your new sources have begun to provide much the same information as your old ones—that is, your search is not yielding much data that you don't already have.

Find a large work surface and sort your note cards into categories according to the headings you've given them. Some stacks will probably contain only one or two notes. Reclassify these under your larger categories if you can, but be careful not to force them under headings where they don't really belong. When you finish, the stacks of cards will correspond with the main sections of your paper. If one stack is much larger than the others, try dividing it into two (or more) different subdivisions. If one stack is significantly shorter than the others, you may want to go back to your sources and take additional notes. Look again at the odd notes; perhaps you can now see that they belong with one of the larger stacks. If not, put them aside; it's normal to accumulate some notes you don't include in the final paper. Don't discard them, however; during the drafting stage you may discover a place for the information they contain.

After you've sorted your cards, shift the stacks until you find a logical sequence for your material. Keep asking "In what order should I present this information to make my paper as clear as possible to my readers?" Once you're satisfied with your organization, copy your headings down in order and use this list as a working outline. If necessary, adjust your thesis to match the new organizational scheme.

*K*eeping a research log, writing a research question, choosing an interesting topic, and devising a search strategy are important steps in beginning the difficult task of writing a research paper. Learning to use library resources such as the card catalogs, reference books, bibliographies, and data bases is indispensable in implementing a search strategy. Potential sources should be evaluated to ensure that they are up to date, reliable, and *usable. In addition, well-conducted interviews can yield useful material for research papers. Index cards should be used for paraphrases and summaries, which express ideas from sources in a researcher's own words, and quotations, language borrowed directly from sources. A research paper's organization should be developed by grouping note cards according to their subject headings.*

CHAPTER EXERCISE

I. MATCHING

Directions: Match each term on the list below with its definition by writing the correct letter in the space provided. Some of the terms on the list will not be used.

TERMS:

A. abstract
B. annotate
C. bibliography
D. call number
E. card catalog
F. closed stacks
G. data base
H. index
I. note card

J. open stacks
K. paraphrase
L. primary source
M. research log
N. scan
O. search strategy
P. secondary source
Q. source card
R. works cited section

DEFINITIONS:

_____ 1. notebook containing a cumulative record of work done on a research project

_____ 2. systematic approach to selecting and using sources

_____ 3. index card containing data needed for a research paper's works cited section

_____ 4. concluding part of a research paper that lists information about the sources used in the paper

_____ 5. record of a person's own experiences or observations

_____ 6. file containing author, title, and subject cards for the books in a library

_____ 7. combination of letters and numbers indicating a library book's location

_____ 8. shelving where library users can locate materials for themselves

_____ 9. list of books, articles, and other material on a particular subject

_____10. list of articles that have appeared in certain periodicals over a specific period of time

_____11. collection of information stored by computer and organized to speed its retrieval

_____12. restatement in one's own words of ideas from a source

_____13. brief summary of an article or book

_____14. glance over printed material to find particular items of information

_____15. underline key passages and add comments in the margins

II. MULTIPLE CHOICE

Directions: On the line at the left write the letter of the phrase that best completes each item.

_____16. Writing a research question

    A. eliminates the need for a preliminary thesis statement.

    B. is a good way to focus a promising general topic.

    C. encourages a researcher to make summaries of source materials.

_____17. One of the advantages of using reference books is that they are always

    A. kept on closed stacks.

    B. very brief and up to date.

    C. available because they can't be checked out.

_____18. When evaluating whether or not to use sources, researchers should always look for materials that are

    A. popularized accounts because such articles and books are easiest to understand and use.

    B. available free or are inexpensive to photocopy.

    C. up to date, reliable, and usable.

_____19. A well-conducted interview

    A. can yield current material not available in published sources.

    B. must follow a list of preplanned questions exactly and must be tape recorded.

    C. should be based mostly on questions that can be answered yes or no.

_____20. Making notes on index cards helps a researcher

    A. devise an effective thesis sentence.

    B. organize his or her notes more easily.

    C. skim and scan for material that can be used to support the research paper's thesis.

12

Using Sources in a Research Paper

Jenny sat at a table in the cafeteria leafing through a pile of word processed pages fastened with a paper clip. "Hi, Jen," said Mario, sitting down next to her. "What's that?" Mario, Jenny's neighbor, was taking his first courses at the university where she was a sophomore.

"My research paper," said Jenny.

"What's all that stuff in parentheses?"

"Citations," Jenny explained. "My sources are all listed in the back. In the parentheses I give the names of the authors I used and the numbers of the pages where I found material."

"Isn't that what footnotes are for?"

"Footnotes are out," Jenny answered. "This is the modern style." She cast a knowing glance at Mario—he had a lot to learn.

Unlike Mario, Jenny has already mastered the strategies needed to write a good research paper. This chapter explains how you can follow the same steps Jenny did to incorporate material from sources and provide documentation. It also includes her completed paper to use as a model for your own research projects.

INCORPORATING MATERIAL FROM SOURCES

A good research paper is far more than a collection of other people's words and ideas. Your paper will be shaped by each decision you make—your choice of a thesis, your evaluation of source materials, your organization of facts and ideas, and your own writing and editing. To develop a coherent argument, you'll present reasons supporting your thesis, backed by authoritative information from articles, books, and other sources. Each time you use words or ideas from a source, you'll make clear exactly why you do so. This means learning to incorporate paraphrases, summaries, and quotations into your paper as smoothly and accurately as you can.

Including Paraphrases and Summaries

Although paraphrases and summaries both restate ideas from sources, a paraphrase can be as long as (or even longer than) the original while a summary, which contains only key points, is much shorter. Writing good paraphrases and summaries demonstrates that you understand your sources. However, you must also explain (or clearly imply) the role you intend such source material to play in your paper.

Readers ordinarily assume that a paraphrase or summary following a topic sentence is intended to support it. Before relying on this familiar pattern, however, remember that your argument is much more familiar to you than to people encountering your views for the first time. Therefore, you may need to provide some guidance for your readers. One approach is to introduce paraphrases or summaries with transitional words or phrases (*for example, for instance*). Another strategy is to use wording that states the relationship between the point you're making and the material supporting it. The following example is drawn from an essay maintaining that workers have been unfairly blamed for the United States' unfavorable balance of trade:

> Other advances have been won only at the cost of endangering some members of the work force. Carson Bender supports this view by arguing that recent productivity increases have resulted from driving workers so hard that their safety and well-being are imperiled.

Here the phrase *supports this view* shows that the summary of Bender's ideas is intended to back up the researcher's own conclusion, expressed in the opening (topic) sentence of the paragraph.

Another use of paraphrase and summary is to express opposing views in order to refute them. When writers introduce ideas they don't accept, they must include wording that makes their own viewpoints clear. Imagine an essay written to maintain that U.S. workers are largely to blame for the nations's economic woes:

> Union activists have tried to protect unproductive workers by exploiting groundless fears about their safety. For example, Carson Bender wrongly claims that recent productivity increases have resulted from driving workers so hard that their safety and well-being are imperiled.

Here the phrase "wrongly claims" shows that the writer does not accept Bender's opinion.

Using Quotations

A research paper that contains a large proportion of quoted material, some of it undistinguished or even pointless, suggests that the person who wrote it padded the paper just to meet an instructor's length requirements. At least three quarters of your research paper should consist of your own views supported by paraphrases and summaries of your sources. Add quotations only when they are so distinctive, memorable, or authoritative that reproducing their exact wording is essential. To decide whether or not you have a compelling reason to include a quotation, ask if readers who skipped it would miss anything. In other words, if a quotation merely restates a point you've already made or contains dull or overly abstract language, don't use it.

The following suggestions should help you choose effective quotations.

TIPS ON CHOOSING QUOTATIONS

1. Select distinctive passages that would lose much of their impact if they were paraphrased.

2. Use some quotations from well-known authorities to show you're familiar with the work of experts on your subject.

3. Introduce material directly from primary sources to provide immediacy and credibility.

4. Reproduce the language of passages so specialized or technical that you could not paraphrase them without distorting their meaning.

5. Quote rather than paraphrase when you want to give your opponents a chance to express or defend their views in their own words.

INCORPORATING QUOTATIONS SMOOTHLY

Suppose that in a paper about the negative effects of television talk shows you quote American artist Andy Warhol's remark about fame: "In the future everyone will be famous for fifteen minutes." The quotation marks at the beginning and end assure readers that you have reproduced Warhol's comment just as it occurs in your source, the catalog of his exhibition in Stockholm, Sweden, in 1968.

To include this quotation in your paper, you would usually add an introductory or explanatory phrase before, after, or in the middle of the quoted material:

> As Andy Warhol explains, "In the future everyone will be famous for fifteen minutes."

> "In the future everyone will be famous for fifteen minutes," Andy Warhol cynically predicts.

> "In the future," Andy Warhol claims, "everyone will be famous for fifteen minutes."

Notice that the quotation marks enclose only the wording borrowed directly from your source, enabling readers to distinguish Warhol's language from yours. Even though the quoted words were written in the past, the present tense (*explains*, *predicts*, *claims*) is often used to introduce or explain quotations.

You can also combine quotations with paraphrases or summaries, perhaps quoting only a few of the original writer's words to add flavor:

> American artist Andy Warhol was so cynical about the kind of instant celebrity offered by the modern media that he predicted everyone would achieve fame "for fifteen minutes."

A common way to incorporate a quotation is by naming its author or source (or both) in an introductory phrase:

> In *Henry Ford and Grass-Roots America* Reynold M. Wik states, "Those of us who drove the intrepid Model T realize that the machine impressed us more than any other car we ever drove."

INDENTED QUOTATIONS

Any quotation of four typed lines or less is considered short and can be included without changing the indentation in your text. However, if the quoted passage is longer than four typed lines, you should set it off by indenting it. Start a new line and indent the quoted material ten spaces, as in the following example:

The continuing necessity for civil disobedience is eloquently explained in Martin Luther King's "Letter from Birmingham Jail." In it King offers a brief historical sketch relating the civil rights marchers in Birmingham to a long tradition of resistance to tyranny:

> Of course there is nothing new about this kind of civil disobedience. It was evidenced sublimely in the refusal of Shadrach, Meshach, and Abednego to obey the laws of Nebuchadnezzar on

the ground that a higher moral law was at stake. It was practiced superbly by the early Christians, who were willing to face hungry lions and the excruciating pain of chopping blocks rather than submit to certain unjust laws of the Roman Empire. To a degree, academic freedom is a reality today because Socrates practiced civil disobedience. In our own nation the Boston Tea Party represented a massive act of civil disobedience.

Notice that the indented material is not enclosed within quotation marks; indentation alone is enough to identify it as a quotation.

PUNCTUATING QUOTATIONS

Observe the rules below for punctuating quotations.

Put a comma or a period INSIDE closing quotation marks:

"Whoever wants to know the heart and mind of America had better learn baseball," remarks essayist Jacques Barzun.

Put a colon (:) or a semicolon (;) OUTSIDE closing quotation marks:

"Tribalism is the strongest force at work in the world today"; these words, which appear in *Custer Died for Your Sins* by Lakota author Vine Victor Deloria, Jr., were powerfully illustrated by events in eastern Europe during the 1990s.

Put a question mark or exclamation mark INSIDE closing quotation marks if it belongs to the quoted passage and not to the sentence as a whole:

In their 1966 song "Eleanor Rigby" the Beatles ask the poignant question, "All the lonely people, where do they all belong?"

Put a question mark or exclamation mark OUTSIDE closing quotation marks if it punctuates the whole sentence:

Can anyone remember without irony Nikita Khrushchev's grim threat, "We will bury you"?

When quotation marks are used in material you want to quote, use single quotation marks for the quotation within the quotation. The sentence below is taken from Robert Goldston's book *The Great Depression*:

So desperate were conditions in New York City that from faraway Africa, the natives of the Cameroons collected $3.77 which they sent to the city authorities "for the relief of the starving."

Here is the same sentence included in the text of a research paper:

According to Robert Goldston, "So desperate were conditions in New York City that from faraway Africa, the natives of the Cameroons collected $3.77 which they sent to the city authorities 'for the relief of the starving.'"

Use only one end mark (a period, question mark, or exclamation mark) to conclude a sentence:

NOT: In confusing situations it's tempting to ask Pontius Pilate's famous question "What is truth?".

In the correct version the final period is omitted:

In confusing situations it's tempting to ask Pontius Pilate's famous question "What is truth?"

MAKING CHANGES IN QUOTATIONS

The omission of unneeded material from a quotation is indicated by an **ellipsis** (. . .), which consists of three dots with a space before and after each one. The following example is taken from a paper quoting a 1962 interview with former Supreme Court Justice Hugo Black:

My view is . . . that freedom of speech means that you shall not do something to people either for the views they have or the views they express or the words they speak or write.

Here is Black's complete answer to the interviewer's question. The words omitted from the first version are italicized:

My view is, *without deviation, without exception, without any ifs, buts, or whereases,* that freedom of speech means that you shall not do something to people either for the views they have or the views they express or the words they speak or write.

The writer chose to omit the italicized words because Black's meaning is entirely clear without them. Including them would have lengthened her paper unnecessarily.

When an ellipsis comes at the end of a sentence, it includes a fourth dot to serve as a period. The following passage is taken from "Where College Fails Us" by Caroline Bird:

But college has never been able to work its magic for everyone. . . . College graduates are selling shoes and driving taxis; college students sabotage each other's experiments and forge letters of recommendation in the intense competition for admission to graduate school.

The first full sentence of this passage is "But college has never been able to work its magic for everyone." Between it and the next quoted sentence, a complete sentence has been omitted.

You may change a quoted passage slightly to make it fit into your paper. If the grammar of your own sentence requires it, you may change the final punctuation mark (from a period to a comma, for example). Any other changes in a quotation should be clearly indicated to your reader. To emphasize a word or phrase, you may italicize it (italic type is indicated by underlining in typewritten texts). However, you should indicate that you've added italics by providing an explanation in parentheses such as (emphasis added) or (italics added).

Use square brackets to indicate a change in a quotation or an addition to it. For example, suppose you're quoting Franklin D. Roosevelt's comments on the power of the printed word: "Books cannot be killed by fire. People die, but books never die. No man and no force can abolish memory. . . . In this war, we know books are weapons." To identify the war to which Roosevelt refers, you could add an explanation within square brackets: "In this war [World War II], we know books are weapons." Square brackets are also used to indicate a change from a small letter to a capital: "[A]nimal research is leading to dramatic progress against AIDS and Alzheimer's disease," John G. Hubbell claims. Here the bracketed letter shows that words have been omitted from the beginning of the quotation.

The word **sic** (a Latin word meaning "thus") may be used to show that a passage is being quoted correctly, despite appearances to the contrary. Adding *sic* allows you to quote a passage containing a mistake without giving the impression that you made the mistake yourself, as in this example:

> The Santa Barbara Savings and Loan Association announced that for a Visa credit account, "the annual fee for the card is $10 per year, or $25, whichever is greater [*sic*]."

EXERCISE 1

Directions:

1. Identify each item below by using the following code:

   C   correct   I   incorrect

2. Correct the incorrect items.

Example: __I__ "A child is the root of the heart⌣, Carolina Maria de Jesús rightly observes.

_____ 1. "I was a fantastic student until ten," Grace Paley reports, "and then my mind began to wander".

_____ 2. "True leaders have to be totally free." Shirley Chisholm claims.

_____ 3. "It was so cold I almost got married," Shelly Winters jokes.

_____ 4. "My father was not a failure," Harry S Truman asserted. "After all, he was the father of a president of the United States."

_____ 5. "Never go to bed mad," Phyllis Diller advises. Stay up and fight."

_____ 6. Jean Kerr complains that she's "tired of all this nonsense about beauty being only skin-deep," asking, "What do you want—an adorable pancreas"?

_____ 7. Janet Flanner, who for fifty years wrote letters to the *New Yorker* from Paris, explains, "I keep going over a sentence. I nag it, gnaw it, pat and flatter it."

_____ 8. "The sad truth is that excellence makes people nervous," Shana Alexander complains.

_____ 9. In *A Sand County Almanac* Aldo Leopold states:

> We face the question whether a still higher "standard of living" is worth its cost in things natural, wild, and free. For us in the minority . . . the chance to find a pasqueflower is a right as inalienable as free speech."

_____10. According to James William Fulbright, "We must dare to think "unthinkable" thoughts."

UNDERSTANDING DOCUMENTATION

Documentation informs readers about the sources of ideas and language a writer has taken from other authors. A properly documented research paper requires both citations in parentheses and a works cited section or references list. A researcher who doesn't supply this documentation is guilty of plagiarism, the unacknowledged use of other writers' ideas or wording.

Providing documentation is mostly a matter of imitating models such as the ones in this chapter, which illustrate the documentation style recommended by the Modern Language Association (MLA) and the American Psychological Association (APA). MLA documentation style is used in academic writing in English, history, philosophy, and foreign languages while APA style is used in the social sciences, education, and business.

Why Documentation Is Provided

Accurate documentation assures readers that a writer has researched a subject carefully, provided credible, verifiable support for his or her claim, and followed the conventions of academic writing. **Parenthetical citations**, references enclosed in parentheses, indicate where a writer found each item of information. In MLA style, a parenthetical citation usually contains an author's last name and a page number. An APA citation for a paraphrase or summary ordinarily contains an author's last name and a publication date; for a direct quotation APA style requires a page number as well.

Each citation in the text of a research paper corresponds to an entry in the works cited section or references list. Readers encountering the parenthetical citation (Gray 5) in the text of a paper can turn to the back of the paper for information about the original source. In an MLA-style paper they would find the following related entry in the works cited section:

> Gray, Denis. "Koala Mania." International Wildlife. May–June 1986: 4–10.

In APA style the author's last name is often mentioned in the text of the paper, followed by the year of publication in parentheses: "According to Gray (1986), koalas . . ." The references list would contain the following related entry:

> Gray, D. (1986, May/June). Koala mania. International Wildlife, pp. 4–10.

Each new idea or quotation obtained from a source must be cited separately. As a result, a typical research paper contains many citations, usually several on every page. The tips in the list below will help you decide when to supply parenthetical references.

WHEN TO INCLUDE PARENTHETICAL CITATIONS

Use citations when you take the following material from sources:

Every quotation, whether a single distinctive word or a lengthy paragraph

Every paraphrase

Every summary

Every visual aid (such as a map or diagram)

However, not everything in your paper needs to be cited. Your own ideas (your thesis, your topic sentences, and all the sentences providing your own interpretations, evaluations, and explanations) do not need citations. Nor does **common knowledge**—facts that most readers can be expected to know. For example, the date when the U.S. Declaration of Independence was signed (1776) is so well known it doesn't require a parenthetical citation. Common knowledge also includes information easily found in a variety of sources, such as the date of former President Jimmy Carter's birth (1924), even though this information may not be widely known. Your sense of what can be classified as common knowledge will develop as you research a particular topic.

In general, if you're not sure whether or not to provide a citation, you're better off doing so. Including unnecessary citations is merely awkward, but omitting necessary ones leaves you open to a charge of plagiarism. Try to look at each of your sources as if you were its original author. If you'd feel annoyed to see your idea in someone else's paper without receiving credit for it, cite the source.

**How to
Prepare
Citations**

Writing an entire paper first and adding documentation later can lead to numerous mistakes. Instead, include needed parenthetical citations as you draft your paper. This will be easy if you've made careful note cards, each containing all the information you need (the author and page number for MLA style; the author, date, and page number for APA style). Writing complete publication data on any photocopies you make also helps ensure accuracy. In addition, following a regular work schedule will help you avoid documentation errors that result from rushing to finish a research paper before a deadline.

USING MLA (AUTHOR/PAGE) STYLE FOR PARENTHETICAL CITATIONS

When following MLA style, space once after short quotations, paraphrases, and summaries, add a citation, and put a period after it: (Sedgwick 320). End an indented quotation of four typed lines or more with a period, space twice, and add the citation. In either case, don't use a comma between an author's name and a page number or include "p." or "pp." or the word "page(s)." If you've already mentioned an author's name in a way that makes clear whose work is being cited, use only a page number in the citation: (320).

For a work by two or three authors, include all the authors' last names: (Gilbert and Gubar 147). For a work by more than three authors, use only the last name of the first author and **et al.**, an abbreviation of the Latin phrase *et alia*, "and others": (Moreno et al. 79).

If you cite more than one work by the same author, add a short title so readers know which source you're referring to: (Brookner, Watteau 203). Use only the author's name (no page number) for a reference to a one-page article or a nonprint source such as an interview or videotape: (Sowter).

Cite unsigned works by their titles. Use complete titles if they are brief but shorten long titles, beginning with the word under which the source will be alphabetized in your works cited section. Underline book or pamphlet titles; use quotation marks for titles of articles: (Soybeans 13); ("Industrial nations" 56).

Use *qtd. in* (for "quoted in") to indicate that material you're quoting or paraphrasing has come to you secondhand. Suppose, for example, that a book by Cruz contains a quotation from a second author named Greene. You like what Greene has to say and quote it in your own paper. The citation (qtd. in Cruz 225) means that you found the passage not where it first appeared but in the book by Cruz. On your works cited list you would include information about Cruz's book, not Greene's.

USING APA (AUTHOR/DATE) STYLE FOR PARENTHETICAL CITATIONS

In APA style, when you quote an author directly without naming him or her, include the author's last name, the year of publication, and the page number in the citation: (Sedgwick, 1988, p. 320). Notice that APA style includes the abbreviations p. for "page" and pp. for "pages." Citations for paraphrases and summaries require authors' names and publication dates, but not page numbers: (Sedgwick, 1988). If you mention an author's last name in a sentence, add the date of the work in parentheses: "According to Sedgwick (1988) zoos . . ." A quotation of forty words or more is indented five spaces. End an indented quotation with a period, space twice, and add the citation.

The publication date normally indicates which of two or more works by the same author is being cited. If the works were published in the same year, distinguish them by adding small letters: (1989a), (1989b). For works by two authors, name both, joining them with an ampersand (&) in the citation: (Gilbert & Gubar, 1992). Use *and* within the text: "Gilbert and Gubar (1992) point out . . ."

For a source with up to six authors, use all the authors' last names in the first citation. In later citations use only the last name of the first author followed by et al. (Moreno et al., 1990). Use the et al. format for all references to works by more than six authors, but include every author on the references list. When a work is unsigned, cite it by its title if the title is short. If not, use a shortened version: (Soybeans, 1979, p. 13); ("Industrial nations," 1986, p. 56).

Use *cited in* to indicate that material you're quoting comes from another source: (cited in Cruz, 1990, p. 225). Be sure your references list includes the source you're citing, not the work in which the passage first appeared.

TRY IT OUT

In December 1988 an ironworker named Calvin Davis was tightening a bolt on a girder sixty-five feet above the ground. When the head of the bolt came off, Davis lost his balance, fell off the girder, and was killed. The bolt turned out to be a counterfeit—a cheap imitation of the high-quality carbon steel bolt called for on the job. Counterfeit bolts have been discovered in bridges, cars, trucks, airplanes, and even nuclear power plants.

The three excerpts below discuss the safety hazard posed by counterfeit bolts. Following the excerpts is a student's paragraph based on these sources but lacking necessary quotation marks and citations. First, study the sources below. Then try your hand at revising the plagiarized paragraph. Sample revisions are provided in both MLA and APA styles at the back of this book.

SOURCE 1

For the past several years, U.S. suppliers have had to import increasing numbers of fasteners because of the declining number of domestic manufacturers. This decline has forced domestic consumers to become dependent on the quality control procedures and ethics of foreign manufacturers and importers. During the investigation of a single case, the U.S. Customs Service discovered eight Japanese trading houses and one Japanese manufacturer involved in producing and marketing counterfeit bolts. (From page 55 of "Report Cites Increase in Substandard Fasteners." <u>Aviation Week & Space Technology</u> 12 Sept. 1988: 55–57.)

SOURCE 2

How these counterfeit bolts got into the system is a tale of greed and deceit that begins with U.S. bolt importers. U.S. Customs investigators say the importers, beginning in the late 1970s, contacted foreign producers, principally in Japan, and asked them to manufacture counterfeits. Because bolts are a commodity item—bought largely on price and until recently rarely tested for quality—low-cost counterfeits offered tempting profit margins even when their suppliers underbid purveyors of legitimate bolts. (From page 56 of John Merwin's article "The High Cost of Cheap Bolts." <u>Forbes</u> 13 June 1988: 56–57.)

SOURCE 3

What all parts dealers offer are faster delivery and usually cheaper prices on an odd-lot order of, say, two hydraulic pumps or one [end of p. 81] de-icer than their customers could get from the original manufacturer. As a result, carriers can sometimes end up with bogus parts bought unwittingly from unscrupulous dealers. Says C. O. Miller, the head of Systems Safety Inc., an aviation consulting firm: "Maintenance is a critical item; cost is a critical item. Put the two together and that opens the door to bogus parts."(From pages 81 and 82 of Anna Cifelli Isgrò's article "The Hidden Threat to Air Safety." <u>Fortune</u> 13 April 1987: 81–84.)

Using either MLA or APA documentation style, add quotation marks, insert parenthetical citations, and change the wording where necessary to eliminate the plagiarism in the paragraph below. Provide citations for both wording and ideas borrowed from the three sources.

STUDENT'S PLAGIARIZED VERSION:

> As the number of U.S. producers of fasteners has decreased in recent years, dependence on importers has increased. Because bolts are a commodity item—bought largely on price and until recently rarely tested for quality—domestic manufacturers are tempted by inexpensive counterfeits. Lured by the prospect of faster delivery and usually cheaper prices than original manufacturers offer, carriers can sometimes end up with bogus parts bought unwittingly from unscrupulous dealers. Much of the counterfeiting began in the late 1970s when the greed and deceit of U.S. importers led them to ask foreign producers, mostly Japanese, to make counterfeits for the U.S. market. In a U.S. Customs investigation of one case, nine Japanese firms were found to be manufacturing and selling fake bolts. As C. O. Miller, an aviation consultant, explains, "Maintenance is a critical item; cost is a critical item. Put the two together and that opens the door to bogus parts."

Listing Your Sources in a Works Cited Section or References List

To ensure accuracy when compiling your list of sources, take the information you need directly from books or periodicals, not from card catalogs or published bibliographies. If several cities are listed as places of publication, use only the first one. Add the name of the state (for U.S. cities) or country (for cities outside the U.S.) if the city isn't well known. Finally, check to see that every source you've cited in your research paper is included in the works cited section or references list and that every item in the works cited section or references list is cited in the paper.

The works cited section or references list should be double spaced between and within items. Alphabetize the entries by authors' last names. If a work is unsigned, include it in the alphabetical listing according to the first word in its title (disregarding *a*, *an*, and *the*).

PREPARING A WORKS CITED LIST (MLA STYLE)

If you're following MLA style, provide information about each item in your works cited list in the following order: author, title, and publication data, with the date of publication last. Include both the first and last names of authors. When a work has more than one author, reverse the first author's first and last names and use "and" between the names of the last two authors. If you list two or more works by the same author, substitute three hyphens and a period (- - -.) for the author's name at the start of each entry after the first one.

Begin typing the first line of each entry at the left margin and indent each additional line five spaces. In titles of books and articles, capitalize the first word, the last word, and all nouns, verbs, adjectives, adverbs, pronouns, and subordinating conjunctions, regardless of how they are capitalized in the original. Underline the titles of books and periodicals and enclose article titles within quotation marks.

Refer to publishing companies by shortened forms of their names ("Norton" for W. W. Norton and Co., Inc.; "Harcourt" for Harcourt Brace & Company, and so on). Use "UP" for a university press. When an article begins on one page in a periodical and continues on a later one with unrelated material in between, give the first page number followed by a plus sign: 4+.

PREPARING A REFERENCES LIST (APA STYLE)

When you're using APA style, include information about each item in your references list in the following order: author, date (in parentheses), title, and publication data. Use initials for authors' first and middle names. When a work has more than one author, reverse the order of all authors' names. Add an ampersand (&) between the names of the last two authors. List works by the same author in the order in which they were published and repeat the author's name each time. If two works by the same author were published in the same year, add letters to their publication dates to distinguish them: 1989a, 1989b. If a work is unsigned, begin with its title followed by the date in parentheses.

Start each entry at the left margin, indenting additional lines three spaces. Capitalize only the first words of titles and subtitles of books and articles (except for words that are always capitalized such as names of people and places). Underline the titles of books and periodicals but do not underline or use quotation marks for article titles. Use the complete names of publishers, except for descriptive words such as *Publishers* and *Inc.*, which you should omit. When an article begins on one page in a periodical and continues on a later one with unrelated material in between, list all the page numbers and separate them with commas.

Sample Items for Works Cited and References Lists

Examples of the common types of works cited (MLA) and references (APA) follow. For more information consult the *MLA Handbook for Writers of Research Papers* and the *Publication Manual of the American Psychological Association.*

A Book by One Author

MLA style:

> Harrison, Barbara Grizzuti. Italian Days. New York: Ticknor, 1989.

APA style:

> Harrison, B. G. (1989). Italian days. New York: Ticknor & Fields.

A Book by Two Authors

MLA style:

> Parry, Tom, and Deb Preusch. <u>The Soft War: The Uses and Abuses of U.S. Economic Aid in Central America</u>. New York: Grove, 1988.

APA style:

> Parry, T., & Preusch, D. (1988). <u>The soft war: The uses and abuses of U.S. economic aid in Central America</u>. New York: Grove.

An Article Reprinted in a Book

MLA style:

> Stent, Angela. "The One Germany." <u>Foreign Policy</u> 81 (1990–91): 53–70. Rpt. in <u>The Reunification of Germany</u>. Ed. Robert Emmet Long. New York: Wilson, 1992. 107–23.

APA style:

> Stent, A. (1992). The one Germany. In R. E. Long (Ed.), <u>The reunification of Germany</u> (pp. 107–123). New York: H. W. Wilson.

An Article in a Monthly Periodical

MLA style:

> Halfpenny, James C. "The Cold Facts of Winter." <u>Natural History</u> Dec. 1991: 50–61.

APA style:

> Halfpenny, J. C. (1991, December). The cold facts of winter. <u>Natural History</u>, pp. 50–61.

An Article in a Weekly Magazine

MLA style:

> Allman, William F. "The Mental Edge." <u>U.S. News & World Report</u> 3 Aug. 1992: 50–56.

APA style:

> Allman, W. F. (1992, August 3). The mental edge. <u>U.S. News & World Report</u>, pp. 50–56.

An Unsigned Article

MLA style:

> "Bubble Gum in a Tube: Will It Stick?" <u>Business Week</u> 29 Aug. 1983: 30.

APA style:

> Bubble gum in a tube: Will it stick? (1983, August 29). <u>Business Week</u>, p. 30.

An Article in a Scholarly Journal in Which Issues Are Numbered Continuously throughout the Year
MLA style:

> Shore, Chris. "Virgin Births and Sterile Debates: Anthropology and the New Reproductive Technologies." <u>Current Anthropology</u> 33 (1992): 295–314.

APA style:

> Shore, C. (1992). Virgin births and sterile debates: Anthropology and the new reproductive technologies. <u>Current Anthropology, 33</u>, 295–314.

An Article in a Scholarly Journal That Starts Each Issue with Page 1
MLA style:

> Sue, Stanley. "Ethnicity and Mental Health: Research and Policy Issues." <u>Journal of Social Issues</u> 48.2 (1992): 187–205.

APA style:

> Sue, S. (1992). Ethnicity and mental health: Research and policy issues. <u>Journal of Social Issues, 48</u>(2), 187–205.

A Newspaper Article
MLA style:

> Kang, Grace. "Asian-Americans Surge into Law, Tripling Their Ranks in a Decade." <u>Wall Street Journal</u> 29 July 1992, eastern ed.: B2.

APA style:

> Kang, G. (1992, July 29). Asian-Americans surge into law, tripling their ranks in a decade. <u>The Wall Street Journal</u>, p. B2.

A Government Publication
MLA style:

> United States. Dept. of Education. <u>America 2000: An Education Strategy</u>. Washington: GPO, 1991.

APA style:

> U.S. Department of Education. (1991). <u>America 2000: An education strategy</u> (Publication No. ED/OS91–13). Washington, DC: U.S. Government Printing Office.

EXERCISE 2

Directions: For each work described below prepare an entry for a works cited page (MLA style) or a references list (APA style).

Example: "The Best Schools in the World," an article by Barbara Kantrowitz and Pat Wingert published on pages 50–52 in the December 2, 1991, issue of *Newsweek*.

MLA style:

> Kantrowitz, Barbara, and Pat Wingert. "The Best Schools in the World." Newsweek 2 Dec. 1991: 50–52.

APA style:

> Kantrowitz, B., & Wingert, P. (1991, December 2). The best schools in the world. Newsweek, pp. 50–52.

1. *Reviving the American Dream: The Economy, the States and the Federal Government*, a book by Alice Rivlin published in 1992 by The Brookings Institution, located in Washington, D.C.

   _____

   _____

   _____

2. A book by Jill Duerr Berrick and Neil Gilbert, *With the Best of Intentions: The Child Sexual Abuse Prevention Movement*, published in 1991 in New York and London by Guilford Press.

   _____

   _____

   _____

3. "They Want to Take Our Guns," an article by Joe Foss on pages 175–178 in *The Informed Argument: A Multidisciplinary Reader and Guide*, edited by Robert K. Miller and published in 1992 by Harcourt Brace Jovanovich, Inc., in Fort Worth, Texas. The article was originally published in the September 1988 issue of *Conservative Digest* on pages 103–106.

   _____

   _____

   _____

4. *What Works: Schools without Drugs*, publication 1987–178–865 of the U.S. Department of Education, printed in 1987 at the Government Printing Office in Washington, D.C.

_____

_____

_____

5. "Humane Chemistry or Scientific Barbarism? American Responses to World War I Poison Gas, 1915–1930," an article by Hugh R. Slotten in *The Journal of American History*, a scholarly journal that is numbered continuously throughout the year. The article appears on pages 476–498 in Volume 77, Number 2, which was published in September 1990.

_____

_____

_____

6. *Backlash: The Undeclared War against American Women*, a book by Susan Faludi published in 1991 by Crown Publishers, Inc., in New York, New York.

_____

_____

_____

7. "Afro-American Studies Get New Life at Harvard," an article by Fox Butterfield in the *New York Times* published on Wednesday, June 3, 1992, on page B7.

_____

_____

_____

8. "Your Daily Bread," an unsigned article published on pages 611–614 in the October 1988 issue of *Consumer Reports*.

_____

_____

_____

9. An article on pages 78–110 in the October 15, 1990, issue of the *New Yorker* entitled "Reflections: The Old Way" and written by Elizabeth Marshall Thomas.

_____

_____

10. "Exercise and Weight Loss: The Uncertain Connection," an article by Steven R. Hawks in *Health Education*, a scholarly journal that renumbers each issue starting with page one. The article appears on pages 11–15 in the August–September 1989 issue, which is Volume 20, Number 4.

_____

_____

_____

EXAMINING A SAMPLE RESEARCH PAPER

When Jenny Rodriguez's instructor told her English Composition students to write a research paper on a controversial topic, Jenny at first wished that she'd been assigned a specific subject. However, she remembered a television show on Native Americans she'd seen recently and realized that the paper could provide an opportunity to learn more about the issues discussed in the program. Her first idea was to write about the controversy over whether the skeletons of Native Americans in museum collections should be returned to their descendants for burial.

Checking the *Library of Congress Subject Headings*, she discovered that material on Native Americans could be found in card catalogs and indexes under the heading "Indians of North America." Several articles she found listed in computerized indexes were available in her college library. From them she learned that many museums had already agreed to return the skeletons in their collections to Native American tribes for reburial. Since this issue no longer seemed controversial, she needed a new idea. A reference librarian with whom she spoke suggested looking for recent articles on Native Americans in *Editorial Research Reports (CQ Researcher)*. Reading the articles gave Jenny an idea for a new research question: What can be done to protect Native American sacred sites from treasure seekers? *Editorial Research Reports* included a list of sources on her new topic, and a return to her library's computerized indexes provided more. The result, after three weeks' research and much rewriting, is the paper below. Her paper illustrates the MLA documentation style.

1

Jenny Rodriguez
Professor Barkowitz
English Composition II
1 May 19XX

America's Past for Sale

At the annual Indian relic show in Owensboro, Kentucky, collectors search for bargains among thousands of Native American artifacts, ranging from fifty-cent arrowheads to jewelry and blankets costing thousands of dollars. The most valuable objects, however, are not on public view: "You won't find much of the really good stuff out in the open," one vendor confides. "That's kept in vaults. You gotta be serious before they'll show it to you" (Arden 390). The "really good stuff" can be very expensive indeed: in 1990 a pot from the southwestern United States was sold in Paris for $250,000 (Landers 35). Before dismissing this curious phenomenon as just another ex- ample of the modern mania for collec- tibles, it is worth reflecting that what is really for sale at this so-called "In- dian Relic Show of Relic Shows" is America's prehistoric past.

Before 1971 Native American ar- tifacts were of interest only to ar-

chaeologists and a small number of collectors. However, in that year a collection
sold at the Parke-Bernet auction house in
New York that was expected to yield between $40,000 and $67,000 brought in more
than $161,000 (Landers 36). The sale sent
prices for native American artifacts on
an upward spiral that led to a growth industry in looting graves and other sites.
In recent years the thievery has worsened
as prices have continued to rise. Unless
the people of the United States are willing to see an invaluable legacy vanish
forever, the federal government must pass
and enforce a strong law to protect Native American sites from destruction.

Because Americans have prided themselves on being a forward-looking people,
they have often shown little concern for
the past. Moreover, many of them believe
that their own history began about 500
years ago with the European discovery of
the New World. Both views are short-
sighted. The first is refuted by Karl E.
Meyer in his book The Plundered Past:

> [I]f the remains of the past
> should disappear, our lives
> will be poorer in ways that the
> statistician can never measure—
> we will live in a drabber
> world, and will have squandered
> a resource that enlivens our ex-
> istence, offers a key to our

Rodriguez 3

> nature, and, not least, acts as
> a psychic ballast as we venture
> into a scary future. (208-09)

The second view ignores the story of
people who migrated to an unpopulated
hemisphere from Asia at least 12,000
years ago. At a time when ethnic
divisions threaten to tear this country
apart, all our heritage is precious. We
cannot afford to turn the cultural legacy
of any Americans into a mere commodity.

In some ways, attitudes toward Native Americans and their heritage have
changed for the better in recent years.
Not only has the movement for Native
American rights, fueled by several important court victories and successful
negotiations, gained considerable momentum, but the public as a whole has also
become aware of the need to protect what
remains of the prehistoric past. Nevertheless, the struggle to preserve ancient
sites has never looked more hopeless.
"[I]f the unchecked looting continues to
increase," writes archaeologist George E.
Stuart, "there will be no archaeology to
do by the turn of the century" (393). The
situation has become so serious that the
long-running battle between Native
Americans and archaeologists over the
rights to remains and artifacts seems in-
significant compared with the threats

posed by those who plunder for profit.

Native American sacred places continue to face the threat of destruction
from a wide variety of commercial interests. In December 1990 Woodruff Butte, a
site sacred to the Hopi, Zuni, and Navajo
peoples for over 1,000 years, was
bulldozed by a company seeking gravel for
road construction ("After Mining"). In
Bells Bend, Tennessee, an area containing
thousands of Cherokee graves was sold to
a company proposing to dig fill dirt for
an adjoining sanitary landfill (Marshall). Other locations throughout North
America have been menaced by miners and
developers (Gibbs 19).

Distressing as it is, however,
destruction to exploit the land for its
natural resources is less offensive than
destruction motivated by the desire to
loot artifacts from graves. Despite new
laws, little has been done to prevent
reckless pillage. For example, archaeologists have known since 1858 that
the area of Slack Farm near Uniontown,
Kentucky, was occupied some time between
A.D. 1450 and 1650 by people of a culture
known as Late Mississippian, which once
dominated much of the eastern United
States (Arden 385-86). According to archaeologist Bruce Fagan, "The farm was of
special importance, for it straddled the

Rodriguez 5

vital centuries of first European contact
with the New World" (15).

The Slack family had long forbidden
any digging on their land, but after the
farm was sold, people hoping to discover
salable artifacts paid the new owner
$10,000 for excavation rights. Fagan nar-
rates what happened next:

> They rented a tractor and began
> bulldozing their way through
> the village midden [garbage
> dump] to reach graves. They
> pushed heaps of bones aside,
> and dug through dwellings and
> the potsherds, hearths, and
> stone tools associated with
> them. Along the way, they left
> detritus of their own--empty
> pop-top beer and soda cans--
> scattered on the ground
> alongside Late Mississippian
> pottery fragments. Today, Slack
> Farm looks like a battlefield--
> a morass of crude shovel
> holes and gaping trenches.
> Broken human bones litter the
> ground, and fractured ar-
> tifacts crunch underfoot. (15)

When archaeologists excavate a
site, they take extensive measurements
and numerous photographs, recording
precisely where and at what depth in the

ground each object was discovered. They
take great care to preserve everything--
bones, small fragments of pottery and
cloth, refuse, even ash from long-dead
cooking fires. Looters, on the other
hand, seek only intact objects they can
sell; the rest, from their point of view,
is trash. Even the objects they preserve
can tell scientists little because they
have been wrenched from their original
settings. "The artifact out of context,"
explains Stuart, has "as little use as
the beached plank of a wrecked ship"
(393).

Grave robbing is as old as antiq-
uity. When the tomb of the Egyptian king
Tutankhamen was discovered in 1922, its
finders were astonished because the contents were untouched; all the other tombs
in the Valley of the Kings had been
robbed many centuries before (Woolley
85). Documents from as long ago as the
Egyptian twentieth dynasty (c. 1200-1090
B.C.) report the deliberations of a committee appointed to investigate tomb rob-
beries (Edwards 243-44).

Ancient looters usually did little
damage to the graves they ransacked
either because they had to work quietly
to avoid detection or because they feared
the spirits of the dead. The noted
British archaeologist Sir Leonard Woolley
describes one excavation in which the
tombs remained intact except that he

Rodriguez 7

could find no objects in them made of a
precious metal; holes in the back walls
just large enough to admit a person's arm
provided a clue to what had happened (86).
Modern tomb robbers, however, seem to fear
neither the living nor the dead, so they
cause far greater problems for archaeologists than ancient ones ever did.

They certainly have little to fear
from present state or federal laws. In
1979 Congress passed the Archaeological
Resources Protection Act, making the
removal of artifacts from federal lands illegal. However, prosecutions under the act
have been few, and those convicted have
mostly received light sentences. For example, Derek V. Goodwin, author of the New
York Times Magazine article "Raiders of
the Sacred Sites," reports that in 1984
Earl Shumway of Blanding, Utah, was arrested for stealing more than two million
dollars worth of Native American art objects from federal land. He pleaded guilty
to charges that could have brought a maximum sentence of ten years in jail and a
$20,000 fine. In fact, the judge put him
on probation (87). People charged under
state law have even less to worry about.
In an article in National Geographic, Harvey Arden reports the outcome of the Slack
Farm case: the ten men arrested were
charged under Kentucky law with a misdemeanor carrying a maximum penalty of a

year in jail or a $500 fine. Since four
of the ten were residents of Illinois and
Indiana and could not be extradited to
face misdemeanor charges, they could not
be prosecuted (378-80). These outcomes
have demonstrated to looters that they
have excellent chances of escaping lightly from brushes with the law.

Another obstacle to adequate enforcement of the present federal law is the
vastness of federal lands. The most spec-
tacular native American sites lie in the
Four Corners region, where the states of
Utah, Colorado, Arizona, and New Mexico
meet. There the Anasazi, ancestors of the
Zuni and Hopi, built huge communal dwell-
ings now preserved in Mesa Verde National
Park, Chaco Canyon, Canyon de Chelly, and
other locations. Three government agencies (the Bureau of Land Management, the
Forest Service, and the National Park Service) together manage about 104 million
acres of federal land in this region,
only about six million acres of which
have been surveyed for archaeological
sites (Landers 43). In a recent auction
at Sotheby's in London, an Anasazi basket
brought $152,000 (Landers 37). The high
prices for artifacts make the area a
prime target for looters at a time when
the enforcement resources of federal agencies are shrinking steadily because of
budget cuts.

Rodriguez 9

Grave sites on public land are difficult to protect, but many people feel
that graves on private lands should not
be protected at all. When Bruce Fagan
described the crime at Slack Farm to some
people he knew, he was at first
astonished by their indifference:

> "So what?" shrugged one coffee
> shop acquaintance. "It's a free
> country." He expressed what
> turned out to be a widely held
> view: it's up to the landowners
> what they do with their proper-
> ty. I had forgotten that many
> people see nothing wrong with
> private landowners ravaging the
> past for profit--as long as
> laws are not broken. (16)

No wonder average people who sit on
juries in cases brought under the Archeological Resources Protection Act
often take an extremely tolerant view of
defendants' activities. Only two jury trials so far have resulted in felony convictions under this act. The defendant in
the first case was convicted in 1987 of
trying to sell the mummified remains of
an infant from a cave in Utah (Landers
40). Then in March 1990 Newall Charlton
of Elizabethtown, Tennessee, was found
guilty of grave robbery in the Cherokee
National Forest in Tennessee. He was

Rodriguez 10

fined and sentenced to twenty-two years in
jail (Landers 34).

Apart from these two cases, judges
and juries have found reasons to let defendants off lightly. Before 1988, for the
government to charge a defendant with a
felony rather than a misdemeanor, the
value of the artifacts stolen or the cost
of repairing damage to the site had to be
$5,000 or more. Kristine Olson Rogers, a
former lawyer in the U.S. Attorney's office in Portland, Oregon, describes a typical trial:

> A case is indicted accompanied
> by headlines touting massive
> damage estimates and then the
> jury convicts of a misdemeanor,
> utterly disregarding the
> experts' staggering damage to-
> tals. (qtd. in Landers 40)

Behind such attitudes lies the experience of walking through a field as a
child and picking up an arrowhead or fragment of ancient pottery. Sometimes such
discoveries lead to a lifelong fascination
with Indian artifacts and an innocent-seem-
ing hobby of collecting them. One collec-
tor, Bob Brown, an automobile salesman in
Deming, New Mexico, argues that the problem has been blown out of proportion:
"Even if you are a qualified amateur and
you love prehistoric culture," he says,

Rodriguez 11

"you are still considered a grave robber
and a vandal or worse" (Cowley 59). Collectors often suggest that they are preserving artifacts that would otherwise be
destroyed. "If it weren't for collectors,"
argues Art Gerber, an organizer of shows
at which relics are sold, "a lot of this
stuff would be totally lost--plowed into
pieces by farmers, washed away by floods,
paved over for parking lots and housing
projects" (Arden 383). "To allow the
looters and gravediggers to call themselves amateurs and hobbyists," counters
Ray Apodaca, director of the Texas Indian
Commission, "is like allowing Jack the Rip-
per to call himself an amateur surgeon"
(Cowley 59).

     In fact, the worst vandalism is com-
mitted not by amateurs but by professional
diggers whose interests are entirely financial. Peter Hester, owner of the art gal-
lery Fourth World, expresses their
viewpoint:

> This [excavating Native American
> sites] is not a crime. . . . I
> excavated over a hundred ruins,
> big deal. I dug 185 pots in
> Arizona last year. When it comes
> to Southwest archeology, I'm the
> best. I'm one of the last out-
> laws, man. (Goodwin 86)

Rodriguez 12

"Few in the know would disagree with
him on either point," Goodwin comments
dryly (86).

The Archaeological Resources Protection Act was amended in 1988, lowering
the amount of theft or damage needed for
a felony prosecution from $5,000 to $500.
Many states have also passed laws protecting archaeological sites on state-owned
land and graves even on private land.
None of these laws, however, has succeeded in solving the problem. Providing
more money to educate the public about
the value and fragility of archaeological
sites and to enforce the present laws
would help, but not enough. A new federal
law is needed, making it a felony to excavate or otherwise disturb any Native
American site without the approval of
both a state government and any Native
American tribe concerned. This new law
would not solve enforcement problems but
would make it easier to punish criminals
who are now let off lightly by lenient
judges and juries. More importantly, it
would hinder the continuing desecration
of Native American graves on private
property. Archaeologist Keith Kintigh accurately describes the present situation:

> In the United States, which is
> not true of other countries, if
> you own a site, you can go out

Rodriguez 13

> with dynamite and blow it to
> kingdom-come, you can go out
> there with a backhoe, you can do
> whatever you want, pretty much.
> (Landers 37)

Newspaper and magazine articles on this issue have often asked "Who owns the past?" treating the question as if it cannot be answered. The answer, however, is simple: we all own the past, not to possess but to preserve for future generations. If the American past is not to be looted and vandalized, we must act quickly to assert our stewardship.

Rodriguez 14

Works Cited

"After Mining, a Furor Over a Shrine."
New York Times 3 Jan. 1991: A12.

Arden, Harvey. "Who Owns Our Past?" National Geographic Mar. 1989: 376-92.

Cowley, Geoffrey et al. "The Plunder of the Past." Newsweek 26 June 1989: 58-60.

Edwards, I. E. S. The Pyramids of Egypt. Harmondsworth, Eng.: Penguin, 1976.

Fagan, Brian. "Black Day at Slack Farm." Archaeology July-Aug. 1988: 15+.

Gibbs, Nancy. "This Land Is Their Land." Time 14 Jan. 1991: 18-19.

Goodwin, Derek V. "Raiders of the Sacred Sites." New York Times Magazine 7 Dec. 1986: 65+.

Landers, Robert K. "Is America Allowing Its Past to Be Stolen?" Editorial Research Reports 18 Jan. 1991: 34-47.

Marshall, Brenda K. "Native American Grave Sites at Risk." Progressive Jan. 1991: 14.

Meyer, Karl E. The Plundered Past. New York: Atheneum, 1973.

Stuart, George E. "The Battle to Save Our Past." National Geographic Mar. 1989: 392-93.

Woolley, Leonard. Digging Up the Past. 1930. Harmondsworth, Eng.: Penguin, 1937.

EXERCISE 3

Directions: Refer to the research paper above ("America's Past for Sale") to answer the following questions.

1. What is the thesis of the paper? _____

   _____

   _____

2. What is the meaning of the citations in parentheses in the first paragraph of the paper: (Arden 390) and (Landers 35)? _____

   _____

   _____

3. Why are some of the quotations indented? _____

4. Explain the square brackets ([]) around the first letter of the indented quotation on page 2. _____

   _____

   _____

5. What does ("After Mining"), on page 4, mean? _____

   _____

   _____

6. Why are no page numbers included in ("After Mining") and (Marshall) on page 4? _____

   _____

   _____

7. What is the main point of the paragraph that starts at the bottom of page 10? _____

   _____

   _____

8. Why is no citation provided for the proposed federal law described on page 12?

   _____

   _____

9. How many articles from periodicals are listed on the works cited page? ____ How many books are listed? ____

10. What does "15+" at the end of the citation for Brian Fagan's "Black Day at Slack Farm" signify? _____

_____

_____

A good research paper consists of a writer's own ideas supported by paraphrases and summaries of source material along with occasional well-chosen quotations. Material from sources should be incorporated smoothly into the paper, and documentation should be provided. In the documentation styles recommended by the Modern Language Association (MLA) and the American Psychological Association (APA), parenthetical citations within the body of a research paper refer to a works cited section (MLA) or references list (APA) included at the end of the research paper.

CHAPTER EXERCISE

I. MATCHING

Directions: Match each term on the list below with its definition by writing the correct letter in the space provided.

TERMS:

A. common knowledge

B. documentation

C. ellipsis

D. et al.

E. parenthetical citation

F. sic

DEFINITIONS:

_____ 1. dots indicating an omission from a quotation

_____ 2. a Latin word meaning "thus" which is added to a quotation to indicate that a mistake appears in the original

_____ 3. parenthetical citations and a works cited section or references list

_____ 4. information in parentheses about the source of wording or of an idea used in a research paper

_____ 5. information generally known or easily found in a number of sources

_____ 6. an abbreviation of a Latin phrase meaning "and others"

II. MULTIPLE CHOICE

Directions: On the line at the left write the letter of the phrase that best completes each item.

_____ 7. Quotations should take up

    A. one quarter or less of a research paper.

    B. about half of a research paper.

    C. at least three quarters of a research paper.

_____ 8. To punctuate a quotation, a writer should

    A. put a comma or period inside closing quotation marks.

    B. put a colon or semicolon inside closing quotation marks.

    C. put a period, question mark, or exclamation mark inside the closing quotation marks and add another period, question mark, or exclamation mark if the sentence as a whole requires it.

_____ 9. To indicate a quoted passage within a quotation,

    A. use double quotation marks to enclose both the quotation and the quotation within it.

    B. use single quotation marks to enclose the entire quotation and double quotation marks to enclose the quotation within the quotation.

    C. use single quotation marks for the quotation within the quotation and double quotation marks for the quotation as a whole.

_____ 10. Documentation is provided in order to

    A. demonstrate that a researcher is not including any of his or her own ideas in a research paper.

    B. indicate where a researcher found each item of information.

    C. prove that a researcher knows how to use a library.

_____ 11. An unsigned article

    A. should not be used in a research paper.

    B. should be alphabetized in a works cited section or references list under the first important word in its title.

    C. should not be mentioned in parenthetical citations.

_____12. In both MLA and APA styles, titles of books and periodicals listed in works cited sections or references lists

A. are enclosed in quotation marks.

B. are underlined.

C. are neither underlined nor enclosed in quotation marks.

III. TRUE OR FALSE

Directions: On each line at the left write T if an item is true and F if it is false.

_____13. To include a quotation in a paper, a writer can add introductory or explanatory wording before, after, or in the middle of the quoted material.

_____14. One good reason to use a direct quotation rather than a paraphrase or summary is the quotation's distinctive language.

_____15. Long quotations should be indented and enclosed in quotation marks.

_____16. Every citation within a research paper should have a corresponding entry in the works cited section or references list.

_____17. In both MLA and APA styles a parenthetical citation includes an author's last name and a publication date.

_____18. Items in a works cited section or references list should be given in the order in which they are cited within a paper.

_____19. In APA style an entry on a references list ordinarily begins with an author's name followed by the publication date.

_____20. In works cited sections or references lists, articles from weekly or monthly magazines are listed in the same format as articles from scholarly journals.

Glossary

Abstracts are brief summaries of articles and books; abstracts are available in data bases and printed sources such as *Biological Abstracts*.

An *ad hominem* **attack** is a way of arguing against a claim by attacking the person who made it. *Ad hominem*, which is Latin for "to the person," generally describes a personal attack on anyone, male or female, but *ad feminam* is sometimes used to describe a personal attack on a woman.

An *ad misericordiam* **appeal** is a way of playing on people's compassion instead of supplying evidence to support a claim. *Ad misericordiam* is Latin for "to pity."

An *ad populum* **appeal** is an emotional appeal to a group's shared beliefs and prejudices. *Ad populum* is Latin for "to the people."

Aesthetics is a branch of philosophy concerned with determining standards of beauty and excellence in the arts.

Agreement is correspondence in person, number, and gender. A subject and verb agree when they are both singular or both plural. Pronouns should agree with their antecedents in person, number, and gender.

An **analogy** compares objects or ideas that are not ordinarily associated with one another.

Analyzing means breaking up a whole into its parts, identifying the parts, and describing how they relate to each other.

Annotating a source involves underlining its key passages and jotting notes in the margins.

Antecedents are the words to which pronouns refer.

An **appeal to anonymous authorities** is a claim that one or more unidentified experts hold a particular view.

A statement is **arguable** if it expresses a controversial point of view that a person can support (or argue against) by providing evidence.

Arguing from ignorance is suggesting that a claim must be true because no one can prove that it is false or false because no one can prove that it is true.

Argument is a form of persuasion; it is the process of making a point and trying to convince other people that the point is worthy of belief by providing support for it.

Backing, according to Stephen Toulmin, is support that justifies a warrant.

The **bandwagon** technique is the suggestion that a product, candidate, or cause merits support because large numbers of other people already support it.

Begging the question is taking for granted a point that is open to dispute. Here *begging* means "evading" or "dodging" the responsibility to support an assumption.

Bias is prejudice.

A **bibliography** is a list of books, articles, and other materials on a particular subject; bibliographies range in size from a few items at the end of an encyclopedia entry to a large volume.

Brainstorming is a prewriting technique that involves jotting down a list of ideas on a particular issue in order to focus thinking, reveal possible topics for further writing, and gather support for general ideas.

The **burden of proof** is the obligation to support a claim with evidence. For example, a prosecuting attorney must prove that someone accused of a crime is guilty; that is, the burden of proof rests on the prosecution.

A **call number** is the combination of letters and numbers that indicates a book's location in a library.

A **card catalog** is a file containing at least one index card for every book and periodical a library owns. Typically a book is listed under its author's name, its title, and one or more subject headings.

A **cause-effect argument** explains why something has happened or probably will happen.

Chronological order is organization based on the time sequence in which events occurred.

A **claim** is an arguable statement.

A **claim of fact** is an arguable statement about information that can be proven true or false.

A **claim of policy** is a proposal that something should either be done or not done.

A **claim of value** is a judgment about whether something is good or bad, right or wrong, or worthwhile or not worthwhile.

Classifying is grouping objects and ideas into categories based on characteristics they have in common and labeling the groups.

Clichés are expressions such as "blind as a bat" that have been used so often they have lost their freshness and power to communicate precisely.

Closed stacks are library shelves researchers cannot search through themselves; to obtain needed materials, they must fill out call slips and submit them to a library employee.

Clustering is a way of gathering thoughts by drawing a diagram that illustrates the relationships between groups of ideas; since the finished diagram looks like a spider web or a road map, clustering is also known as webbing or mapping.

Coherent means containing clear connections between ideas. Adding transitional words and phrases, repeating key words, and using parallel sentence structure ensure coherence.

A **colloquialism** is a word or phrase such as *giveaway* which is appropriate to casual speech.

Common knowledge includes facts most readers would know as well as information readily found in a variety of sources. In a research paper, information classified as common knowledge does not need to be cited.

Comparing and contrasting involve showing how two or more objects or ideas are similar and different. Comparison emphasizes similarities and contrast emphasizes differences, but comparisons and contrasts are usually intertwined so that similarities, differences, and equivalences are discussed within a single argument.

Concise writing conveys information briefly.

A **conclusion**, in deductive reasoning, is the part of a syllogism that follows logically from the premises.

A **conflict of interest** is a clash between an authority's responsibility to seek the truth and his or her personal benefit.

Connotations are the positive or negative feelings associated with a word.

A **counterclaim** is an expression of opinion that directly contradicts a claim. Being able to state a strong counterclaim is an indication of having written an arguable thesis.

Criteria are standards used as the basis for an evaluation.

Critical listening and reading involve looking carefully at both the strengths and weaknesses of arguments and evaluating the arguments conscientiously and impartially.

Data is another term for evidence used to support a claim.

Data bases are collections of information stored by computer and organized to make searching for and retrieving data as rapid as possible.

A **debate** is a formal discussion in which people (or teams) with opposing views appeal to third parties (voters or judges) to determine which side has argued a public question more effectively.

Deduction is the process of drawing conclusions based on the relationship between premises.

Defining is establishing what a word or phrase means. It is often an essential first step that establishes the boundaries within which an argument will take place.

Denotation is the meaning of a word independent of its emotional associations.

Digressions are passages unrelated to a main idea.

A **discovery draft** is a very rough version of an argument intended to help its author determine what he or she wants to say.

Documentation informs readers about the sources of all ideas and wording a writer has obtained from other authors. A research paper requires two types of documentation: citations in parentheses and a works cited section or references list.

Doublespeak is intentionally misleading language.

Drafting is writing a preliminary version (a rough draft) of a paper.

Editing is making writing as clear and correct as possible.

Editorials are short argumentative essays presenting and supporting the opinions of a publication's editors or editorial board.

An **either-or dilemma** (also known as a false dilemma) suggests that there are only two possibilities when more than two exist.

An **Ellipsis**, three dots with a space before and after each one (. . .), is used to indicate the omission of unneeded material from a quotation. When an ellipsis comes at the end of a sentence, a fourth dot is included to serve as a period.

Emphatic order is the organization of main points according to their importance, either from least to most important or from most to least important.

An **enthymeme** is a syllogism in which one of the premises or the conclusion is not stated.

Equivocation means using a term in two senses. The use of the word *faithful* in the statements "I promise that I will be faithful to you. I'll always give you a faithful account of my activities, no matter what they are" is an example of equivocation.

Essays are short works of nonfiction expressing personal viewpoints.

Et al. is an abbreviation of the Latin phrase *et alia*, which means "and others." Et al. is used in research papers in parenthetical citations and in works cited sections and references lists.

Ethics are standards of conduct that apply in a particular kind of activity, for example, in business or professions such as medicine and law.

Ethnocentrism is the assumption that the values of one's own culture apply throughout the world.

Etymology is the history of words. The word *etymology* comes from two Greek words, *etymos* ("true") and *logos* ("word").

A **euphemism** (derived from the Greek words *eu*, meaning "pleasant," and *phēmē*, meaning "speech") is a word or phrase that takes the place of a term with unpleasant or offensive connotations.

Evaluating means judging what something is worth. Evaluations are based on moral, ethical, aesthetic, or practical considerations.

Expert testimony consists of judgments and interpretations of data by qualified people.

A **fact** is an item of information that can be proven true.

A **fallacy** (from the Latin word *fallere*, "to deceive") is a mistake in reasoning that distracts from careful analysis of issues and hinders problem solving.

A **false analogy** is a comparison between situations that are similar only in trivial or irrelevant ways.

A **formal definition** consists of putting a word into a class or category and then telling how it differs from others in the same class.

A **formal outline** is a balanced, carefully written plan consisting of progressively indented elements labeled with a standard sequence of roman and arabic letters and capital and lower case numbers.

Freewriting is a prewriting technique that consists of putting down words without pausing to think; it summons up half-forgotten incidents and ideas and helps writers make sense out of new events and unfamiliar concepts.

Glittering generalities are vague positive words or expressions such as *great* or *healthy* used as part or all of the evidence intended to support a claim.

A **hasty generalization** is a conclusion based on too few specific examples.

A **hypothesis** is a tentative assumption that will be tested by collecting evidence.

A **hypothetical example** is an incident or circumstance that did not occur but might have occurred or could occur at any time.

Immediate causes are causes close in time to the effects they produce. For example, the immediate cause of a forest fire might be a dropped match.

Incubating is taking time away from writing so that new ideas and solutions to writing problems can evolve.

Indexes are lists of articles that have appeared in a particular range of periodicals or in a particular field over a specific period of time. The *Readers' Guide to Periodical Literature* and the *Humanities Index* are examples.

Induction is the process by which people reach general conclusions based on particular facts, examples, or other evidence.

Inferences are interpretations of facts. Inferences are arguable.

An **informal outline** is an indented list of main ideas and key supporting details arranged as they will appear in an argument. Because it is strictly a planning tool, it need not be labeled with letters and numbers and can contain complete sentences as well as phrases and single words.

Jargon is specialized vocabulary (such as *myocardial infarction*) understood by people who have studied a particular discipline but not necessarily clear to outsiders.

A **journal** is a record of someone's thoughts about events and issues; journal entries are often informal, personal, and experimental.

A **judgment** is an evaluation based on ideals or philosophical beliefs. Judgments are arguable.

To **justify** text is to space it so that the ends of the lines are even. The left margin but not the right margin of a typed or word processed paper should be justified.

A **loaded question** is a question based on an assumed answer to another, unasked question. An example is "Have you stopped beating your spouse?"

Loaded words and phrases, such as "Only a fool would believe . . . ," have unfair implications that make it difficult to disagree with the claims in which they appear.

A **major premise** is the more general of the two statements that begin a syllogism. In a valid syllogism the major premise always contains the word or words in the predicate (the last part) of the syllogism's conclusion.

A **mean** is an amount found by adding a group of numbers and dividing the sum by the number of items in the group.

A **median** is the middle number in a series of numbers.

A **minor premise** is the second statement in a syllogism. It is more specific than the major premise, and it contains the grammatical subject of the syllogism's conclusion.

A **mode** is the number that occurs most frequently in a group of numbers.

Moral evaluations are judgments about whether particular kinds of conduct, especially the conduct of individuals, are right or wrong.

Negation is pointing out what something is not. In a definition, negation can be used to correct commonly held but limited or erroneous views of a word's meaning.

A **non sequitur** is a response that does not follow logically from what has previously been said or written.

Note cards are 3 x 5-inch or 4 x 6-inch index cards used mostly to record paraphrases and summaries of resource material. Each card should include a subject heading, the last name of the author of the source being used, and the page number on which material was found.

Occam's Razor is the principle that of two good explanations for an event or situation, the simpler one is better. It is attributed to the English philosopher William of Occam (c. 1290–c. 1349), who wrote, "It is vain to do with more what can be done with fewer."

The **op-ed** or commentary page is the newspaper page opposite the editorial page. It is devoted to columnists and other contributors of interpretative essays.

Open stacks are library shelves researchers can browse through to locate materials.

An **overview** is a general idea of what to expect in a written argument. To get an overview of an argument, read its preface or introduction, glance through the argument itself to determine its main points and general organization, and look at illustrations and other special features.

Parallel means expressed in the same grammatical form. Using parallel form makes ideas easier to understand and remember.

Paraphrases are restatements in a researcher's own words of ideas from source materials.

Parenthetical citations are references in parentheses indicating where information used in a research paper was found. In MLA style, a parenthetical citation usually contains an author's last name and a page number; an APA citation includes an author's last name and the date of publication along with a page number if a direct quotation is being cited.

Peer critics are fellow students or colleagues who read or listen to written work and usually respond to it by suggesting additional support for a thesis, providing leads to new supporting evidence, or pointing up flaws in reasoning.

Person is a grammatical term that indicates the distinction between a person speaking (first person), a person being spoken to (second person), and a person or people being spoken about (third person). First-person pronouns (such as *I* and *we*) and second-person pronouns (such as *you* and *your*) are common in informal writing.

A **personal preference** is an opinion based entirely on an individual's tastes. It is not arguable.

Persuasion is convincing someone that a point of view is sound (and perhaps that action should be taken based on that view). It can be carried out through manipulation and trickery as well as through argument.

A **persuasive definition** is an argument that a term should have a particular meaning.

Plagiarism (from the Latin word *plagium*, which means "kidnapping") is presenting another person's words or ideas as one's own. Deliberate plagiarism is highly unethical and can lead to severe penalties.

Plain folks is the strategy of associating products, ideas, or candidates with seemingly ordinary people who recommend them.

Poisoning the well is a type of personal attack in which someone suggests at the beginning of an argument that any evidence coming from a particular source will be contaminated like water that comes from a poisoned well.

A *post hoc* **fallacy** (based on *post hoc, ergo propter hoc,* a Latin phrase meaning "after this, therefore because of this") is the assumption that because one event happened before another, the first event caused the second one.

A **precedent** is a past occurrence that can be used to justify a recommendation.

Premises are sentences which state points that are the basis for an argument.

Prewriting, the first stage of the writing process, involves thinking about a subject and gathering material. Keeping a journal, talking about writing, freewriting, brainstorming, asking questions, and drawing diagrams are prewriting techniques.

A **primary source** is a record of a person's own experiences or observations. The diary of a Civil War soldier, an interview with a police officer, and a creative work are primary sources.

Proofreading is checking to make sure no errors appear in the final form of a paper.

A **qualifier** is a word such as "probably" or "many" that limits the scope of a claim.

A **question-begging definition** is an arguable definition presented as if it were a statement of fact.

Rationalization is finding reasons to justify what we want to believe and tricking ourselves into thinking the reasons are good ones.

Reciprocal cause-effect relationships are situations in which effects act upon their causes. For example, a school may influence a community at the same time that the community influences the school.

Recommending means proposing changes in people's attitudes or actions. A recommendation usually includes a description of what is wrong, a proposal for action to solve the problem, an explanation of the benefits that would result from adopting the proposal, and a refutation of possible objections to the proposal.

A **red herring** is a remark that causes a discussion to head in an irrelevant direction.

Reductio ad absurdum (Latin: "reduction to absurdity") is a way of demonstrating the unreasonableness of an opponent's claim by pretending to accept the claim and then extending it to nonsensical lengths.

Redundancy is unneeded repetition.

Reference books are publications such as encyclopedias, dictionaries, atlases, and yearbooks that are consulted to find facts or brief summaries of information quickly and easily; they cannot be checked out of libraries.

A **references list** is the concluding part of a research paper written in APA documentation style. It provides information about the paper's sources.

Refutation provides reasons for rejecting all or part of an opponent's argument.

Regionalisms are terms such as *goober* ("peanut") and *tonic* ("soft drink") that are common only to limited geographical areas; they are considered acceptable in the speech of particular regions but not in writing.

Register refers to the varieties of language that fit particular occasions or subjects. The three registers (formal, middle, and informal) require different kinds of vocabulary, punctuation, and sentence and paragraph length.

Remote causes are causes distant in time from their effects.

A **report** presents information on a specified topic but usually not the writer's own opinion. It is often based on sources.

A **research log** is a notebook containing a cumulative record of work done on a research project; the log is not used for material that will be included in the paper itself.

A **research paper** is a long formal paper that supports a thesis and is based on a variety of sources.

Restrictions, according to Stephen Toulmin, are statements of exceptional conditions under which claims do not apply.

Revising is a stage in the writing process based on an overall analysis of a draft's effectiveness. Revising is likely to involve changes that affect an argument's content while editing is concerned with particulars such as sentence completeness and correct spelling.

A **rough draft** is an early version of a written argument.

A **run-on sentence** consists of two separate sentences (independent clauses), each with its own subject and verb, that are incorrectly punctuated to suggest that they form a single sentence.

Scanning is glancing quickly over printed material to find particular items of information such as names, dates, and key words.

A **search strategy** is a systematic approach to selecting and using sources.

A **secondary source** is the work of a researcher who has analyzed and evaluated primary sources or other secondary sources. A historian's book about the Civil War, a criminal justice textbook, and an essay on the Mona Lisa are secondary sources.

A **sentence fragment** is an incomplete sentence. To correct a sentence fragment, add the missing words or attach the fragment to the preceding or following sentence.

A **sentence outline** is a formal outline in which all the elements are complete sentences.

Sexist language is wording (such as *mankind* instead of *humanity*) that reveals a bias against one sex, usually females, by implying that only males or females ought to fill certain roles or possess certain characteristics; sexist language can cause offense and should be avoided.

Sic, a Latin word meaning "thus," may be added to a quotation containing a mistake to show that the error occurs in the original.

Signs are indications assumed to accompany certain events. For example, a flock of geese flying overhead is assumed to be a sign of the changing seasons.

Slang is a very informal colloquialism such as *humongous* or *freaked out*. In written argument, slang can make writing seem dated or confusing.

Slanting is distorting information to reflect a particular point of view.

The **slippery slope fallacy**, also known as "the domino theory," is a faulty assumption that an early error (like a false step at the top of a slippery slope) will inevitably lead to a bad outcome.

Source cards are index cards on which researchers record the data needed for a research paper's works cited section or references list.

Spatial order means organization in terms of space.

Special pleading is presenting only favorable information while ignoring equally valid material that would weaken a case.

Statistics represent information in the form of numbers (either totals or percentages).

Stereotypes are oversimplified generalizations based on insufficient evidence.

A **stipulative definition** is an announcement that a speaker or writer will use a term in a specific way. Such a definition is not explained or defended.

A **straw man** (or straw figure) is a weak argument attributed to an opponent and attacked as if it had really been made; it can also be an unimportant aspect of an opponent's argument attacked as if it were the main point.

Style consists of a writer's characteristic decisions about what words to use and how to combine them in sentences and paragraphs.

A **subtitle** is a secondary, explanatory title that limits or expands upon a title. In academic writing a subtitle follows a colon, not a semicolon or dash.

A **sufficient cause** is a cause adequate by itself to produce an effect. When a sufficient cause occurs, its effect necessarily follows.

Summaries are very condensed statements in a researcher's own words of main ideas from sources.

A **syllogism** is a concise form of deductive argument in which two statements (premises) lead logically to a third statement, called a conclusion.

Synthesizing (which comes from a Greek word meaning "put together") creates new meaning by restructuring information in terms of broad connections among its parts.

Tenses are verb forms (such as the past tense or the present tense) that indicate when actions take place.

Terms are the grammatical subjects or predicates of the statements in a syllogism. In a valid syllogism each term appears twice.

A **testimonial** is an endorsement of a product or viewpoint, often by a prominent person.

A **thesis** is a clear statement of an argument's claim; it is either stated directly or strongly implied.

Tone is the quality of speech and writing that reveals people's attitudes toward their subjects, their audiences, and themselves.

A **topic outline** is a formal outline consisting of words or phrases, not complete sentences.

A **topic sentence** is a general sentence that limits and controls the material in a paragraph. A topic sentence usually begins a paragraph, but it can appear in the middle or at the end or be omitted entirely.

Transfer is the association of a product or idea with an image that people already feel strongly about.

Transitional words and phrases (such as *however*, *for example*, and *on the other hand*) are terms that explicitly point out the relationships between ideas.

Tree diagrams (also known as issue trees or topic trees) are drawings in which words and branching lines illustrate the relationships between ideas.

A *tu quoque* **argument** is the claim that someone is guilty of the same bad behavior he or she criticizes. *Tu quoque* is Latin for "you [do it] too."

Turning the tables is using the same evidence an opponent does but showing that it leads to a very different conclusion.

An **unqualified generalization** is a statement without such limiting words as *probably* or *usually*. An unqualified generalization allows for no exceptions, so it is not always accurate. The Latin phrase *dicto simpliciter* ("something said [too] simply") refers to an unqualified generalization.

A **usage label** is a term or abbreviation included in a dictionary entry to indicate that a word or a particular use of a word is not standard.

Valid, when applied to a syllogism, means that the syllogism contains premises that must lead to its conclusion. A valid syllogism is logically correct.

Verification is the process of confirming that a statement is true.

A **warrant** is a general statement that provides a link between an argument's data and its claim.

A **working title** is a preliminary designation that establishes the boundaries of a writing topic. After a paper is finished, the working title is often replaced by a more accurate or more interesting title.

A **works cited section** is the concluding part of a research paper written in MLA documentation style. It provides information about the paper's sources.

Writer's block is a temporary inability to put words on paper.

The **writing process** is a series of mental and physical steps (prewriting, drafting, revising, editing, and proofreading) that lead to a finished piece of writing.

Resources for Writers

The books listed below provide additional help for writers.

Barnet, Sylvan, and Hugo Bedau, eds. *Current Issues and Enduring Questions: Methods and Models of Argument*. 2nd ed. Boston: Bedford, 1990.

Cook, Claire Kehrwald. *Line by Line: How to Improve Your Own Writing*. Boston: Houghton, 1985.

Damer, T. Edward. *Attacking Faulty Reasoning*. Belmont, CA: Wadsworth, 1980.

Daniels, Barbara J., and David I. Daniels. *English Grammar*. New York: Harper-Collins, 1991.

Elbow, Peter. *Writing with Power: Techniques for Mastering the Writing Process*. New York: Oxford UP, 1981.

Fahnestock, Jeanne, and Marie Secor. *A Rhetoric of Argument*. 2nd ed. New York: McGraw, 1990.

Fisher, Alec. *The Logic of Real Arguments*. Cambridge: Cambridge UP, 1988.

Fowler, H. Ramsey, and Jane E. Aaron. *Little Brown Handbook*. 5th ed. New York: HarperCollins, 1992.

Gibaldi, Joseph, and Walter S. Achtert. *MLA Handbook for Writers of Research Papers*. 3rd ed. New York: MLA, 1988.

Govier, Trudy. *A Practical Study of Argument*. 2nd ed. Belmont, CA: Wadsworth, 1988.

Huff, Darrell. *How to Lie with Statistics*. New York: Norton, 1954.

Johnson, Jean. *The Bedford Guide to the Research Process*. 2nd ed. Boston: Bedford, 1992.

Kahane, Howard. *Logic and Contemporary Rhetoric: The Use of Reason in Everyday Life*. 5th ed. Belmont, CA: Wadsworth, 1988.

Lutz, William. *Doublespeak*. New York: HarperCollins, 1989.

Miller, Casey, and Kate Swift. *The Handbook of Nonsexist Writing*. 2nd ed. New York: HarperCollins, 1988.

Miller, Robert K. *The Informed Argument: A Multidisciplinary Reader and Guide*. 3rd ed. Fort Worth: Harcourt, 1992.

Publication Manual of the American Psychological Association. 3rd ed. Washington: APA, 1984.

Strunk, William, Jr., and E. B. White. *The Elements of Style*. 3rd ed. New York: Macmillan, 1979.

Toulmin, Stephen Edelston. *The Uses of Argument*. Cambridge: Cambridge UP, 1964.

Troyka, Lynn Quitman, Emily R. Gordon, and Ann B. Dobie. *Simon & Schuster Handbook for Writers*. 2nd ed. Englewood Cliffs, NJ: Prentice-Hall, 1990.

Waldrep, Tom, ed. *Writers on Writing*. New York: Random, 1985.

Weidenborner, Stephen, and Domenick Caruso. *Writing Research Papers: A Guide to the Process*. 3rd ed. New York: St. Martin's, 1989.

Willard, Charles Arthur. *A Theory of Argumentation*. Tuscaloosa: U of Alabama, 1989.

Answers

Chapter 1

Try It Out
Answers will vary.

Exercise 1

1. NA	6. A
2. A	7. A
3. NA	8. NA
4. A	9. A
5. NA	10. NA

Exercise 2

1. W	6. S
2. S	7. W
3. S	8. S
4. W	9. S
5. W	10. W

Exercise 3
Answers will vary. Sample questions follow.
1. What problems do tumbleweeds cause? In what sense can they be considered an ally?
2. What is the tough law? How is this law being tested?
3. Who are the outcast Americans? How can their rightful place in society be restored to them?
4. What will the second space age involve? How will it be different from the first space age?
5. Who was Paul Gauguin? In what ways was Gauguin a rebel?
6. What kinds of hate are found on college campuses? What can be done about hatred on college campuses?
7. What are school vouchers for? What doubts have been raised about them?
8. Who are the black poet and white critic? What is the relationship between them?
9. Why do investors need relief? What kind of relief will they get?
10. In what sense is justice blinded? What should be done about it?

Exercise 4
Answers will vary. Sample answers follow.
1. a. I think wolves are fierce, dangerous animals uncommon in North America. I haven't heard about the controversy over reintroducing them to Yellowstone.

    b. Why should wolves be reintroduced to Yellowstone? How do the people who live near Yellowstone feel about the reintroduction of wolves?
2. Despite the occasional problems this reintroduction may cause, it deserves vigorous public support.
3. I'd back up this thesis with information on how wolves aren't as dangerous as people think they are.

    I'd explain that wolves would restore the balance of nature.

    I'd try to find experts who support bringing wolves back to Yellowstone.

5. Underlined transitions: *however* (paragraph 2), *first* (paragraph 3), *therefore* (paragraph 3), *second* (paragraph 4), *third* (paragraph 5), *however* (paragraph 5), *for example* (paragraph 6), *As a result* (paragraph 6), *However* (paragraph 7), *Nevertheless* (paragraph 7), *however* (paragraph 8), *On the other hand* (paragraph 8), *In fact* (paragraph 9)

6. Section 1: paragraph 1—introduction and thesis

Section 2: paragraphs 2 and 3—historical justification

Section 3: paragraph 4—benefits to prey species

Section 4: paragraph 5—ecological benefits

Section 5: paragraph 6—precedents for reintroduction

Section 6: paragraph 7, 8, and 9—refutation of opposing views

Section 7: paragraph 10—conclusion and restatement of key points

7. The author basically does what I expected but did not refer to very many experts. I'd rely more on experts' opinions, but I don't think there are serious problems in the essay. I didn't anticipate the author's historical argument or the ideas about benefits to prey species. I wouldn't have thought of these ideas myself.

8. Yes. Describing the reintroductions in North Carolina and Minnesota is a good way to respond to opponents. Paragraphs 7, 8, and 9 do a good job of responding to objections by hunters, ranchers, and other nearby residents.

9. yes, yes, yes, yes

10. After studying the essay I somewhat agree with the author's thesis (paragraph 1). I disagree with the idea that wolves should be returned to the park just because they were once there (paragraph 3). I thought the ideas on wolves benefiting the deer, elk, and bison were the best part of the argument (paragraph 4). Paragraph 5 seems weaker. It's based more on vague generalities, not specific facts. Paragraphs 6, 7, and 8 do a good job of responding to opposing views. I basically accept the ideas in them, but I'm not sure how I'd feel if I were one of the people directly involved.

11. Yes. The essay is effective because it contains so much specific information about wolves. I also think it's clearly organized.

Chapter Exercise

1. A		11. M
2. K		12. L
3. E		13. C
4. P		14. B
5. J		15. A
6. F		16. A
7. G		17. B
8. D		18. C
9. B		19. A
10. O		20. B

Chapter 2

Exercise 1

1. is learning to play a musical instrument
2. has a double wedding ring pattern
3. People who have traveled abroad several times are sophisticated.
4. Martin is a member of a fraternity.
5. Divorced people are lonely.

Try It Out

Answers will vary. Sample answers follow.
1. Almost certainly
2. presumably
3. probably
4. Most
5. seem to
6. often
7. usually
8. somewhat
9. main
10. apparently

Exercise 2

1. P		6. F
2. V		7. P
3. F		8. V
4. P		9. V
5. P		10. F

Exercise 3

1. L		6. E
2. K		7. A
3. I		8. F
4. D		9. M
5. C		10. J

Chapter Exercise

1. I	11. K
2. E	12. A
3. H	13. L
4. N	14. M
5. J	15. G
6. P	16. C
7. F	17. C
8. C	18. B
9. D	19. A
10. Q	20. A

Chapter 3

Try It Out

Answers will vary. Sample claims follow.
1. Drunk drivers who kill people should be given long sentences.
2. The governor's new reform proposals should be rejected.
3. Cuts in federal funding for effective crime-fighting programs are responsible for our city's increase in crime.
4. Women should allow men to make their decisions for them.
5. People should pay more attention to children's needs.
6. This country should establish a voluntary national service program.

Part II Answers will vary.

Exercise 1

1A. claim	6A. warrant
1B. warrant	6B. data
1C. data	6C. claim
2A. data	7A. data
2B. warrant	7B. warrant
2C. claim	7C. claim
3A. claim	8A. warrant
3B. data	8B. claim
3C. warrant	8C. data
4A. data	9A. claim
4B. claim	9B. warrant
4C. warrant	9C. data
5A. claim	10A. data
5B. data	10B. warrant
5C. warrant	10C. claim

Exercise 2

Answers will vary. Sample answers follow.
1. Explain that one person's experience with astrology is not enough evidence to prove that astrology is legitimate. Point out that "certainly" is too strong.
2. Give examples of effective lectures. Provide evidence that college students do learn from lectures.
3. Point out that making such a large, sudden change in the minimum wage is not practical. Suggest that an increased minimum wage might require many businesses to fire workers.
4. Show that legalizing drugs may lead to more addiction, that the high cost of illegal drugs is not the only cause of the high crime rate, and that the power of organized crime does not depend entirely on illegal drugs.
5. Point out that ridiculing one's opponents by calling them idiots offends readers. Instead, ask the arguer to provide supporting evidence for the claim that car theft can't be stopped.
6. Suggest that bringing all nonparticipants to court at once would overburden the court system and create an image problem for the recycling program.
7. Show that the national anthem is not hard to sing or that even if it is, mere difficulty is not a good enough reason to defy tradition by changing the time-honored national anthem.
8. Give other reasons mothers of young children work, such as that single parents must support their children and that some couples cannot pay for necessities on a single income.
9. Point out that prohibiting traffic in central business districts might lead to a decline in business for stores and restaurants and would overcrowd mass transit systems. Also suggest that the lack of traffic on shopping streets might lead to increased crime, especially at night.
10. Show that the arguer's criteria for judging the music of today is flawed or that today's music fits his or her criteria better than the music of the fifties does.

Chapter Exercise

1. D	11. K
2. J	12. C
3. C	13. B
4. E	14. C
5. F	15. B
6. G	16. C
7. B	17. A
8. A	18. B
9. I	19. C
10. H	20. C

Chapter 4

Try It Out

Answers will vary.

Exercise 1

Answers will vary. Sample answers follow.

1. immediate: <u>S</u> Lightning struck a tree in the forest. Too little water was available to fight the fire.
   remote: A drought had made the forest very dry. Budget cuts had prevented local fire companies from replacing outdated equipment.
2. immediate: <u>S</u> The driver was too drunk to control the vehicle. <u>S</u> The van's steering mechanism was defective.
   remote: The curve was too sharp because the road had been poorly planned. Bad design made the van unstable.
3. immediate: The student studied hard for the exams. The student cheated.
   remote: The student had an excellent background from past math courses. The student had taken calculus before.
4. immediate: The man ignored a "Beware—Dangerous Dog" sign. The man kicked the dog.
   remote: The man had gotten in the habit of crossing his neighbor's lawn when previous owners had lived there. <u>S</u> The dog had been trained to attack trespassers.
5. immediate: The two members of rival gangs quarreled. Both gang members were carrying guns.
   remote: <u>R</u> Previous shootings had led to a desire for revenge. Illegal guns were easy to obtain in the gang members' city.

6. immediate: <u>S</u> An accidental chemical spill polluted the river. <u>S</u> A devastating illness attacked the fish.
   remote: The laws against transporting and disposing of dangerous chemicals were poorly enforced. The level of pollution in the river was already high, making the fish vulnerable to any additional risk.
7. immediate: The teenager just received money for a birthday present. The teenager needs the shoes for a big game tonight.
   remote: <u>R</u> Most of the teenager's friends have new shoes of the same brand. Advertising for this type of shoe had created a desire for the shoes in the teenager.
8. immediate: <u>S</u> A workman knocked down a supporting wall. <u>S</u> A massive earthquake caused the ground underneath the building to cave in.
   remote: Inferior concrete had been used in the original construction. Construction adjacent to the building had weakened its foundation.
9. immediate: The pitcher threw a no-hitter. <u>S</u> The opponents failed to appear and lost by forfeit.
   remote: <u>R</u> A series of excellent seasons made it easy to recruit top players. Years of playing on community teams had given the local players excellent softball skills.
10. immediate: <u>S</u> A major newspaper featured a very enthusiastic review of the restaurant. The owner recently cut prices for most food items.
   remote: <u>R</u> Satisfied customers told their friends how much they liked the restaurant. The chef received excellent training at a cooking school in Italy.

Exercise 2

1. analysis	6. synthesis
2. analysis	7. synthesis
3. synthesis	8. analysis
4. synthesis	9. synthesis
5. analysis	10. synthesis

Exercise 3

1. must	6. should (not)
2. should	7. urges
3. endorses, proposal	8. must
4. support	9. ought
5. ought	10. should (not)

Chapter Exercise

1. E
2. B
3. D
4. P
5. I
6. N
7. O
8. C
9. Q
10. H
11. G
12. J
13. A
14. F
15. M
16. A
17. B
18. A
19. C
20. C

Chapter 5

Exercise 1

1. -, +, +, -
2. +, +, -, +
3. +, +, -, -
4. -, -, +, +
5. -, -, -, +
6. -, +, +, -
7. +, -, +, -
8. -, +, -, +
9. -, -, +, +
10. -, -, +. +

Try It Out

Answers will vary. Sample answers follow.

Synonym

1. A good synonym for *dedication* is "commitment."

Examples

2. Some examples of dedication are a student studying all night for an exam, a lawyer worrying about a client's case during a dinner party, an artist working for years on a single painting, and parents nursing their child through an illness.

Attributes

3. Some attributes (qualities) associated with dedication are caring, self-sacrifice, loyalty, faithfulness, and diligence.

Negation

4. Although some people think differently, dedication is not mindless commitment to a person or a cause.

Etymology

5. The word *dedication* comes from the Latin language and originally meant an act of proclaiming one's devotion (usually to a god).

yes

Stipulation

6. If I needed a stipulative definition of *dedication* to use in an argument, I would define it as a constantly renewed commitment to achieve a goal that one values highly.

Formal Definition

7. Dedication is an attitude of complete devotion.

Evaluation

Answers will vary.

Exercise 2

1. D
2. D
3. A
4. D
5. C
6. A
7. D
8. A
9. C
10. A

Exercise 3

1. bird, (egret), heron, ibis, spoonbill
2. game, bridge, (canasta), cribbage, hearts
3. (insect), fly, grasshopper, lace-wing, midge
4. mineral, diamond, garnet, (mica), quartz
5. fish, carp, flounder, (grayling), haddock

Exercise 4

1. B
2. A
3. D
4. A
5. B
6. C
7. D
8. C
9. D
10. A

Chapter Exercise

1. C
2. D
3. B
4. G
5. F
6. J
7. E
8. H
9. I
10. A
11. B
12. C
13. A
14. B
15. T
16. T
17. F
18. T
19. F
20. T

Chapter 6

Try It Out

Answers will vary. Sample answers for Part I
follow.

1. slender	6. touchy
2. nosy	7. pretty
3. careless	8. original
4. gaudy	9. rigid
5. cheap	10. determined

Part II Answers will vary.

Exercise 1

1. A	6. B
2. C	7. A
3. A	8. B
4. A	9. A
5. C	10. B

Exercise 2

1. C	6. A
2. C	7. A
3. A	8. B
4. B	9. A
5. B	10. B

Exercise 3

1. A	6. A
2. B	7. C
3. A	8. B
4. A	9. A
5. C	10. B

Exercise 4

1. B	6. A
2. A	7. C
3. C	8. A
4. A	9. A
5. B	10. A

Exercise 5

1. The speaker is using a key term in two different senses. The first time the word *liberty* is used it means "personal freedom." The second time it means "violation of standard practice."
2. A discussion of one issue (racism) should not be sidetracked by a discussion of another issue (mass transportation).
3. A weak hypothetical argument is attributed to an opponent (an attack on the Olympic logo)

while stronger arguments against U. S. participation in the Olympics go unanswered.
4. Although a knowledge of science is important, knowledge of how to read and write is far more basic. The two kinds of knowledge aren't as similar as the speaker is suggesting they are.
5. Appealing to nameless authorities is less convincing than identifying them and letting readers judge whether they really are leading experts in their field.
6. A candidate's previous experience is relevant only if it will enable him or her to perform well in office. While Byler's previous work experience may make him sympathetic to working people, he appears to have no managerial or governmental experience.
7. Perhaps this situation can be resolved through negotiations in which some of the workers' demands are met. There needn't be only two possibilities.
8. In a contest restricted to people from a particular area, an outsider, however good, should not be eligible for a prize.
9. Ms. Rainer's proposal should be judged on its merits. The speaker's personal attack on her isn't relevant to the issue.
10. Other explanations may account for the decline in Billy's grades, such as unhappiness at home or some other distraction.

Chapter Exercise

1. J	11. E
2. G	12. L
3. M	13. N
4. P	14. Q
5. F	15. I
6. K	16. A
7. A	17. C
8. S	18. A
9. C	19. C
10. D	20. A

Chapter 7

A Writing Questionnaire

Answers will vary. Probably no one will answer "always" to every question, but the more "often" or "always" answers you have, the more comfortable you feel with the writing process. Try retaking the questionnaire after completing the remaining chapters of this book to check your progress.

Exercise 1

Answers will vary. Sample answers follow.

I think now that both opinions were based on hasty generalizations. Probably consumer groups, such as the publishers of *Consumer Reports* magazine, have done some real research on this issue. I don't think that any single consumer could compare enough generic products with name brand products to argue knowledgeably one way or the other.

1. The woman's side might be easier to support. Since generic products are often manufactured by the same companies that make the corresponding name brand products, the main difference between the two may be in price, not in quality.
2. Consumers should consider buying more generic products than they do now since many of these products are just as good as the name brand equivalents, only cheaper.
3. I would want to find magazine articles comparing the two kinds of products. I would also want to compare the prices of equivalent generic and name brand products in my local supermarket.
4. Generic Products: Cheaper but Just as Good.

Try It Out

Answers will vary.

Exercise 2

Answers will vary. Sample answers follow.

1. A local issue that has interested me is the question of how to restrict the apparently endless population growth in this county because it now seems out of control. Since we moved here five years ago, the number of people in our own neighborhood has more than doubled. Large wooded areas that looked really appealing when we came have been cut down and large housing developments built on those sites. Traffic is a lot worse than it used to be—roads that were like quiet country lanes a short time ago now need lights at every intersection. Local taxes have gone up, schools are overcrowded, and I can't even run simple errands anymore without standing in long lines

everywhere. Some growth is fine, but there needs to be intelligent management so that the people who already live here don't face inconveniences due to overcrowding. <u>We need to elect people to local offices who are both aware of the problems caused by unrestricted growth and prepared to do something about them.</u>

2. We need to elect people to local offices who are both aware of the problems caused by unrestricted growth and prepared to do something about them. The present officeholders seem to think the more growth the better. But they have made few attempts to make life easier for people—the procedure to get a new traffic light installed is as complex as ever. It involves a petition, an impact study, and three separate hearings—total time, six months to a year. Too long. I know, because the light on our corner was installed only after nine separate accidents had occurred there, one of them almost fatal. <u>We need to streamline these procedures so that local government can move faster to get needed things done.</u> More people means more traffic, but I suppose it also means more business for local merchants, and five of the present officeholders own retail stores. <u>We need to set a limit on future growth and keep to it firmly.</u> Rezoning large areas of the county would probably be the best way to accomplish this.
3. We must elect local officials who will work to make life safer and easier for the people who now live in this county and who will restrict future population growth.

Exercise 3

Answers will vary.

Exercise 4

Answers will vary. Sample answers follow.
Topic: job rights of the disabled
2a. Which aspect of this topic interests me the most? Why?
I would like to know how widespread discrimination against the handicapped really is. It's important to give equal opportunities to all people who can take advantage of them—both for their sake and to ensure that precious human resources are not squandered through prejudice.

b. How can this issue be stated as a problem? What are some alternative ways of expressing this problem?

The problem is to make sure that everyone who can do a particular job has an equal opportunity to be hired for that job. Partially disabled people are still refused jobs because of their handicaps, but their disabilities have little or nothing to do with their ability to do those jobs. We must make sure that this sort of thing no longer happens.

c. What have I heard people say about this topic? <u>I overheard a conversation once in which someone said he didn't like to work around handicapped people because they made him feel uncomfortable.</u> He also said something about wheelchairs being safety hazards, but I think he was only trying to rationalize his prejudices.

d. How have the key issues related to this topic changed over the years? How might they change in the future?

People are becoming increasingly aware of the rights of handicapped people to employment, and laws have recently been enacted to protect these rights. I would expect the trend to continue, with more laws passed prohibiting discrimination. I also expect growing public support for handicapped people who are able to work.

e. What disagreements are there about this topic?

Employers argue that hiring the handicapped will increase their costs, which will then have to be passed on to the consumer. They talk about having to build ramps and rest rooms to accommodate handicapped workers. Workers argue that if laws are passed favoring the handicapped, able-bodied people will suffer from reverse discrimination.

f. What do both sides agree on? <u>I think they agree that everyone has a right to the fulfillment and feeling of self-worth that holding a job can bring.</u>

Exercise 5

Answers will vary.

Chapter Exercise

1. H	11. B
2. D	12. A
3. J	13. A
4. F	14. T
5. I	15. F
6. E	16. F
7. A	17. T
8. B	18. F
9. A	19. T
10. C	20. F

Chapter 8

Exercise 1

1. Q	6. N
2. F	7. B
3. B	8. SF
4. A	9. OK
5. OK	10. F

Try It Out

Answers will vary. Sample answers for Part I follow.

1. 2, 1, 3; chronological
2. 3, 2, 1 or 1, 2, 3; spatial
3. 2, 3, 1; most familiar to least familiar
4. 2, 3, 1; most likely to happen to least likely to happen
5. 3, 2, 1; least controversial to most controversial
6. 2, 3, 1; most familiar to least familiar

Part II Answers will vary.

Exercise 2

4. Lowered IQs
II. Exposure to lead more widespread than previously thought
2. Misdiagnosis due to low academic expectations for ghetto children
B. Middle-class and upper-class children
B. Use of qualified contractors to remove lead paint

Exercise 3

1. A	6. A
2. A	7. B
3. B	8. A
4. A	9. B
5. B	10. A

Exercise 4

1. C	6. D
2. B	7. A
3. F	8. B
4. A	9. E
5. G	10. G

Chapter Exercise

1. J	11. C
2. C	12. A
3. A	13. A
4. I	14. C
5. D	15. A
6. M	16. B
7. E	17. A
8. G	18. C
9. K	19. C
10. B	20. B

Chapter 9

Try It Out

Answers will vary.

Exercise 1

Answers will vary. Sample answers follow.
1. Please remove your belongings before Mr. Leithauser loses his temper.
2. All the employees remember the good party Mr. Bingham gave at his apartment.
3. Because drunk driving is so dangerous, I do not drink and drive.
4. Some employees like working overtime but most do not.
5. Certain state prison inmates have television and telephone privileges.
6. Another reason college students may decide to live off campus is the annoying behavior of some dormitory residents.
7. Surgeons' exploitation of women who have received breast implants angers me.
8. Bill wants to get an A in his chemistry class, but so far he is barely passing.
9. Norma likes reggae music very much as does one of my neighbors.
10. Establishing a neighborhood watch program is preferable to demanding increased police patrols.

Exercise 2

Answers will vary. Sample answers follow.
1. In Maine tourism should be more important than the lumber industry by the year 2000.
2. The best way to stabilize Latin American economies is to make loans more easily available to small businesses.
3. William Ewart Gladstone was one of the most illustrious and controversial of Great Britain's prime ministers.
4. At the beginning of the twentieth century Italian intellectuals hoped to establish a new, inclusive national culture.
5. Pigs are believed to be more intelligent than dogs.
6. A key element in congressional campaigns today is the amount of money candidates spend.
7. The restoration of the Sistine Chapel's ceiling reflects Michelangelo's intentions.
8. Free speech is threatened on this country's college campuses today.
9. Profit-making hospitals unfairly monopolize wealthy patients, burdening nonprofit hospitals with the care of the poor and uninsured.
10. Children should be given yearly increases in their allowances but be required to buy more for themselves each year.

Exercise 3

1. bat	6. bull
2. hills	7. doornail
3. iceberg	8. dog
4. surely	9. music
5. bee	10. swim

Answers will vary. Here are possible new versions of sentences 2 and 5:
2. My car is so old Henry Ford drove it as a test model.
5. She's as busy as an umbrella peddler in a downpour.

Exercise 4

1. K	6. F
2. I	7. D
3. G	8. B
4. C	9. E
5. J	10. L

Chapter Exercise

1. L	11. J
2. I	12. A
3. B	13. E
4. K	14. D
5. N	15. A
6. H	16. B
7. M	17. A
8. G	18. C
9. F	19. C
10. C	20. C

Chapter 10

Try It Out

Answers will vary.

Exercise 1

Corrections of the sentence fragments and run-on
  sentences may vary.
1. Change *then* to *than.*
2. Add to the sentence fragment to make it complete: The efforts to discredit myths about the
   origins of AIDS have not been entirely successful.
3. Change *is* to *are.*
4. Correct the run-on sentence by adding a
   period and capital letter or a semicolon after
   brutality.
5. Change *you* to *they* or omit the first comma
   and *you.*
6. Change *their* to *they're* or *they are.*
7. Change *he* to *they* and *benefits* to *benefit.*
8. Change *destroy* to *destroyed.*
9. Make the sentence fragment into a complete
   sentence: U.S. airlines need to simplify fare
   structures.
10. Change *fail* to *fails* or *failed.*

Exercise 2

1. NH	6. H
2. H	7. NH
3. NH	8. H
4. H	9. H
5. NH	10. H

Exercise 3

line 1: of

line 2: tele vision

line 6: off

line 9: accurally

line 10: then accuracy scientific work Attracting

line 11: kind

line 12: more graphic

line 13: (to)

line 14: We're

line 18: the the

line 19: to

Chapter Exercise

1. D	11. M
2. H	12. K
3. C	13. E
4. G	14. C
5. I	15. A
6. J	16. A
7. L	17. B
8. A	18. C
9. B	19. A
10. F	20. B

Chapter 11

Exercise 1

Answers will vary. Sample answers follow.
1. How can urban mass transit systems be made
   safer?
2. Is taking estrogen safe and effective for
   postmenopausal women?
3. Should AIDS testing be mandatory for health
   care workers?
4. How can the nomination process for U.S.
   Supreme Court justices be improved?
5. How widespread is racial bias in the granting
   of home mortgages?
6. Has seizing the property of suspected drug
   dealers been an effective weapon in the war on
   drugs?
7. What are the long-term effects of plastic pollution in oceans?
8. Can support groups be helpful to parents
   whose children have died due to sudden infant
   death syndrome?
9. Can city parks be revitalized?

10. Should the terms of elected officials be limited?

Try It Out

Answers will vary.

Exercise 2

Answers will vary somewhat.

1. A (This account is by a person whose practical experience qualifies her as an expert.)
2. A (This is an evaluation by a highly trained expert.)
3. B (Zabrisky is clearly biased on this issue, but he is probably very well informed.)
4. C (The book is long out of date. Both organized crime and law enforcement have changed a great deal since 1952.)
5. B (The editors probably offer only their own viewpoint, defending their own rights and those of their colleagues to strike, but they have probably presented their side of the case clearly and backed it up with the best evidence at their disposal.)
6. B (This is advertising for a specific college, but it probably includes information relevant to other colleges as well.)
7. B (Lindow is no expert on censorship, but he does have some inside information about the music business.)
8. A (The author is an expert, so the essay is probably very useful. If the language she uses is too technical, however, this source might need to be downgraded to a B or even a C.)
9. C (The article is out of date, and the author is probably not an expert on the subject.)
10. C (This is the work of a biased group, capable of distorting evidence to win points with readers.)

Exercise 3

Answers will vary. Sample answers follow.
1. Pioneers who participated in the Oklahoma land rush in 1889 each received 160 acres of land from the U.S. government. They showed courage and stamina by reaching Oklahoma any way they could. But injustices were committed, too. Most blacks and women were denied the chance to stake claims, and some native Americans were driven out of territories the government had previously ceded to them.
2. The large body of information collected by spy satellites during the Cold War is now being used by scientists to study global warming. However, some people are afraid that intelligence agencies will try to keep their budgets high by arguing that they are now needed to gather data on the environment.
3. The U.S. divorce rate has been increasing since the early 1970s. Children whose parents get divorced are more likely to get divorced themselves than children who grow up with both their natural parents. Over a million children in 1990 alone were caught up in their parents' divorces; this suggests that the divorce rate will continue to rise in the years to come.
4. Some people suspect President Franklin Delano Roosevelt knew in advance that the Japanese were going to bomb Pearl Harbor. They think that Roosevelt wanted to get the United States into the war to fight alongside the British and therefore did not pass along intelligence information about the attack. However, others maintain that the reports Roosevelt had at his disposal were unclear. Moreover, they argue that even if the base had been warned, the Japanese attack would have brought the United States into the war.
5. Locating the genome, a guide to a person's genetic inheritance, will make it possible to determine what diseases have been passed down to newborn infants by their parents. However, no one is sure whether it is ethical for doctors to tell people that they have inherited incurable illnesses.

Chapter Exercise

1. M	11. G
2. O	12. K
3. Q	13. A
4. R	14. N
5. L	15. B
6. E	16. B
7. D	17. C
8. J	18. C
9. C	19. A
10. H	20. B

Chapter 12

Exercise 1

1. I   wander."
2. I   free," Shirley
3. C
4. C
5. I   "Stay
6. I   pancreas?"
7. C
8. C
9. I   speech.
10. I   'unthinkable'

Try It Out

Answers will vary. Sample answer (MLA style):

As the number of U.S. manufacturers of fasteners has decreased in recent years, dependence on importers has increased ("Report Cites" 55). "Because bolts are a commodity item—bought largely on price and until recently rarely tested for quality," domestic manufacturers are tempted by inexpensive counterfeits (Merwin 56). Anna Cifelli Isgrò points out that low costs and quick deliveries mean "carriers can sometimes end up with bogus parts bought unwittingly from unscrupulous dealers" (81–82). Much of the counterfeiting began in the late 1970s when unscrupulous U.S. importers asked foreign producers, mostly Japanese, to make counterfeit bolts for the U.S. market (Merwin 56). In a U.S. Customs investigation of only one case, nine Japanese firms were found to be manufacturing and selling fake bolts ("Report Cites" 55). As C. O. Miller, an aviation consultant, explains, "Maintenance is a critical item; cost is a critical item. Put the two together and that opens the door to bogus parts" (qtd. in Isgrò 82).

Sample answer (APA style):

As the number of U.S. manufacturers of fasteners has decreased in recent years, dependence on importers has increased ("Report cites," 1988). "Because bolts are a commodity item—bought largely on price and until recently rarely tested for quality," (Merwin, 1988, p. 56) domestic manufacturers are tempted by inexpensive counterfeits. Isgrò (1987) points out that low costs and quick deliveries mean "carriers can sometimes end up with bogus parts bought unwittingly from unscrupulous dealers" (p. 82). Much of the counterfeiting began in the late 1970s when unscrupulous U.S. importers asked foreign producers, mostly Japanese, to make counterfeit bolts for the U.S. market (Merwin, 1988). In a U.S. Customs investigation of only one case, nine Japanese firms were found to be manufacturing and selling fake bolts ("Report cites," 1988). As C. O. Miller, an aviation consultant, explains, "Maintenance is a critical item; cost is a critical item. Put the two together and that opens the door to bogus parts" (cited in Isgrò, 1987, p. 82).

Exercise 2

1. MLA style:

Rivlin, Alice. Reviving the American Dream: The Economy, the States and the Federal Government. Washington: Brookings, 1992.

APA style:

Rivlin, A. (1992). Reviving the American dream: The economy, the states and the federal government. Washington, DC: Brookings Institution.

2. MLA style:

Berrick, Jill Duerr, and Neil Gilbert. With the Best of Intentions: The Child Sexual Abuse Prevention Movement. New York: Guilford, 1991.

APA style:

Berrick, J. D., & Gilbert, N. (1991). With the best of intentions: The child sexual abuse prevention movement. New York: Guilford Press.

3. MLA style:

Foss, Joe. "They Want to Take Our Guns." Conservative Digest Sept. 1988: 103–06. Rpt. in The Informed Argument: A Multidisciplinary Reader and Guide. Ed. Robert K. Miller. Fort Worth: Harcourt, 1992. 175–78.

APA style:

Foss, J. (1992). They want to take our guns. In R. K. Miller (Ed.), The informed argument: A multidisciplinary reader and guide (pp. 175–178). Fort Worth: Harcourt Brace Jovanovich.

4. MLA style:

United States. Dept. of Education. <u>What Works:
Schools without Drugs</u>. Washington: GPO,
1987.

APA style:

U.S. Department of Education. (1987). <u>What
works: Schools without drugs</u> (Publication
No. 1987–178–865). Washington, DC: U.S.
Government Printing Office.

5. MLA style:

Slotten, Hugh R. "Humane Chemistry or Scientific Barbarism? American Responses to
World War I Poison Gas, 1915–1930." <u>Jour-
nal of American History</u> 77 (1990): 476–98.

APA style:

Slotten, H. R. (1990). Humane chemistry or scien-
tific barbarism? American responses to World
War I poison gas, 1915–1930. <u>The Journal of
American History</u>, <u>77</u>, 476–498.

6. MLA style:

Faludi, Susan. Backlash: <u>The Undeclared War
against American Women</u>. New York:
Crown, 1991.

APA style:

Faludi, S. (1991). <u>Backlash: The undeclared war
against American women</u>. New York: Crown.

7. MLA style:

Butterfield, Fox. "Afro-American Studies Get
New Life at Harvard." <u>New York Times</u> 3
June 1992: B7.

APA style:

Butterfield, F. (1992, June 3). Afro-American
studies get new life at Harvard. <u>The New
York Times</u>, p. B7.

8. MLA style:

"Your Daily Bread." <u>Consumer Reports</u> Oct.
1988: 611–14.

APA style:

Your daily bread. (1988, October). <u>Consumer
Reports</u>, pp. 611–614.

9. MLA style:

Thomas, Elizabeth Marshall. "Reflections: The
Old Way." <u>New Yorker</u> 15 Oct. 1990: 78–
110.

APA style:

Thomas, E. M. (1990, October 15). Reflections:
The old way. <u>The New Yorker</u>, pp. 78–110.

10. MLA style:

Hawks, Steven R. "Exercise and Weight Loss:
The Uncertain Connection." <u>Health Educa-
tion</u> 20.4 (1989): 11–15.

APA style:

Hawks, S. R. (1989). Exercise and weight loss:
The uncertain connection. <u>Health Education</u>,
<u>20</u>(4), 11–15.

Exercise 3

1. Unless the people of the United States are willing to see an invaluable legacy vanish forever,
the federal government must pass and enforce a
strong law to protect native American sites
from destruction. (found at the end of the
second paragraph)
2. The quotation and paraphrase immediately
preceding the parenthetical citations are from
works by Arden and Landers respectively; 390
and 35 are the page numbers where the information was found.
3. Quotations longer than four typed lines are indented.
4. Square brackets mean that a change has been
made in a quotation. The [I] shows that the
word *if* was not capitalized in the original, indicating that one or more words were omitted
from the beginning of the quoted sentence.
5. This citation refers to the first entry on the
works cited page: "After Mining, a Furor Over
a Shrine." <u>New York Times</u> 3 Jan. 1991: A12.
"After Mining" is used in the parenthetical citation because the article is unsigned.
6. No page numbers are needed because the references are to one-page articles.
7. The paragraph is a statement of opposing
views and a refutation of those views.
8. No citation is needed because the proposal to
pass a new law is the writer's own idea.
9. 9 articles, 3 books
10. The article starts on page 15 and skips to an
additional page or pages later in the periodical.

Chapter Exercise

1. C	11. B
2. F	12. B
3. B	13. T
4. E	14. T
5. A	15. F
6. D	16. T
7. A	17. F
8. A	18. F
9. C	19. T
10. B	20. F

Index

Index

A

Abstracts, 258, 303
Academic writing, 13
Ad hominem attack, 130–31, 303
Ad misericordiam appeal, 132, 303
Ad populum appeal, 132, 303
Aesthetics, 88–89, 303
Agreement, subject-verb, 227–28, 303
American Psychological Association style, 236, 273
   citations in, 275–76
   references in, 279–81
Analogy, 72, 102, 303
   false, 139, 306
Analysis, 161, 303
   synthesis and, 84–86
Annotation, 259, 303
Anonymous authorities, appeal to, 134–35, 303
Antecedents, 228, 303
APA. *See* American Psychological Association.
Apology, 30
Appeals
   to authority, 134–36, 303
   bandwagon, 135
   emotional, 131–32
   plain folks, 136
   to tradition, 135
Aregood, Richard, 14
Arguable statements, 7–8
Arguing from ignorance, 121–22, 304

Argument, Uses of, 36
Argument(s)
   analysis of, 20–21
   cause-effect, 77–80, 304
   classification of, 110–11
   comparison, 72
   definition of, 2–3, 102, 304
   drafting of, 185–94
   evaluation of, 89
   key terms in, 99
   models for, 29–46
   purpose of, 3–4
   reevaluation of, 222–23
   sign, 79
   spoken, 12
   thesis in, 173–74
   tu quoque, 131
   written
      plan for, 170–96
      spoken vs., 9–11
      types of, 12–14
Aristotle, 32, 46, 102, 118
Articles, in bibliography, 280–81
Attacks, *ad hominem*, 130–31, 303
Attribution, 101
Audiences, types of, 6–7
Author/date citations. *See* American Psychological Association style.
Authority, appeal to, 134–36, 303
Averages, in statistics, 52–53

B

Backing, of warrants, 38–39, 304
Bandwagon appeal, 135, 304
Barnet, Sylvan, 102
Bedau, Hugo, 102
Begging the question, 126–28, 304, 309
Benefits, 91–92
Bibliography, 251, 304. *See also* References.
Bird, Caroline, 271
Black, Hugo, 271
Boétie, Etienne de La, 12
Books, in bibliography, 279–80
Brainstorming, 157, 304
Burden of proof, 121, 304
Burke, Edmund, 61

C

Call number, 250, 304
Card catalog, 249–50, 304
Categories, 110
Cause-effect arguments, 77–80, 304
    questioning for, 161
Cause-effect relationship, 78–79, 309
Cause(s)
    immediate, 78, 307
    remote, 78, 310
    sufficient, 78, 311
Chronological order, 175, 304
Circular reasoning, 126–28
Citations. *See also* References.
    parenthetical, 273–76, 308
    preparation of, 275–76
Claims, 304
    in argument, 36
    facts and, 50
    refutation of, 61–62
    types of, 40–42
Classification, 109–11, 304
    questioning for, 161
Clichés, 210–11, 304
Cluster diagrams, 164–65
Clustering, 164, 304
Coherence, 188–90, 305
Collaboration, 230–31

Colloquialism, 201, 305
Columbus, Christopher, 160
Common knowledge, 274, 305
Comparatives, 76–77
Comparisons, 305
    contrasts and, 71–72
    diagrams for, 73–74
    questioning for, 161
Conclusions, 194, 305
Conflict of interest, 55, 305
Connotation, 99–100, 305
Contrast, 71–72, 305
    diagrams for, 73–74
    questioning for, 161
Copernicus, Nicolaus, 85
Counterclaim, 172–73, 305
Criteria, 88, 305
Critical listening, 14–16, 305
Critical reading, 16–21, 305
Criticism, peer, 230–31, 308
Current Issues and Enduring Questions, 102

D

Data, 49–55, 305
    evaluation of, 53–55
    as evidence, 36
Data bases, 305
Debate, 2, 305
Deduction, 31–35, 305
Definition, 98–105, 305
    formal, 100
    methods of, 100–4
    persuasive, 104–5
    question-begging, 127–28, 309
    questioning for, 161
    stipulative, 102–3, 311
Denotation, 99–100, 305
Description, questioning for, 161
Diagrams
    cluster, 164–65
    tree, 180–81, 312
Dialogue, Socratic, 30
Dickens, Charles, 89
Dictionary, usage labels in, 201, 312
Dicto simpliciter, 119

Digressions, 12, 305
Dilemma, either-or, 119–20, 306
Discovery drafts, 305
Documentation, 273–81, 305
Doublespeak, 215–16, 305
Draft. *See also* Writing process.
 of argument, 185–94
 of conclusions, 194
 discovery, 146, 305
 of introductions, 192–94
 of paragraphs, 186–87
 rough, 146, 305, 310
Dutch treat, 213

E

Editing, 146, 306. *See also* Proofreading *and*
 Revising.
 guide to, 228–29
 for precision, 226–29
Editorials, 14, 306
Einstein, Albert, 104
Either-or dilemma, 119–20, 306
Elbow, Peter, 148
Elements of Style, 226
Ellipsis, 271, 306
Emotional appeals, 131–32
Emotional language, 212
Emphatic order, 176, 306
Enthymeme, 35, 306
Equivocation, 103, 126, 306
Essays, 12, 306
Et al., 275, 276, 306
Ethical standards, 224–26
Ethics, 88, 306
Ethnocentrism, 44, 306
Etymology, 101–2, 306
Euphemism, 214–15, 306
Evaluation(s), 88–90, 306
 argumentative, 89
 moral, 307
 questioning for, 161
 of sources, 253–54
Examples
 as definitions, 100–1
 evaluation of, 54

facts and, 50
 hypothetical, 50–51, 307
Expert testimony, 53, 306
 evaluation of, 54–55
 reliance on, 104

F

Facts, 306
 claims of, 40–41, 50, 304
 evaluation of, 54
 verification of, 7
Fallacy(ies), 306
 definition of, 117–18
 post hoc, 120
 slippery slope, 120–21, 311
False analogy, 139, 306
Faulty generalizations, 118–19
Faulty reasoning, 117–40
Fear, appeals to, 132
Flexible categories, 110
Formal definition, 100
Formal outline, 181–82, 306
Formal register, 201
Fragment, sentence, 227, 310
Franco, Francisco, 14
Frankenstein, 119
Freewriting, 155–56, 306

G

Gable, Clark, 1
Generalities, glittering, 125–26, 307
Generalization
 hasty, 118–19, 307
 unqualified, 119, 312
Government publications, in bibliography, 281
Gypped, 213

H

Hemingway, Ernest, 127, 206
How to Lie with Statistics, 51
Huff, Darrell, 51

Hypothesis, 31, 245, 307
Hypothetical example, 50–51, 307

I

Ignorance, arguing from, 121–22, 304
Impersonal tone, personal vs., 204–6
Inappropriate language, 210–16
Incubating, 146, 220–22, 240, 307
Index cards, 247–48, 308, 311
Indexes, 252, 307
Induction, 31–35, 307
Inference, 8, 307
Inflexible categories, 110
Informal outline, 181, 307
Informal register, 202
Informal writing, 179–80
Intentional vagueness, 125–26
Interest, conflict of, 55, 305
Interviewing, 256
Introductions, drafting of, 192–94
Irrelevance, 138–39

J

Jargon, 206–7, 307
Jefferson, Thomas, 43–44
Journals, 149–51, 307
    hints for, 151
    topics for, 151–52
Judgment, 307
    as arguable statement, 8
Justification, 307

K

Key words, repetition of, 192
King, Martin Luther, 109, 269–70
Knowledge, common, 274, 305

L

La Boétie, Etienne de, 12
Labels, usage, 201, 312

Language
    emotional, 212
    inappropriate, 210–16
    offensive, 212–14
    sexist, 213–17, 310
Leigh, Vivien, 1
Library, use of, 249–50
Like, 202
Listening, critical, 14–16, 305
Loaded question, 127, 307
Loaded words, 127, 307
Log, research, 244
Lutz, William, 215

M

Manuscript, preparation of, 235–37
Mapping, 164
Marx, Karl, 104
Mean, 52, 307
Median, 52, 307
Middle register, 201–2
Mill, John Stuart, 3
MLA. *See* Modern Language Association.
Mode, 52, 307
Modern Language Association style, 236, 273
    citations in, 275
    references in, 278–81
Montaigne, Michel de, 12
Moral evaluations, 88, 307

N

Negation, 103, 308
Newspaper articles, in bibliography, 281
Non sequitur, 138, 308
Note cards, 308
Notes
    organization of, 262
    tips on, 256–58

O

Occam's razor, 85, 308

Offensive language, 212–14
Op-ed page, 13, 308
Order
  chronological, 175
  emphatic, 176, 306
  spatial, 176, 311
Orwell, George, 215
Outline(s)
  advantages of, 183–84
  formal, 181–82, 306
  informal, 181, 307
  sentence, 182, 310
  topic, 181–82, 311
Overviews, 308

P

Paper. *See specific types, e.g.,* Research paper.
Paragraphs
  drafting of, 186–87
  revision of, 223
Parallelism, 183, 308
Paraphrases, 257, 259–60, 267–68, 308
Parenthetical citations, 273–76, 308
Pasteur, Louis, 55
Peer criticism, 230–31, 308
Person (grammatical), 227, 308
Personal attacks, 130–31
Personal preferences, 7, 308
Personal pronouns, 205–6
Personal tone, 204–6
Persuasion, 2, 6–7, 308
Persuasive definition, 104–5, 308
Phrases. *See* Words.
Pity, appeals to, 132
Plagiarism, 226, 309
Plain folks appeal, 136, 309
Plato, 30, 46
Pleading, special, 122, 311
Poisoning the well, 131, 309
Policy, claims of, 41–42, 304
Pornography, 100–1
Post hoc fallacy, 120, 309
Practical evaluations, 89
Precedents, 91, 309
Preferences, personal, 7, 308
Premises, 32, 307, 309

Prewriting, 146, 148–67, 309. *See also* Writing process.
  strategies for, 149
  tips for, 166–67
Pronouns
  antecedents of, 228
  personal, 205–6
Proof, burden of, 121, 304
Proofreading, 146, 309. *See also* Editing.
  symbols for, 238
  tips for, 237
Proposals, 91–92

Q

Qualifiers, 37, 309
Quarrel, definition of, 2
Question
  begging the, 126–28, 304, 309
  loaded, 127, 307
Questioning, 159–63
Questionnaire, for writing, 147–48
Quotations
  changes in, 271–72
  choice of, 268
  incorporation of, 268–69
  indented, 269
  punctuation of, 270–71

R

Rationalization, 7, 309
Reading
  critical, 16–21, 305
  preparation for, 16–17
  steps in, 19–20
Reasoning
  circular, 126–28
  faulty, 117–39, 139–40
Reciprocal relationship, 78–79, 309
Recommendations, 90–92, 161, 309
Red herring, 138, 309
Reductio ad absurdum, 62, 309
Redundancy, 207, 309
Reference books, 251–52, 309
Reference cards, 247–48
References, 251, 309

References (*cont.*)
   primary, 249
   secondary, 249
   styles for, 278–81
Refutation, 60–65, 309
   of opposing views, 92
   tips for, 64–65
Regionalism, 202, 310
Register(s), 310
   formal, 201
   informal, 202
   middle, 201–2
   types of, 200–1
Remote causes, 310
Reports, 13, 310. *See also specific types, e.g.*, Research
      paper.
Research, 243–63
   log of, 244, 310
   strategy for, 247–49
Research paper, 13, 310
   organization of, 175–77
   sample of, 284–98
   sources for, 266–85
Restrictions, 38, 310
Revising, 146, 222–23, 310. *See also* Editing.
Rhetoric, 30
Rise and Fall of the Third Reich, 233
Rogers, Carl, 16
Roosevelt, Franklin D., 272
Rough draft, 310
Run-on sentence, 310
Russell, Bertrand, 31, 104

S

Scanning, 258–59, 310
Scientific method, 31
Search strategy, 247–49, 310
Sentence fragment, 310
Sentence outline, 182, 310
Sentence(s)
   editing of, 228
   run-on, 226–27, 310
   topic, 186, 311
Sexist language, 213–17, 310
Shelley, Mary, 119
Shirer, William L., 233
Sic, 272, 310

Sign arguments, 79
Signs, 310
Slang, 201, 310
Slanting, 13, 311
Slippery slope fallacy, 120–21, 311
Socrates, 30, 46
Source cards, 247–48, 311
Sources. *See also* References.
   evaluation of, 253–54
   incorporating of, 267–72
   listing of, 278–81
   primary, 249, 309
   for research papers, 266–85
   secondary, 249, 310
Spatial order, 176, 311
Spelling, 228
Stacks, library, 250, 304, 308
Statements, arguable, 7–8
Statistics, 51–52, 311
   evaluation of, 54
Statistics, How to Lie with, 51
Stereotypes, 44, 311
Stipulative definition, 102–3, 311
Straw man, 138–39, 311
Strunk, William, 226
Style, 311
   American Psychological Association, 236, 273
      citations in, 275–76
      references in, 279–81
   choice of, 199–217
   definition of, 199–200
   Modern Language Association, 236, 273
      citations in, 275
      references in, 278–81
Subconscious, drawing on, 146, 220–22, 240
Subject-verb agreement, 227–28, 303
Subtitle, 234, 311. *See also* Titles.
Sufficient cause, 78, 311
Summaries, 267–68, 311
Sun Also Rises, 127
Superlatives, 76–77
Support, refutation of, 62–63
Swear words, 213
Syllogism, 32–35, 311
   invalid, 34–35
   unsound, 34
Synonyms, 100
Synthesis, 84–86, 311

T

Tables, turning the, 63, 312
Tense, 311
  shifts in, 227
Terms, in syllogism, 33, 311
Testimonial, 54, 311
Testimony
  expert, 53, 306
    evaluation of, 54–55
    reliance on, 104
Thesis, 170–74, 311
  errors in, 171–72
  of essays, 12
  preliminary, 246–47
Titles
  effective, 103, 233
  format for, 234–35
Tolstoy, Leo, 104
Tone, 204–6, 311
Topic, choice of, 91, 244–45
Topic outline, 181–82, 311
Topic sentence, 186, 311
Toulmin, Stephen, 36, 46, 304, 310
Tradition, appeal to, 135
Transfer, 135–36, 312
Transitional words, 188–91, 312
Tree diagrams, 180–81, 312
Tu quoque argument, 131, 312
Turning the tables, 63, 312
Twain, Mark, 120

U

Unity, 188–90
Usage label, 201, 312
Uses of Argument, 36

V

Vagueness, intentional, 125–26

Valid, 312
Value, claims of, 41, 304
Verification, 7, 312

W

Warhol, Andy, 268–69
Warrants, 36, 312
  backing of, 38–39
  refutation of, 64
  stated, 43–44
  unstated, 44
Webbing, 164
Welsh rabbit, 213
White, E. B., 226
Winn, Marie, 104
Words
  editing of, 229
  key, 192
  loaded, 127, 307
  sexist, 214
  swear, 213
  transitional, 188–91, 312
Working title, 312
Works cited, 278–81, 312. *See also* References.
Writer's block, 185–86, 312
Writing
  academic, 13
  clear, 206–7
  concise, 207
  precise, 226–29
  talking about, 153–54
Writing process, 312. *See also specific stages, e.g.,*
    Prewriting.
  approaches to, 147
  plan for, 179–80
  questionnaire for, 147–48
  revision in, 222–23
  stages of, 146